Also by Alex Fynn and Lynton Guest:

The Secret Life of Football
Heroes and Villains: The Inside Story of the 1990/91
    Season at Arsenal and Tottenham Hotspur
Out of Time: Why Football Isn't Working

Also by Alex Fynn

Dream On: A Year in the Life of a Premier League Club
    (with H. Davidson)
Cantona on Cantona (with Eric Cantona)

Alex Fynn wrote the commercial section of the FA's
Blueprint for the Future of Football which led to the forma-
tion of the Premier League and its contract with BSkyB.
He has advised the FA, the Football League, Tottenham
Hotspur, Arsenal, Manchester United and Celtic on
media and marketing.

Lynton Guest is probably the only sportswriter to have
made a number-one hit record when he played
keyboards on the Love Affair's 'Everlasting Love'. He
has been writing on football since 1988 for publications
including the *Sunday Telegraph*, the *Observer* and *World
Soccer*.

FOR LOVE OR MONEY

MANCHESTER UNITED AND ENGLAND – THE BUSINESS OF WINNING

Alex Fynn and Lynton Guest

André Deutsch

First published in hardback in 1998
This revised edition published in 1999 by
André Deutsch Limited
76 Dean Street
London W1V 5HA
www.vci.co.uk

A catalogue record for this title is available from the British Library

ISBN 0 233 99755 5

Typeset by
Derek Doyle & Associates, Liverpool
Printed and bound in the UK by
Caledonian International Book Manufacturing Ltd, Glasgow

To Tamara

ACKNOWLEDGEMENTS

It will be apparent that this book could not have been produced without the considerable cooperation of many people. A debt of gratitude is owed to Martin Edwards, Michel Platini and Glenn Hoddle for their invaluable insights. In Glenn's case, it must be mentioned that some of these were gained during the course of helping him with his World Cup diary. Although he was told at the outset that his advisor would also be producing a book and further, after the World Cup, that its tone would be critical, it only belatedly dawned on him that in listening to an alternative point of view he was exposing himself to a situation that might backfire on him. The knowledge gained has not been used to embarrass him, rather to try to convey to the reader a better understanding of Hoddle, the man and the manager.

In addition to those quoted in the book, many as a result of specific interviews, special thanks are owed to Harry Lansdown, Greville Waterman, Gerrard Tyrrell, John Bick, Rob Bagchi and Andy Mitten, who read the manuscript and who were constructively critical, as was John Sinnott, who also acted as friend and researcher. Background information was also provided by Pam Kemmey and Katie Camy and Gerry Boon and Reem Rahmatalla of the Deloitte & Touche Football Industry Team.

Discussions with colleagues in media, marketing and football were always instructive. Thanks are due to

Edward Freedman, Marcela Mora y Araujo, Patrick Harverson, Kevin Morton, David Dein, Jon and Phil Smith, James Freedman, Austin Lally, Mel Goldberg, Claude Ruibal, Ken Goldman, Daniel Wolf, Barrie Pierpoint, Phil Carling and David Lacey. Thanks also to *Red Issue*, *Red News*, *United We Stand* and *Red Attitude* for their informed opinions on the object of their affections.

Along the way, friends gave enormous help and encouragement. These include Aurora Menon, Jason Tomas, Peter Suchet, Pat Barker, Cliff Francis, Mark Whitford, Simon Jones, Monty Fisher, Peter Law, Marek Wystepek, Simon Aldis, Stepak, and The Unknown Soldier.

Jenny Olivier was an indefatigable and considerate editor. Thanks are also due to Tim Forrester, Louise Dixon, Nicky Paris, Michael Crick, Callum Murray and Philip Cornwall.

Contents

FOREWORD

What Price Glory?

THE CREATION OF the Premier League and the Champions' League, and the expansion of the World Cup, have changed the face of football for ever. We have come a long way from the early days when football was played purely for the enjoyment of fans and players. Money men have learned that the dedication of fans means a willingness to spend. Where there's passion, there's profit.

The game today is part of showbusiness. Its top-of-the-bill stars attract fabulous money from the ambitious or the fearful – the impresarios and the backers who make up the ranks of club chairmen. The whole show is under-written by global businesses and presided over by administrators who have transformed their amateur organizations into conduits for the new riches.

The fans, as ever, want glory. For the players, clubs and national sides, winning brings not just glory but potentially huge financial rewards. In an ever more competitive environment, success takes not just the skill of eleven men on the pitch but also the strategy and business acumen of those behind the scenes.

In order to try to make sense of the new order for all

football supporters, we have tracked the paths of Manchester United and England through the 1997/98 season and beyond, all the way to the World Cup in France, the biggest sporting event the world has ever seen.

We have been inside chairmen's offices, we have felt the atmosphere in boardrooms and we have attended private meetings in hotels and official gatherings of the game's power brokers. We have watched matches from directors' seats, from press boxes and corporate boxes and the seats behind the goals.

This is not a match-by-match account, but an unfolding tale of the journeys undertaken by Manchester United and England to attain their respective goals. Games have been used as signposts to the key issues, the behind-the-scenes manoeuvres and the people who made the headlines on and off the pitch. What you read will be what we found at the time, since we have made every effort to resist any temptation towards hindsight.

As this book goes to press, revolution is once again in the air. A European Super League and pay-per-view television are fast appearing over the horizon. Anyone who is interested in football should be aware of the ramifications of these and other proposed changes.

Above all, we think the story revealed in these pages is relevant to all supporters. The future is uncertain but it is not entirely in the hands of those whose interests are essentially financial. We hope this book will show how the lifeblood of the greatest game can be sustained.

Alex Fynn & Lynton Guest
London, August 1998

INTRODUCTION

Now and Then

THE FORLORN FIGURE trudging towards the tunnel at Wembley was headed for football oblivion. Sir Alf Ramsey, the General at England's finest hour, was now revealed for all to see as a spent force. Needing to beat Poland to qualify for the 1974 World Cup finals, Ramsey's England team was foiled by a combination of defensive error, failure to finish, sheer bad luck and the antics of Jan Tomaszewski, a goalkeeper publicly derided as a clown by Brian Clough. Consequently, England could do no better than draw 1–1 and were eliminated from the competition. For Ramsey's 'wingless wonders' it was a campaign too far. The 100,000 fans crammed into the old Empire Stadium and the twenty million more who followed the drama live on BBC television were stunned. Two games later Ramsey was gone and his era came to a stuttering end.

The Secretary of the Football League at the time, Alan Hardaker, had said before the game, 'If we do lose . . . it will be a terrible thing for six weeks and then everyone will forget about it.' How wrong can one man be?

Twenty-four years later, in October 1997, England faced another World Cup qualifier of equal significance.

A draw this time, against Italy in Rome, would suffice to take the coach, Glenn Hoddle, and his confident England squad to France 98. However, in the build-up to the day of reckoning, it emerged that there would be no shared experience for the millions of armchair fans desperate to watch events unfold on live television. The quarter of the population who had paid their subscriptions to Sky Sports would be catered for but everyone else would either have to go to the pub or be content with Radio Five Live.

The years between the two encounters had seen cataclysmic change in the way football is structured, financed and supported, exemplified by the role of television, which has gone from grateful servant to overbearing master. It was the result of a revolution driven not by idealism but by money.

When the Football Association (FA) published its *Blueprint For The Future Of Football* in 1991, it argued that optimum commercial revenue would only be produced through the central marketing of the three key components of English football: the about-to-be-created Premier League, England internationals, and the FA Cup (this was a point not lost on UEFA, which has strengthened its hold over its member federations and clubs through its creation of the Champions' League). However, the FA failed to follow the advice of its own blueprint, so concerned was it with breaking the power of the Football League, which had challenged the FA's authority over English football with a power-sharing proposal.

Left to their own devices while the FA vacillated, those running the embryonic Premier League (club chairmen and Premier League Chief Executive, Rick Parry), couldn't believe their luck. The FA had strongly hinted that it would enforce an eighteen-club Premier League and exercise its right to a 'special share', effectively a right to veto, in order to control television rights, but had not actually laid down any rules to that effect, so the Premier League quickly sold out for Sky's pot of gold. Manchester United's Chief Executive and Chairman, Martin Edwards, showed where the power now resided, saying, 'The (Premier League) clubs could decide their own future. They had the TV and sponsorship income in their own hands and that made those clubs a lot wealthier in their own right.'

The rest of the media aped Sky's hype and the platform for the commercial revolution was born. Football became two games: one with all the money and the focus of attention as played in the Premier League; the other, everything else. Part of 'everything else' included England internationals, which had to be fitted around the needs of the showcase top division and its television schedule. It was only through the insistence of FIFA, the world governing body, that the juggernaut had to come to a temporary halt from time to time for what FIFA determined were to be sacrosanct international-only days. Even FIFA could only rule the roost intermittently, though. Weeks that were devoid of Premier League matches because of internationals were invariably followed by spates of three or four games in ten days to restore impetus to the Sky schedules. To mitigate any extraneous influence on its scheduling, Sky soon bought up live rights to the rest of English football, including Wembley internationals.

A couple of weeks before the Rome date the FA suddenly realized it had a problem. Although a clause in the contract with Sky permitted the FA to insist that an international played at home must be broadcast live on 'free-to-air' television if it were deemed to be of national importance, the FA's negotiators had forgotten that matches of 'national importance' are sometimes played on foreign soil. The television rights to these away matches, of course, belong to the host federation. The FA therefore had no control over which television company in England would buy the rights to the Italian game. At the same time there was mounting pressure from politicians and public for universal free access.

The Italian television rights to the first game against Italy at Wembley were bought by RAI, the state broadcaster, with backing from the Italian federation. The rights sale was handled by the FA's representative for such deals, the TV sports marketing company CSI. Had the FA thought about it, it could have instructed CSI to negotiate a reciprocal arrangement – the Wembley game for the Rome game. At a stroke this would have ensured the widest possible audience for the October encounter. Such deals had been common in the past, before the Sky revolution, and the Rome game was, after all, the last in the group and had been seen from the start as the potential decider.

The FA, of course, hadn't thought about it. Sky, in the meantime, had thought about it long and hard. Sky wanted to buy rights for all the England away games in the World Cup but had been outmanoeuvred for one of the matches, the game against Poland, by Channel 5, assisted by CSI. Sky was determined not to lose out again, particularly for the Italy game. Accordingly, six months before the match was due to take place, Trevor East, Sky's Executive Director for Sport, flew to Milan and concluded a deal with RAI, which held the rights for home Italy internationals. The following morning, as he left the hotel, CSI arrived, twenty-four hours too late.

At the eleventh hour, desperate to retrieve the situation, David Davies, the FA's Head of Public Affairs, went public by asking Sky, through the media, to share the broadcast with a terrestrial partner. 'It would be nice,' he said, 'to think the largest number of people could see it.' Davies then tried to seize the moral high ground when he added, 'as far as the FA is concerned the public interest has always been there and will continue to be there,' thus differentiating the request from 'the exclusive deals that are done to benefit the whole grassroots of the game'. There would be less of a problem with this 'good for the game' stance if there was any hard evidence to support it. Ask the fans of Brighton or Bournemouth and they might have something forceful to say on the subject. Moreover, the FA conveniently ignored Sky's business philosophy. As Russell Boynan, a leading media buyer, said, 'It would be a dangerous precedent for broadcasters like Sky if it bid for prestige events but then when their value increased were told it couldn't carry them any more.'

Sky was now in a corner. Any compromise to its exclusive deal would be at the expense of its advertisers, sponsors and subscribers, who, for their differing reasons, had committed themselves to the network on the basis of live and exclusive coverage. On the other hand, not sharing what Sky had bought in a free market might unleash the forces of Parliament against the company. After Sky made inroads into the mass market in the early 1990s, a backlash began which sought to curb the network's growing ability to buy exclusive rights to big sporting events and protect the FA Cup Final and the World Cup finals. Sky executives were terrified that any failure on their part to cooperate over the Italian game could lead to encroachment into their portfolio by extending the number of 'listed' events (major sporting events secured for free-to-air television as being in the national interest) to include others, like golf's Ryder Cup and England's home rugby internationals, which were also Sky exclusives.

In the end Sky screened the match live. But in a major concession, it allowed ITV to show the whole game at 10pm, half an hour after it had finished and while the post-mortem was still in full flow on the satellite channel.

When the referee blew the final whistle in Rome after a 0–0 draw, Glenn Hoddle was engulfed by his coaching staff and players. The exuberant rejoicing was in dramatic contrast to the dejection which had enveloped their predecessors back in 1973. This time around everyone, it seemed, was a winner. Commercial revenue from the combined satellite, cable and terrestrial audience of almost twelve million (excluding pubs and clubs), brought in more than £4 million, easily covering the television companies' outlay, which was the largest rights fee ever paid by broadcasters for an England international. The players' earnings would start to crank up yet another notch, making them even more like Hollywood stars than they were already. Lucrative friendlies and FA junkets beckoned, while the Premier League, the media and the sponsors could bask in the reflected glory of the national team.

Glory – it used to be the *raison d'être*. Glory for owners and administrators, glory for players, glory, if they were lucky, for fans as a reward for their love. Now money calls the shots and the fans are expected to pay, even when they don't attend the match. With demand exceeding supply, spectators are seemingly only tolerated in the role of extras on a film set, there to provide verisimilitude and a backcloth for the television spectacular. If they don't like it, too bad. It is a seller's market and there are plenty waiting outside the gates to get in whatever the price. Gone for ever is the notion that before football is a business it is a game. That was then, this is now. We are in a hall of mirrors where illusion is still presented as a search for glory. It is no longer the glory game, it is the money game.

CHAPTER ONE

Money Makes the World Go Round

THE STRETFORD END at Old Trafford always used to produce a fearsome wall of sound. To supporters and players alike, the atmosphere in the stadium was fashioned by the level of noise generated by the hard-core faithful behind the goal. In common with many Premiership grounds, the conversion to all-seat stadia has changed that atmosphere in recent years, from raucous intimidation to something a little more sedate; 'Cold Trafford', according to some disenchanted United fans.

At Manchester United's home game against Juventus in the 1997/98 Champions' League, something strange happened. Supporters behind both goals remained standing for the whole ninety minutes, in the case of those in the East Stand, all 10,000 of them. Moreover, they were allowed to do so. This was in stark contrast to the first home Premiership game of the season, when heavy-handed stewarding made the point to the 'popular' ends that prolonged standing would not be tolerated. The rule was enforced through a number of indiscriminate ejections.

dnesday night game against Juventus, as a throwback to yesteryear, the intimidating e prompting the Italians' coach, Marcello ...cknowledge the 'exceptional support . . . which would probably even inspire mad cows'. Lippi even felt it was an influential factor in the outcome of the match, which United won 3–2. Perhaps the lungs and voice-box function better from a standing position. Perhaps Alex Ferguson's call for a 'return to a more hostile stadium' had produced its intended effect. Whatever the case, there is no mistaking the revivalist fervour evident when a Champions' League night arrives at Old Trafford.

The atmosphere produced by the crowd must have been music to the ears of UEFA, the governing body of European football. It was, after all, the intention of UEFA when it decided to revamp the European Cup in 1991 that playing more event-like games would recapture the initiative from domestic leagues, fill stadia and ensure the allegiance of television and commercial interests. There could hardly have been a better demonstration of the attainment of all those objectives than the intensity of that October night.

With its distinguished history stretching from the unsurpassed exploits of Real Madrid in the 1950s to the resurgence of AC Milan in the 1980s, the European Cup was, without doubt, the pinnacle of club football. Then, with a number of Italian multimedia entrepreneurs like Silvio Berlusconi, the owner of Milan, becoming involved in the game, UEFA came under heavy pressure to change the knockout format of its premier competition. Berlusconi spoke for a number of vested interests, including the other big clubs, television networks and international sponsors, when he pressed for more guarantees. It was not 'modern thinking', he argued, to put the big clubs at risk from circumstances beyond the control of players, coaches and owners. Bad weather or poor refereeing on one night could see a club out of Europe and millions of dollars could be lost. This, according to Berlusconi, meant that on a given day David could upset Goliath, or two big clubs could be drawn against each other in the early rounds. These vagaries of chance had to be eliminated or at least minimized. The result of Berlusconi's lobbying was the destruction of the old-style European Cup and its replacement in 1991 with the Champions' League.

Each year, with a bit of tinkering here and a touch of trimming there, the structure of the Champions' League gradually evolved. What emerged was something of a hybrid, neither league nor cup. Actually, it owed something both to the National Football League (American Gridiron) model where a regular season is followed by play-offs and a grand final, and to the World Cup, where the early rounds of the finals are played in round-robin groups before the event proceeds to the knockout stages.

While the big clubs pushed for more games, on the basis that more games equals more money, it was, in fact, commercial logic which shaped the new format. By the mid-1980s, one of the most influential sports marketing companies in the world was the Swiss-based International Sport And Leisure Group (ISL), jointly owned by Adidas and a Japanese company, Dentsu, one of the world's largest advertising agencies. ISL held sponsorship rights for the World Cup, the European Championships and the Olympic Games.

The driving force behind much of ISL's success was Jurgen Lenz, an imposing man in his late forties whose native Germanic thoroughness is lightened by a keen sense of humour. In 1990, Lenz broke away from ISL and formed his own company, called TEAM. Lenz was ideally placed to show UEFA how to exploit its commercial potential. He was acutely aware of how the live event could become interdependent with the television spectacular. Using the concept of central control he devised an all-embracing masterplan to fulfil the desires of those clubs for whom Silvio Berlusconi had been lobbying. Lenz informed UEFA that its position as the governing body of European football could only be safeguarded by controlling every aspect of any revamped European Cup. He put a special effort into convincing UEFA that it should be in full charge of the lucrative television rights, which until then had (apart from the final) been owned by the participating clubs.

Lenz insisted that sponsorship become a cornerstone of his proposal but only if, unlike the Premier League in England, the competition did not have a title sponsor. By this method, the matches could be kept 'pure' in television terms. Instead, advertising boards and hospitality in stadia were offered to a select group of sponsors, who were given exclusivity in their product categories. Extending to them the status of 'Official Sponsor' enabled their product promotions to exploit their special association with an event of renown. In addition, by taking advantage of the deregulated European television market, the event sponsors could also become broadcast sponsors and have first call on advertising spots within the television programme. Apart from the obvious advantages of on-screen promotion, it prevented 'ambush marketing' – when a sponsor like Adidas is usurped by another such as Nike (which hasn't paid sponsorship money) buying television advertising spots and reaching the much larger audience television delivers, stealing the kudos of the event sponsor in the process.

Perhaps the most delicate part of Lenz's plan, as far as the clubs were concerned, was for UEFA to take absolute control of television rights. Taking these away from individual clubs might have been a contentious issue but any opposition was silenced by the income produced through TEAM's package which enticed the main networks in the key television markets. Wednesday nights were cleared of other games so that the Champions' League was the only top-flight football available. This meant it could be screened to the widest possible audience and its rarity value to television was precious. Highlights and preview programmes were incorporated as an integral part of the deal and the networks were forced to buy the entire package, for which they received exclusivity in their territory.

TEAM raised commercial considerations to the point where they were an integral part of the Champions' League, rather than an add-on, which is how football traditionally operates in this area. Both were structurally intertwined, each fuelling the other. Amazingly, the ideas were accepted by UEFA with little modification. This was in stark contrast to the FA in England which failed to follow similar advice in its own blueprint. The result for UEFA was instant success, both in gaining widespread support for the proposals and their subsequent speedy implementation. Perhaps it was too successful as no sooner had the Champions' League become reality than there were further rumblings from the clubs that it should be expanded. In 1995, the UEFA President, Lennart Johansson, acknowledged the existence of these opinions but his reaction was to attempt to resist any alteration to the new order. 'I know that certain clubs still dream of changing the Champions' League,' he said, '[but] this competition gives full satisfaction and no modification will occur before five years at least.' The powerful voices would not be stilled, however, and change occurred far earlier than Johansson had anticipated.

As a consequence of creating an elitist showcase, the other UEFA competitions, the UEFA Cup and the Cup Winners' Cup, were inevitably downgraded in comparison. Moreover, they were shoehorned into Tuesdays and Thursdays so as not to encroach on the top-of-the-bill Champions' League. This is where the system fell down somewhat. The runners-up in the Italian league, for example, felt they had as much, if not more, right to enter the premier competition as the champions of lesser leagues, such as the Austrian. Italy was, after all, ranked number one by UEFA while Austria was ranked eleventh. These clubs wanted some of the action and considered they were only being given access to a secondary contest. As the Arsenal coach, Arsène Wenger, put it, 'The UEFA Cup is a consolation prize.'

Johansson and the rest of UEFA had to recognize the inevitable and for the 1997/98 competition, for the first time, the runners-up in the eight top-ranked nations were given the opportunity to enter the Champions' League. This was achieved by allowing them to participate in a new, second qualifying round. The Champions' League was no longer the exclusive preserve of champions. To accommodate these runners-up and the champions of all but the smallest federations (such as Andorra, whose champions play in the UEFA Cup), the Champions' League section was increased from sixteen to twenty-four teams and the qualifying competition expanded. The first qualifying round now consisted of thirty 'minor' champions. The winners joined the champions from the middle-ranked countries, together with the eight second-placed teams from the top-ranked nations. The victors from the second qualifying round went into the Champions' League proper along with the pre-qualifiers, who were the holders and the champions of the top seven ranked countries. Simple it wasn't.

In opening up the Champions' League to clubs that were not champions, UEFA invited criticism from fans and media alike. This was poor public relations. Of course, the competition was no longer a league exclusively for champions. Rather, it was a proto-European league, more representative of merit and wider in scope than anything hitherto. Changing the name would have been more accurate but 'Champions' League' was now an established brand and to alter it would jeopardize its value.

The new version of the Champions' League, while it may have offended purists, certainly made economic sense. There were now two teams to follow in the major markets, increasing the number of attractive fixtures from which television could choose and doubling the possibility of chauvinistic support. In 1997, the first year of expansion, all the runners-up qualified for the league section, which perhaps justified the arguments of the clubs. Once again Arsène Wenger succinctly summed up the fast-changing scenario, when he said: 'The Champions' League is all-important. It is turning into a European League and over the next three or four years that will become more and more clear.'

In fact, the transition towards a fully-fledged European League can now clearly be detected. When the change to allow runners-up was made it was accompanied by a form of relegation as the defeated clubs from the second qualifying round of the Champions' League go into the UEFA Cup. This is how Glasgow Rangers got a second bite of the cherry (though much good it did them, as even with this helping hand they were eliminated straight away by Strasbourg, who had emerged from the much derided Intertoto Cup). Cup winners in the top eight countries who also finish second in their league are allowed into the Champions' League in preference to the Cup Winners' Cup, as happened to Barcelona. In any case, Barcelona were already eligible for the Cup Winners' Cup since they had won the trophy in 1997, beating the holders, Paris St Germain 1–0 in the final, so the 1997/98 Cup Winners' Cup was played without the holders' participation. If they had failed at the qualifying stage of the Champions' League they too would have gone into the UEFA Cup, thus downgrading the Cup Winners' Cup even further.

The next logical step is some form of promotion, perhaps with the winners of the UEFA Cup going into the Champions' League. This would give the UEFA Cup more purpose as it would be a direct feed into the main event. As UEFA at present allows the semi-finalists of the Intertoto Cup into the first round draw of the UEFA Cup (there is no Intertoto Cup final), it would merely replicate at the top of the competition what happens at the bottom, creating a channel of merit from the Intertoto Cup, through the UEFA Cup all the way to the Champions' League. It would keep alive what has always been an important element of the game, the chance for 'smaller' clubs to compete against top European opposition and perpetuate the dream of elevation to the highest level. It is this possibility, however remote, that has enabled professional football to put down roots in every corner of the world.

A measure of what the UEFA Cup can achieve for smaller clubs can be seen in the experience of Leicester City in 1997. Having qualified for the tournament by winning the Coca-Cola Cup Leicester found themselves drawn against one of Europe's bigger clubs, Atletico Madrid, who had been in the Champions' League the previous season. Indeed, Atletico were one of the favourites to win the UEFA Cup, President Jesus Gil having spent in excess of £50 million assembling a squad of stars such as Juninho and Christian Vieri, whose combined transfer fees were more than twice the cost of the entire Leicester team.

For the return leg in Leicester, the club went to extraordinary lengths to make it a true European occasion. The whole city went Spanish for a week and on match day the local paper, the *Leicester Mercury*, set the tone with a front-page headline exhorting the fans to 'Roar Us To Victory'. Outside the stadium there were Spanish bands, Spanish food was available in and around the ground and the PA system played Spanish music. Instead of the usual 'Filbert Fox' mascot, the club re-dressed the character as a flamenco dancer and added a female partner. The match programme, for many years winner of the best programme award in England, entered into the spirit of the night with a cover picture of Ian Marshall, who scored Leicester's goal in the first leg in Madrid, eating paella.

It was no coincidence that what happened at Old Trafford also happened at Filbert Street; the fans behind the goal in the South Stand remaining standing for the whole match. It was a spontaneous gesture born of tremendous excitement and the atmosphere was cranked up several levels higher than for a Premier League game. The *Mercury*, an evening paper, brought out a special edition the following morning to commemorate the event, even though the result, a 2–0 defeat on the night and a 4–1 loss on aggregate, was hardly the outcome hoped for by the Leicester public.

Events in Leicester showed how the UEFA Cup can be a credible competition in its own right and an important adjunct to the Champions' League. For Leicester it was a rare opportunity to share in the dream, for Atletico it enabled them to retain continuity at the European level even though they had failed to qualify for the premier competition. If the links were strengthened between the Champions' League and the UEFA Cup, the secondary competition would have even more purpose.

There can be no doubt that the Champions' League is now a firmly established success story. Whether purists would have preferred to carry on with the traditional knockout format without any entry by second-placed teams is beside the point. In the modern world football no longer has the field to itself, it must compete for the public's support with other sports in a way it rarely had to in the past. Rugby Union, for instance, is now professional and has gone European. For football to retain its pre-eminence, it must evolve.

The Champions' League negotiated new three-year deals with the television networks and sponsors, and these were in place for the 1997/98 competition. It is therefore unlikely that there will be any dramatic change to the format before the millennium, other than a possible increase in the number of clubs participating in the league section. However, the six groups of four system, where the winners and two best runners-up progress to the knockout stage should give way to more groups, with winners and all runners-up going forward. For this to happen, the schedule has to be stretched to accommodate the extra games each team would play in the league section. More games, of course, will mean more income. It is no exaggeration to say that the Champions' League really is the proverbial licence to print money.

The revenue-generating powers of the Champions' League have risen inexorably since its inception, despite, or perhaps because of its continuous expansion. There is now more money available than ever: two million Swiss Francs (£800,000) just for qualifying for the league; SFr 1 million for each win; SFr500,000 for each draw; SFr 3 million for each quarter-finalist; SFr3.25 million for each semi-finalist; SFr4 million for the losing finalist; SFr5 million for the winners. Points most definitely mean prizes. Even when you lose, you win, as failure in the two qualifying rounds brings in up to SFr160,000 and possible entry into the UEFA Cup. The eventual champions, therefore, could earn more than SFr17 million (£7 million) from prize money alone. Add to this the income from gate receipts, club and match sponsorship, corporate hospitality, sale of programmes and catering, which are all owned by the host club and the numbers start to fly off the cash register. Manchester United take well over £1.25 million a match from such sources. But that's not the end of the story. There is a share of the television pool, which earned Borussia Dortmund an extra SFr5.375 million (£2.1 million) when they won the Champions' League in 1997. No wonder the clubs at first welcomed UEFA's control with open arms and with wallets waiting to be filled.

The 1997 version of the Champions' League was without doubt the most important development in European football since the first European Cup more than forty years previously. It has arguably become the biggest sporting competition in the world. Sure, the Olympics and the World Cup finals attract bigger television audiences but they take place every four years and last for a mere four weeks. The Champions' League runs for nine months every year. It is true that only 50,000 can attend Old Trafford and 100,000 the Nou Camp but the television pictures are seen by more than 500 million people around the world every time a match day rolls around. The income from the 1996/97 competition outstripped USA 94 by a third and was more than double that of Euro 96. It has also answered the need for revenue of the biggest clubs and the requirement for increasing market share of television networks and sponsors. For fans, it has provided more games which they want to see. Perhaps most important of all, it has cemented the power and control of UEFA, ensuring that change can now only occur from within, thereby lessening the chances of a breakaway franchise league based on wealth alone for the moment. When the big clubs realize they will need more money to compete with their peers or simply to remain solvent, the agitation will start again.

For Manchester United at the beginning of the 1997/98 season, the income from the team's participation in the Champions' League could not disguise the disappointment engendered by the team's failure to attain European glory. While other clubs hope, Manchester expects. The coincidence of the emergence of a fledgling European league and the development of Alex Ferguson's hugely talented team gave some substance at last to the fans' desire for ultimate glory. It had taken four Premiership triumphs and two 'doubles' to get them to this position. Those successes were achieved while United were themselves being reorganized on a massive scale, a reorganization which caused its own debates and controversies, not all of them amicably resolved.

CHAPTER TWO

There's Only One United

THE FREE-KICK was perfectly struck. It bent round the wall and sailed into the top corner of the net, leaving the keeper stranded on the wrong side of the goal. Such was the virtuosity of the scorer during the previous eighty-nine minutes that those looking on sensed the outcome before the ball was kicked. Always at the heart of the action, he seemingly never wasted a pass. The crowd at Old Trafford and the millions watching on television around the world were privileged to witness a supreme exposition of the art of the modern midfielder as he seamlessly linked defence to attack. Yet Zinedine Zidane was for once on the losing side, his team defeated by one that had absorbed the painful lessons of their encounters during the previous season. That October night, Manchester United, the commercial masters of the universe, outwitted their main rivals where it mattered most, on the field of play.

The 3–2 victory over Juventus marked a turning point for Alex Ferguson's young team. Four Premiership titles in five years had raised expectations, fuelled by Sky television's unremitting hype, which assumed that since the English Premiership was the best league in the world, the

English champions should win the European Champions' League. In this they were assisted by ITV, which screened the Champions' League in the UK. It had not turned out that way, however, and United had suffered some embarrassing excursions as they learned to get to grips with the more subtle demands of their European assignment. It was now apparent that defeats at the hands of Juventus in 1996/97, when United failed miserably, and against Borussia Dortmund, when a plethora of missed chances cost them a place in the 1997 final, had been used by the manager as a learning experience.

When the 1997/98 competition again pitted United against Juventus in the group stage, the two matches became a test of their progress. Moreover, for United, as for Juventus, success in Europe was expected. Europe equalled destiny and had done so ever since the Busby Babes had begun their assault on the European Cup in the 1950s. The feeling persists to this day that United would have become the first British winners but for the Munich tragedy of 1958 and ever since the European Cup has inspired the club and fans with a sense of destiny.

Unlike Juventus, however, the expectations at United lacked real justification. It had taken twenty-six years for United to win the English championship following the success of 1967, during which period Juventus had carried off seven scudettos (Serie A titles). In the years after United's Premiership successes began, Juventus extended their domination at home into Europe, winning the Champions' League in 1996 and the World Club Championship in 1997. It says something for the expectancy in Turin that becoming Champions' League runners-up in 1997 was unacceptable and they, like Manchester United, entered the 1997/98 competition with something to prove. The feeling that the outcome of the group would depend on the matches between the two was reinforced when both won their first games convincingly, Juventus overpowering Feyenoord of Holland 5–1, United brushing aside the Slovakian champions Kosice 3–0.

Juventus, under coach Marcello Lippi, had developed a habit of selling star players, particularly forwards. The Champions' League-winning side of 1996 was broken up with the sale of Fabrizio Ravanelli and Gianluca Vialli, the pattern having been set when Roberto Baggio was transferred in 1995. After losing the 1997 final to Dortmund, Vladimir Jugovic, Allen Boksic and Christian Vieri found themselves surplus to requirements. These sales made a tidy profit for Juventus, despite the purchases of Serie A's leading scorer, Filippo Inzaghi, and Roma's Daniel Fonseca to support Alessandro Del Piero up front. The net outcome of these manoeuvres, however, was a downturn in the team's goal-scoring potential.

The Italian media called it a policy of 'creative destruction'. But there was method behind their madness. The Italians extended the Bosman ruling – which gave freedom of movement to players within the European Union – to their home market. With players signing shorter contracts and with four clubs out of eighteen relegated each season from Serie A, it was a fluid system, with players (and coaches) regularly changing clubs. Juventus's directors determined that they would cash in at the top of the market and stay in profit, without losing strength among the playing staff. The one drawback, of course, was that the onus was on the coach to establish a pattern of play which suited a new squad, and to do it quickly, at the start of the season.

Meanwhile, United, while relying on the development

of their young squad, replaced Eric Cantona, who had retired, with Teddy Sheringham, at the surprisingly low price of £3.5 million. Although Sheringham was the wrong side of thirty, he was probably the only English player who could slot into Cantona's withdrawn role, thereby obviating the need for a tactical upheaval. (Sheringham himself was so surprised at the low fee he initially thought he must be part of a player exchange. Perhaps Tottenham had allowed emotion to cloud their judgement when they became anxious to offload the player.)

There was nonetheless a widespread belief that Ferguson would have liked to augment his squad but his hands were tied by financial constraints imposed by Manchester United plc, whose first duty is to provide profits in the form of dividends for shareholders. The Chief Executive, Martin Edwards, was emphatic in his denial that the plc was guilty of parsimony. 'Last summer,' he argued in autumn 1997, 'we offered up to £60 million in trying to buy different players. We offered £10 million for Zidane. We offered £10 million for two other players in Europe (Barcelona's defender, Miguel Nadal and Gabriel Batistuta, Fiorentina's Argentinian striker) and got turned down. We offered £5 million for (Brian) Laudrup at twenty-nine, with just a year of his contract to go. We had some success because we did get Sheringham, and into the season we got (Henning) Berg (a £5 million buy from Blackburn Rovers). That was £9 million on those two players, so it wasn't as though we didn't spend money but if we'd have been more success-ful we'd have spent a lot more.'

In the absence of superstar signings, United fans, like the manager, can take satisfaction in the incredible progress achieved by the home-grown talent. Paul Scholes, the Neville brothers, Nicky Butt and David

Beckham were, after all, regular members of Glenn Hoddle's England squads (along with Teddy Sheringham and Gary Pallister), while Ryan Giggs could get into any national team (except Wales, which, for some reason, always seems to schedule its games when Giggs is injured). It is also a matter of some pride when jewels like Ole Gunnar Solskjaer are unearthed in the transfer market. However, Ferguson himself admitted in his diary of the 1996/97 season, *Will To Win*, that United's squad did not measure up to the best. 'With the likes of Juve around,' he wrote, 'we need maybe two more top-class players.'

At the pinnacle of club football, spending large amounts of money is the name of the game. The maxim 'speculate to accumulate' has no more apt application than to Europe's top football clubs. The likes of Juventus, Internazionale, Barcelona and Real Madrid, not to mention the teams in American sports which showed them the way, are not held back by such antiquated notions as an equitable wage structure. This is a self-imposed constraint used by many English clubs, more often than not to keep down overall wage bills. Nobody should object to special treatment for true stars if their acquisition works for the benefit of the team. Eric Cantona at United and Jürgen Klinsmann at Spurs fulfilled this role and there would be few supporters, players or officials who would not break any wage structure to have these particular 'Carlos Kickaballs' back. Martin Edwards argued that sometimes a line has to be drawn. 'Batistuta,' he claimed, 'would have cost £12 or £13 million, which in itself may have been acceptable but his personal terms were five times greater than our biggest wage earner. It would not have been responsible for us to have bought Batistuta because the next time . . . our players' contracts came up for negotiation the benchmark would have been Batistuta's wages.'

Edwards was presenting one side of an argument which actually points up the dilemma facing directors of football clubs who also have obligations under British company law to make decisions in the interests of shareholders. Batistuta, according to Edwards, would have cost almost twice as much as United's record signing, Andy Cole, almost three times as much as Henning Berg and almost five times as much as Teddy Sheringham. Surely his wages should reflect this valuation. Not only that, no matter what Batistuta was asking for, it is extremely doubtful if the total, spread over, say, a five-year contract, would be anything approaching the £13 million Edwards was prepared to pay to Fiorentina for his services. Who is deserving of the higher amount? Batistuta himself, who has scored goals at every level of football, including World Cup finals, or Fiorentina, which had already received the benefit of his goal-scoring prowess. As for Edwards's concerns over the renegotiation of the contracts of other players, it would surely be the case that a player at Manchester United would, in the main, only refuse to sign another contract if the wages on offer elsewhere were much higher, which in itself would be an indictment of United's lack of true ambition. Players have, over the years, dramatically improved the serf-like conditions that operated previously. Keeping a so-called wage structure, which is a euphemism for holding down overall wages, is one way in which directors have sought to limit the damage caused by the power shift.

In Martin Edwards's view, 'Getting the wage structure right is the number one priority.' He went on to explain how this is done, saying, 'Every year I sit down with the manager towards the end of the season. We look at all the contracts. In some cases you might renegotiate with two years to go. In a lot of cases it's only one year. As they get older or if someone is coming through to challenge them you might leave it longer. With the youngsters we actually negotiated with three years to go. They were on a very low wage but were doing a first-team job. And as they have continued to do well we will be talking to them well before the end of their existing contracts. It's a judgement we have to make. It's a question of fairness and their worth.'

Fairness, of course, is a relative concept. This is not to say that Edwards is any more unfair than others in similar positions. It is just that fairness has little to do with it. The art of negotiating for a plc requires some canny decisions and a clever deployment of the weapons at your disposal. The benefit to the plc has to be prioritized. Martin Edwards would not last long if he were no good in the hard world of negotiating with players' agents. Edwards recognizes this. 'If you get a salary wrong [i.e. too high],' he said, 'you can add millions to your wage bill with the knock-on effect. Within one year the knock-on effect will start because you are bound to be talking to someone who is coming to the end of a contract, or someone who deserves an increase because of the way they are playing.'

If a club adheres to a wage structure, problems may arise if it wants to compete with the world's best. Few teams can these days be considered among the best unless they have bought the best. This is why Atletico Madrid regularly break the bank, so that they can continue to challenge Barça and Real. The ultimate statement of ambition comes when a club attracts star Brazilians, like Ronaldo and Rivaldo, who (Middlesbrough's brief encounter with Juninho notwithstanding) are consistently bought by the biggest Italian and Spanish clubs. Until Manchester United and other English clubs realize this (along with the Home Office, whose over-stringent rules for non-EU players prevent many potentially great players from obtaining the necessary permit), they will always be at a disadvantage at the very top level. It is not that English coaches fail to recognize the talent of the world's top players. It was, after all, Bobby Robson who took Ronaldo to Barcelona. But when Barcelona lost Ronaldo to Inter in 1997 they immediately spent over £30 million on Sonny Anderson and Rivaldo, going some way to placate the 100,000 members who were up in arms over the loss of the world's best player. It is thus fair to say that as long as the supreme players prefer to practise their craft in Italy, Spain and even Germany rather than England, the Premiership cannot justify Sky's hype that it is the best league in the world. There is some merit in the argument that it is the most entertaining, but even that is inconclusive. Perhaps its most persuasive claim is that it's the best marketed and merchandised.

Apart from the stance taken by Martin Edwards and Manchester United plc, there is a suspicion that even Alex Ferguson too readily swaps football-speak for corporation-speak when it suits him. When Ronaldo was set to leave Barcelona and was being touted around the big clubs of Europe, Ferguson had this to say: 'Now I would love to see Ronaldo playing for Manchester United. I have a gut feeling Old Trafford would be his kind of stage. But can you really justify that kind of outlay when you are a public company?' A supporter may find such a comment surprising coming from a football manager, especially one who has, by dint of his success, become virtually unsackable. And Ferguson could have publicly taken on any board which denied him money for big signings. Instead, he appeared to be going along with an apparent lack of ambition. Commenting on the plc board's discussion of his transfer budget, Ferguson seemed at one moment let down, the next understanding. In *A Will To Win*, he said: 'The outcome of the board meeting is not what I want to hear . . . it's obvious there are going to be some constraints on the amount of cash we can spend and I see a potential area for conflict. There's nothing I can do about the board's decision so I must bite the bullet and get on with it.'

It is often the case that managers seek to blame their boards for a lack of financial support when it is their own indecision which leads to a lack of signings. Such a ploy, if successful, creates the impression that the manager is siding with the fans, leaving the board to take the heat. It is true that Manchester United plc has to give priority to the bottom line but, contrary to the prevailing view in the media, there is substantial financial backing for transfer fees and players' salaries. More to the point is the opinion of a senior colleague, who remarked, 'He [Ferguson] makes up his mind one day, one way, changes the following day and goes back to his original thought. The plc encourages him to spend money but he can't make his mind up on players.'

Ferguson, for instance, admired the talents of Zinedine Zidane while the player was at Bordeaux. Zidane, however, did not perform well in Euro 96 and United's interest cooled. In fact Zidane had been playing continuously for a year, was carrying an injury and, shortly before the tournament, had been involved in a car crash. Ferguson instead went for Karel Poborsky, who did catch the eye when playing for the Czech Republic in Euro 96, but who manifestly failed to live up to expectations at Old Trafford. Meanwhile Zidane moved to the club which had been monitoring his progress for some time and was not put off by one poor tournament – Juventus.

This quixotic nature does not sit well with Ferguson's

supposed ability to assess a footballer but there can be no doubt that Zidane was United's kind of player. Raised in football-mad Marseille, Zidane, confident of his own gifts, had taken himself off to Cannes as a youngster rather than struggle to get into Marseille's team of imported stars. At Cannes, a club which is known for a youth policy that has produced, among others, Patrick Vieira, Zidane blossomed and eventually moved to Bordeaux, where he came to the attention of the big European clubs during Bordeaux's run to the 1996 UEFA Cup final. Despite this, Ferguson passed on the player in 1996 but offered £10 million to Juventus for him in 1997, a bid which was summarily rejected.

On the day before the game against Juventus at Old Trafford, Manchester United reported their financial results for 1996/97. Turnover was up 65 per cent at £88 million. This compares to Juventus's turnover of £52 million for the same period. United's pre-tax profits were up 79 per cent to £27.6 million, whereas Juve managed less than £1 million. While there may not yet be a European Super League, Manchester United undoubtedly top the European financial league and are probably now the richest club in the world. Despite smaller crowds and cheaper ticket prices than Juventus, Manchester United take more money in gate receipts because of the burgeoning corporate hospitality sector. The two clubs received about the same from their mainstream television deals but Juventus make extra money from the Italian subscription and pay-per-view service, Telepiù, and as a result of reaching the Champions' League final. In fact, Juventus's total return from television was just over £20 million, almost twice that of Manchester United. Sponsorship income is comparable at present but United's is set to grow substantially over the next few years. The greatest disparity reveals itself in the merchandising figures, an area where United are world leaders. United's return from this source, at £28 million, is approximately five times greater than that of Juventus and provides almost a third of the club's income. Moreover, this huge sum is likely to increase year on year for the foreseeable future, particularly from the development of overseas markets. Alone among football clubs, United now stand comparison to sports franchises in the USA, which have been doing this sort of thing for many years.

The success of the team, the stadium, the media hype, created the perfect environment for the huge wealth generated by merchandising under the auspices of Edward Freedman, Managing Director of Manchester United Merchandising Ltd from 1991 to 1997. Together with Irving Scholar, Freedman pioneered football's commercial revolution at Tottenham in the late 1980s. After Scholar reluctantly handed Spurs over to Alan Sugar and Terry Venables, Freedman took his expertise north, to a somewhat disbelieving Manchester United. United, like most football clubs at that time, had signally failed to realize their commercial potential. Moreover, while Irving Scholar's reputation was undermined by Tottenham's financial failures, which were largely caused by the acquisition of peripheral businesses, Freedman's merchandising operation always remained a source of profits. In Manchester, Freedman soon began to change the culture, ousting long-held pirating operations and small-scale franchise deals. He then produced a marketing plan and recalls that 'when we [in football] realized we must treat the fan as a customer it was a big step forward'.

Under Freedman's direction Manchester United became adept at maximizing revenue from sales of replica shirts, often at the cost of great, and sometimes deserved criticism. Freedman accepts there is cause for complaint but explained the context and the options available. It transpires that there was a debate within the club over whether to accept a large cash offer from a kit manufacturer, which would result in a loss of control over retailing policy, or invest in their own operation. In Freedman's opinion, the total amount offered (by the shirt supplier, Umbro) should not have been the key factor. He went on to outline what he thought. 'I was very much in favour of doing the shirts ourselves but I understand Martin's [Edwards's] reasoning, which was [that] this particular lump of money [£58 million over five years] would underwrite an enormous number of projects. There would be no headache, no aggravation.' The decision was taken to accept the Umbro deal. Freedman then described what this meant for the fans. 'The supplier has to try and get his money back. Bringing out three shirts is wrong. There should only ever be two shirts. Possibly, instead of changing every two years, the home shirt could change every year. Fans do not buy it in the second year, they are bored with it. They are not unhappy about buying new merchandise if it is more fashionable.'

With his son James, Freedman launched the Manchester United magazine, again in the face of scepticism from the board. The directors eventually decided to back his judgement, profitably, as it turned out. The magazine, and its counterpart for youngsters, soon reached a combined circulation of over 200,000 every month. Other deals with the likes of Umbro and VCI (videos and books) followed and United's commercial income went from a paltry £1.2 million per year to a staggering £28 million in five years, in the process revolutionizing the finances of English football and helping to propel club merchandise into the forefront of the fashion industry.

'I don't understand why you are better than we are,' proclaimed Edward Freedman's counterpart at Juventus when the two met at Old Trafford. If the Italian had bothered to step inside the megastore next door perhaps he would have found enlightenment. Between 6pm and 6.30pm 1,200 people were clicked through the front door of the 5,700 square feet shop and the evening's take approached £70,000 (it's more on Saturdays). Freedman answered the implied question with one of his own. 'The Italians are very good at telling you the negatives. I've heard all the stories about [them] not owning their own stadium so they lose out on hospitality, advertising, etc. but what's that got to do with merchandising?'

To the fans and the media, there is an odious consequence to the drive for profits and that is the refusal to contemplate spending the enormous sums necessary for the world's real star players. Manchester United stands accused of attempting to buy the Champions' League on the cheap. The squad is more than adequate for the hurly-burly of the just-short-of-top-class Premier League, but on-field comparisons with Europe's best have more often than not found them wanting. Umberto Gandini, Director of Football at Milan, while admitting that the Italians could make progress off the field, nevertheless said, 'we have nothing to learn from you about football,' when speaking at a conference.

Surely 1996/97 was the year to invest, in order to meet the likes of Juventus on equal terms. It may be that United's destiny will never be fulfilled if the current strategy persists. This is because Juventus and the rest, unlike United, are football clubs first. Their policies are dictated by what happens on the field. While United never forget that football is their *raison d'être* their first obligation, as a plc, is to their shareholders.

In Italy, a successful coach is still king. In England,

finance rules the roost. Thus the biggest bone of contention within Manchester United in recent times came not with any argument over player transfers but the bad feeling caused by share options when United floated on the stock exchange. All the senior management, including Alex Ferguson, were made the same offer of shares. There was one exception, the more generous terms given to the Finance Director, Robin Launders. Only Ferguson and one other senior staffer, who thought more personnel should have been included in the scheme, failed to take up their allocation and thereby lost, according to one insider, 'an awful lot of money'. Perhaps this missed opportunity continued to fester and was the reason behind a cold spell in relations between Martin Edwards and his manager. Someone who had dealings with both of them told how, on one occasion, the frostiness manifested itself. 'Martin Edwards would not renegotiate his [Ferguson's] salary after the second double. [Edwards] thought he was asking for too much.' The stalemate was only settled by the intervention of the Chairman of the plc, Professor Sir Roland Smith, who arbitrated in the manager's favour. Ferguson came away with a salary of around £750,000 plus bonuses.

The boot is now on the other foot as Martin Edwards probably feels that Ferguson is more than adequately compensated and shouldn't have to pursue other activities. These, of course, can be immensely lucrative for a successful manager but Edwards believes that the time expended on such things as books and videos encroaches upon the day job. However, with the football biography emerging as a best-selling genre and advances for the likes of Kevin Keegan's reaching £500,000, the temptation to climb aboard the gravy train for any British manager, let alone the most successful of the breed in modern times, must be irresistible. The board may have to restrain the Chief Executive from seeking a confrontation with his most important employee over the time Ferguson will have to spend on his autobiography.

These strange goings-on might well have seen the 1997/98 European campaign going the way of previous years had fate not taken a hand. First, Ferguson's midfield linchpin, Roy Keane, destroyed his knee and ended his season in a foul on Alf Inge Haaland of Leeds on the Saturday before the Juventus game. The injury encouraged Ferguson to be more flexible with his midfield selection policy. Then, when United were forced to chase the game against Juventus after going a goal down in the first minute, the manager's perennial misjudgements over selection and tactics in Europe (this time starting with Giggs through the middle and Scholes on the bench) were paradoxically resolved as Giggs tormented Juventus down the flanks and Scholes beefed up the midfield after replacing Butt, who was injured in the first half. Both Giggs and Scholes scored crucial goals. United were further aided by some uncharacteristic indiscipline by Juventus, who were reduced to ten men after Didier Deschamps's dismissal in the second half.

Not everyone saw it this way. David Lacey, writing in the *Guardian*, was not alone in eulogizing the United performance. 'This was Manchester United's graduation ball,' he said. 'The group of freshmen overawed by their surroundings in Turin just over a year ago now wore the gowns and mortarboards of European experience.' Gary Neville, speaking the following week at the England training camp at Bisham Abbey, stressed the importance of the win when he said: 'It was a big thing for us because of the results we had against them last year. There comes a time when we had to win one of these games. We hadn't won against a side of any great importance, one of the real big teams in Europe, and last Wednesday gave us the result we needed. You can't keep telling everyone that you are the best team in Europe when you keep losing to Borussia Dortmund and Juventus. You've got to beat them otherwise you are going to be seen as someone who is shooting their mouth off.'

These views, while understandable in the context of United's bad experience over the previous few seasons, failed to take into account that Juventus were well below their best at Old Trafford. The player who was sent off, Didier Deschamps, put it this way: 'We are still not 100 per cent, which is just as well because if this was our best it would be worrying.' Zinedine Zidane added that when the return match took place in Turin he thought United would find it 'very hard'. Talking after his first season with Juventus, Zidane gave an insight into his club's philosophy. 'To win,' he said, 'is an obligation, it's normal, there's nothing to get worked up about. You must know how to appreciate this culture of winning, this desire to push yourself to the limit. It's this conviction that permits us to achieve the highest objectives.'

Despite the approach outlined by Zidane, Juventus's sale of star players seemed perverse and the team at first lost something in the process. The Rome sports paper, Corriere dello Sport, put the case best, saying, 'We sent great players like Vieri, Boksic and Jugovic to bring wealth to somebody else but we are left with poverty.' Naturally, Marcello Lippi disagreed. 'It's a question of conviction,' he said. 'Everything we do every year happens because we believe in it. If a team has made a mistake with certain choices it is not something you can say after a month . . . we have great players here. In three years they have won everything there is to be won in world football. If this season we need more time or something extra to regain that level of performance it doesn't make me believe we won't get there. It makes me think we have to work a little harder, that's all.'

At the time of the first of the two titanic struggles between Manchester United and Juventus in 1997/98, it was reasonable to suppose that the matches might well decide which of the two would progress to the quarter-final stage of the Champions' League. The win in Manchester saw United in pole position and it was now by no means certain that the second-placed team in the group would qualify. The words of *Corriere dello Sport* would then prove to be prophetic. But there was more at stake than just the head-to-head rivalry between two club teams, however grand their pedigree and however high their ambitions. The two squads provide several players for their respective national teams and England and Italy were in a similar position to United and Juventus – fighting each other for one guaranteed place in a knockout tournament, in this case the World Cup finals. Not long after the Juventus game, England were to face Italy in the most important match of the qualifying phase for both countries. Glenn Hoddle could take heart from the performance of the United youngsters, who formed the backbone of his England squad. Cesare Maldini, recently recalled to rejuvenate a moribund Italy, had more cause to worry, as the Italian team had been below par for some time. By Christmas, the prospects for 1998 for Juventus, Manchester United, England and Italy would be clearer.

CHAPTER THREE

A Night for Villains and Heroes

R OME IS NO stranger to violence at sports events, indeed it was the reason organized sport took place at all in ancient times. The ritual aggression reached its apotheosis in human sacrifice: 'We who are about to die, salute you.' With such a lineage, it is hardly surprising that the modern Roman police force, when faced with marauding hordes of British barbarians, sought retribution in the baton.

When Italy entertained England in the vital, last qualifying game for the 1998 World Cup finals, the Stadio Olympico had lost the capability even to match ticketholders with their designated seats. It was a state of affairs tailor-made for barbarians to exploit. And nobody, however high and mighty, was immune to their malevolence. This much was forcibly brought home to Trevor East, Sky's Director of Sport, when he attended the game as a member of the England travel club with his party of family and friends, which included the Derby County manager, Jim Smith. Their places were already occupied by bellicose Englishmen unwilling to relinquish their seats. Some of the troublemakers were Oxford United fans and their excesses were only curbed when they recognized their former manager, Smith. Unable to garner support from Italian officials, East and his entourage were forced to return to their hotel and, ironically, watch the second half of the game he had secured for his employers on television. Anger and frustration, however, gave way to relief when it dawned on them how lucky they had actually been.

Euro 96 had seen an improvement in the comportment of English fans. The refurbishment of the walkway between Wembley Park station and Wembley stadium incorporated such modern developments as toilet facilities, which reduced the disgusting displays of urination which had hitherto been a feature of the route. The provision of official outlets dispensing food, merchandise and programmes now almost makes the half-mile walk a tolerable experience. However, the same cannot be said for the nightmare tube journey from central London. Passengers invariably have to suffer aggressive and boorish behaviour, apparently a prerequisite of supporting England. For far too long bad behaviour has been tolerated, as long as it stops short of physical violence. Experienced policing and segregation have largely eliminated anarchy from stadia, engendering an air of complacency on the part of the authorities. This is exemplified by former Home Office minister turned football pundit, David Mellor, who said: 'We've got to stop rubbishing ourselves too much. Dutch and German supporters are notoriously violent and more violent than our people.' While this may be true, it is undeniable that no country exports disorder the way England does.

Travelling abroad, of course, gives the worst English supporters far more scope for causing chaos than they get at home. Not only is there a reputation to live up to but also more freedom to engage in mayhem. Generally, when they are arrested, they spend a night or two in prison, itself a mark of pride, before being deported back to these shores. So common have these drunk and disorderly incidents become they are a permanent and defining feature of perceptions of the English football supporter around the world. The syndrome even has a name: the English Disease.

As the Rome game drew near, the implications for England's huge travelling support became apparent. David Mellor was first into the fray. As well as his media profile, Mellor had retained his links with government through being appointed head of a Task Force to examine football's inequities by Sports Minister and fellow Chelsea fan, Tony Banks. Mellor's exalted status led him, on his own initiative, to seek a meeting with the Italian ambassador to ensure that peaceful English fans were not subjected to rough justice. He announced afterwards that he had received assurances from the police in Rome that supporters would be treated as their behaviour warranted.

While the hype intensified, the National Football Intelligence Unit went public with the information that its officers had identified hundreds of potential troublemakers who intended to go to Rome. Furthermore, the Unit said the English authorities were powerless to stop them travelling, as they were EU citizens who had committed no known offence. This news was greeted with apprehension, especially in Italy. By the week of the game, the feeling was one of impending doom.

Unfortunately, the bellicose tendency among England's fans did not disappoint. Large numbers entered Rome on the day before the match, a Friday, giving them ample time to display the full range of their appalling behaviour, which was founded on drunkenness and xenophobia. Amazingly, few were arrested, despite the widespread disorder. This emboldened the English and infuriated the stadium authorities, who determined to prevent any recurrence on match day. To that end, they called up the riot squad. The members of this elite unit were driven by one basic tactic, which was to get their retaliation in first. They were not about to take the time to differentiate between normal, peaceful English supporters and the hooligan element. To them, all the English were incorrigible barbarians, who would only understand refinement if it hit them over the head.

All might not have been lost had there been any kind of organization at the Stadio Olympico. But there was a total breakdown in ticketing and stewarding. Some of the gates were closed and fans were told to sit anywhere. Abuse and coin throwing from the Italian fans elicited a predictable response. The riot police attacked the English and the first half was punctuated by ugly skirmishing in the stands. After the final whistle, most English fans were locked in the stadium for up to three hours, their transport to the city centre and the airport removed.

The English football authorities tend to take action only when forced to by external pressure. The Rome affray, covered as it was by live television, demanded a response, and the FA's was to rush out a report within two weeks which blamed everything on the Italians. The FA's view was supported by David Mellor, who felt personally let down. He proceeded to take the Italians to task for the worthlessness of the assurances they had given him. In his opinion it was simply 'a policing problem' and the Italians had failed to deal with it. 'If the English police had reacted like that, cracking heads indiscriminately, there would have been a public enquiry,' he said. FIFA, under whose auspices all World Cup games are played, later produced their own verdict which largely concurred with the FA.

None of the inquests, however, gave any confidence that such incidents could be avoided in the future. With the World Cup finals taking place less than nine months later in France – the easiest overseas place for the English to travel to – the lack of anything stronger than calls for more sophisticated policing did not bode well. Efforts to keep the worst of the barbarians at home, through wider use and stricter enforcement of existing legislation, such as exclusion orders, were noticeable by their absence. Nor was there to be any review of the workings of the England travel club, even though some of the vandals in Rome openly boasted of their membership. And what on earth is the point of a Football Intelligence Unit if it cannot prevent those it identifies as troublemakers from making trouble? Given that sending English plainclothes police to operate on foreign soil can be a delicate diplomatic issue, the solution must be found at home.

Steve Curry, for many years the chief football correspondent of the *Daily Express* and now with the *Sunday Telegraph*, spoke for many in the media when he tried to ensure that the excesses of the Italian police did not obscure what he saw as the main issue. 'If we are going to try and pretend that we do not have a serious hooligan problem then we are really shutting our eyes,' he warned. Curry's diagnosis was simple. 'We've got to stop these people travelling abroad. Otherwise they are going to do it every time England play.' David Mellor's initial response, while reasonable in itself, starkly demonstrated why a solution has not yet been found. 'This is a serious and substantial point of principle,' he said. 'We decided [when he was at the Home Office and hooliganism was in full flood back in the 1980s] we could not give the authorities the power to remove people's passports without a proper order of the court and a criminal conviction, because in a free society, once you start giving power to the authorities, it can be exercised arbitrarily.' Italian culpability notwithstanding, Mellor, having discussed the problem with Tony Banks, admitted to having second thoughts. 'I now think we've got to revisit that,' he said. 'We've got to see if there is some kind of offence created whereby the police produce what evidence they've got about trouble, there is some kind of adjudication and passports are removed.'

As the law stands, offenders can only be dealt with retrospectively, once any Restriction Order has been breached. In addition, they cannot be prevented from leaving the country earlier than they normally would. Perhaps this is why fewer than a dozen such orders have been imposed since 1990. Legally and practically, it is a pretty pointless exercise. Preventing people travelling abroad on evidence which does not reach meticulous standards can and will lead to injustices. There are already cases going before the European Court because of this issue. Moreover, it is foolish to believe that all troublemakers, or even a significant proportion of them, can be identified and stopped. And anyway, passports within the European Union are no longer needed between certain countries who have signed up to the Schengen Agreement, which seeks to promote total free-dom of movement within the Union's frontiers. Thus a group determined to get around the present system could travel to France via a third country without having to produce any documentation.

It is a pity the English, whose support is founded upon the most unpalatable kind of patriotism, cannot learn from the Scots and Irish, whose unqualified support for their teams does not go beyond the idea of a marvellous adventure. If the problem is to be tackled at all it surely must start at the beginning, with a zero tolerance policy applied at Wembley games when so-called fans partake in the ritual booing of opponents' national anthems. Only by starting at this basic level can the confrontations that are waiting to happen be avoided. From there, domestic policy can be internationalized. English football has, after all, begun to tackle the problem of racist chanting and abuse through grassroots campaigns, which are beginning to make such behaviour socially unacceptable. Much more would be achieved if some of football's millions were used to fund more high-profile schemes, such as a mainstream advertising campaign to supplement the worthy, but largely ineffectual pleas in match-day programmes. Nevertheless, there have been successes and the lessons from them need to be learned and applied. This would be a better bet than attempting to impose unworkable criminal sanctions, which only serve to increase the bravura of the demented.

Immediately after the game, Glenn Hoddle was asked to comment on the violence. Filled with emotions generated by his team's excellent performance, Hoddle was initially dismissive. 'It's not a night to be talking about crowd trouble,' he exclaimed, 'it's a night to be talking about a proud nation that's qualified.' But it was precisely the 'proud nation' mentality, perverted and distorted as it was, that lay behind the trouble in the first place. Moreover, stereotyping by the media incites a confrontational atmosphere; England, represented by the bulldog spirit and the flag of St George, against the Italians, portrayed as cheats, whingers and divers (and don't forget the war).

The trouble in Rome overshadowed what should have been a joyous celebration. After all, the 0–0 draw had consigned the Italians to a play-off which they would have to win to make it to France 98, whereas England had automatically qualified. That situation, reversing some historic failures, deserved all the attention but was caught up in the wake of what happened off the pitch and the arguments afterwards over who was to blame. One point about the shameful incidents, though, was that they obscured somewhat the way the FA used shrewd tactics to gain an advantage before a ball was kicked in Rome.

After England's defeat in the earlier Wembley game against Italy, Glenn Hoddle took stock and saw the encounter as a bench-mark in terms of what not to do. For instance, the coach thought the Italians had been handed a crucial advantage by knowing well in advance what team and formation he intended to deploy. Hoddle became determined to control the situation for the Rome match and in conjunction with the FA's David Davies, devised a strategy of disinformation primarily designed to mislead the Italian coach.

The first ploy was to play to the Italian belief that although English football had improved technically, the English would not be able to resist a deep-seated urge to compete and would go for a win, even though a draw was all that was needed. 'There's a result to get,' Hoddle said, 'and if we go and try to defend to get a draw, I don't think it's our natural instinct to do that. What we have got to say is that we have done reasonably well away from home and we have got to make one more concerted effort to win the group.'

Hoddle and Davies followed this up with a strategy aimed at putting distance between the squad and the media, using set-piece press conferences and selected interviews to control the flow of information. Italian journalists expected greater access, which is exactly what they got with their own team and officials at the Italian training camp. In contrast, England's availability, both at Bisham Abbey before the party left for Rome and when they arrived in Italy, remained restricted.

The media were only allowed to see some basic training, such as shooting practice and twenty-minute mixed team games, which made it difficult to discern Hoddle's thoughts on selection. Journalists were not best pleased that they were forced to hang around in the car park at Bisham when the closed training sessions overran. Attention was diverted by discussion of who the captain was going to be and although it was later denied, the media were steered in the direction of Tony Adams, and a number of stories were published to this effect. This made them even more miffed when it was finally announced that Paul Ince would wear the captain's armband.

These diversions were followed up in Rome when minor fitness problems with Gareth Southgate and David Beckham were exaggerated to lay a false trail. David Davies then tried to bring journalists into the conspiratorial loop, exhorting them, if they found out who was going to be in the team, to 'fray the edges' of their reporting. As a former reporter himself, Davies knew this was against journalistic instinct, so he invoked a version of the wartime 'national interest' to justify his request.

At a key press conference at Bisham on the Monday, it was simply not on Glenn Hoddle's agenda to discuss any specifics concerning the potential team or the tactics it would employ, although he revealed that, even though kick-off was six days away, he knew 'exactly what my team is going to be'. His thoughts, though, were presented in the most general of terms and repeated over and over again, revealing an ability to come up with the right-sounding platitudes. 'We know this is going to be a very tight game again like Wembley was,' he opined. 'I think the team that settles down and can play as naturally as possible to whatever set of tactics they choose will win the game. It's our job all this week to make sure we get the right balance in the team, to make sure the players go out and perform. The players and myself know exactly the task in hand. They are focused and they are up for it but nice and relaxed at the same time.' Totally at ease with his audience, Hoddle talked in a bizarre mixture of metaphysical language and football cliché. There were references to 'inner belief' and coping with pressure, along with the more prosaic opinion that, 'If we don't concede a goal early doors that pressure might turn on them. It's up to me to put my tactics down and play the team that suits those tactics.'

The surroundings at the Bisham press conference mirrored the unreal nature of what was happening. The forty-foot-long, wood-panelled Warwick Room, with its ornate gilt-framed portraits of haughty Jacobean ladies, lent an incongruous context to the plastic table at which Hoddle and Davies sat. Journalists were arranged in eight rows of plastic chairs, about forty in total, and they participated in the ritual by asking questions that could be answered without giving away any hard information.

This 'tell-the-media-nothing' attitude was complemented by those with whom the head coach chose to surround himself. Their primary qualification seemed to be their affinity with Glenn the player, manager or friend, and their ability to remain loyal to the tight circle. The atmosphere was always convivial but this merely made it easier to say nothing and Hoddle's staff, like their boss, were hardly forthcoming with pertinent points. Unlike his predecessor, Terry Venables, who called in Don Howe to organize the defence, Hoddle had made no overtures to experienced international campaigners. Indeed, they couldn't boast any great coaching success between them. John Gorman, for instance, had been an assistant at Bristol City, Hoddle's second in command at Swindon Town and, when Hoddle went to manage Chelsea, the man who oversaw relegation from the Premiership at the west country club. Then there was Glenn Roeder, a failed Watford manager, and Ray Clemence, who hardly set the world alight when he managed Barnet and Tottenham. The Under-21 side was entrusted to Peter Taylor, plucked from the obscurity of non-league club Dartford. No one on this list was in a position to challenge Glenn Hoddle even if they wanted to.

Hoddle, though, is nothing if not a fast learner and has firm ideas of how he expects players under his command to perform. At Swindon and Chelsea, for instance, he brought in a sweeper system and made sure that all of the playing staff, including those in youth teams, understood the system and were comfortable with it. The success he enjoyed at both clubs also showed an ability to communicate his ideas and ensure his players could carry out his instructions, even if they were alien to the traditional English footballer.

Hoddle's way of working helped him maintain an unassailable position. He became cagey and expedient, but presented a friendly, helpful face to the world. Allowances were made for the excesses of Paul Gascoigne and Ian Wright because they were necessary to his plans, whereas the young Rio Ferdinand was dropped from the Moldova squad because of a drink-driving offence, a sacrifice Hoddle could afford to make. He also managed to make a point to the Liverpool Spice Boys, Robbie Fowler and Steve McManaman, by leaving them out after they made themselves unavailable for the summer Tournoi de France due to injury. Commenting on their withdrawal, Hoddle said: 'I don't get annoyed, I get even.' They were soon back in the squad, though, if not in the team.

Glenn Hoddle shares with Alf Ramsey a complete conviction in his own abilities and a total belief in what he is doing, sometimes to the point of stubbornness. This makes him one of a rare breed, a seemingly self-contained person able to cope with the demands of the most pressurized of jobs even while his marriage of eighteen years was disintegrating. His announcement of his separation from his wife was made within a day of World Cup qualification, and not even his closest friends knew it was coming. Yet through it all Hoddle was able to remain personable and affable, while single-mindedly orchestrating 'a performance on the night [that] was as professional as I could ever have hoped for.'

Glenn Hoddle the player was always viewed by his England managers as something of a luxury. Even though he won fifty-three caps, neither Ron Greenwood nor Bobby Robson had sufficient confidence in him to build a team round his extravagant gifts, which said more about their lack of imagination than Hoddle's shortcomings. Their attitude to Hoddle was summed up by Brian Glanville in the *Sunday Times* after England lost to Denmark at Wembley in 1983. 'Now Robson tells us he wants Hoddle, provided he will play more than twenty minutes in each half. That's forty minutes, sports fans! Would that Gregory, Wilkins and Lee had given us forty decent minutes between them.'

The ex-Chairman of Spurs, Irving Scholar, who, like many, idolized Hoddle as a player, never thought he possessed the necessary toughness to succeed as a coach or manager. As a player Hoddle only had to worry about himself. To do his job now he simply extends his 'inner belief' (a favourite maxim) to others. 'I have always been focused,' he says, 'I have always been a guy that's had total belief in my own ability. As a coach you have to get that through to your players. That's the important thing.

The coach can go out there with all the belief in the world but if the players don't want it . . .' The determination to succeed has always been there but now, to fulfil his own expectations as a manager, he has found a different expression of his attributes. Like George Graham, who was also a player of subtlety, Hoddle sees managerial success as a result of putting organization before flair. Hence the transformation into the assured, calculating strategist who demands absolute control in order to do things his way. Ironically, the one flirtation with his past, the selection for the Wembley game against Italy of Matt Le Tissier, the nearest contemporary incarnation of Hoddle himself, was soon consigned to the wastebin of history.

Before the Rome match, the coach of the Italian World Cup-winning team of 1982, Enzo Bearzot, in a prescient intervention, warned his countrymen that Italy would face difficulty if England eschewed their instincts, retained possession and made defence their priority. They could do this, he said, if they flooded the midfield and restricted themselves to counter-attacks. After all, he reminded everyone, England only needed to draw to top the group, whereas Italy had to win.

As it turned out, Hoddle's and Davies's pre-match strategy was justified as the Italians were unprepared for England's tactics, which were exactly as Bearzot thought they might be. A 3–5–1–1 formation put the emphasis on teamwork and possession. Every player stuck to his allotted role. The discipline was maintained for the whole match, which drew the comment from the Blackburn and former Internazionale coach, Roy Hodgson, that 'there were times, especially in the first half, when those three midfield players [Ince, Batty and Gazza], just passed the ball around so well that the Italians could not get near them.'

England had only taken one point in the two games against Italy, yet even the Italian press agreed that they deserved to qualify at Italy's expense. 'Today, Italy is inferior to England,' pronounced the Milan sports daily, *Gazzetta dello Sport*. 'They [Italy] are not as assured, they cannot match their [England's] control of play, nor their adaptability. The lions who once knew only how to launch the ball and run under it, tackle, cross and mix it up, now dribble with skill, take control of the action, take possession with elegance and look for the winning chance.' While the praise was exaggerated, it reflected the widespread surprise that England had matched the Italians at their own game. Indeed, England had surpassed them with away victories in Georgia and Poland, where Italy could only draw.

In a tight and nervous encounter, Italy were shown six yellow cards and had Angelo Di Livio sent off. England's five yellows showed that the fighting qualities of the team mirrored the hostile passion of the crowd. The contest, in fact, went right down to the wire. In a game of few clear-cut chances, either side could have won in stoppage time. Ian Wright hit the post from an acute angle after he had rounded goalkeeper Angelo Peruzzi, then, when Teddy Sheringham lost possession from the rebound, the ball was worked upfield in typical Italian counter-attacking style. Alessandro Del Piero's accurate cross from the left found Christian Vieri perfectly placed. He should have hit the target but headed the ball wide of David Seaman's goal.

England were through and Hoddle, the coaching staff and the team, hugged each other in ecstatic reaction. There appeared to be a genuine rapport between the coach and his squad; together they had succeeded. England were one of nine European group winners who qualified automatically, along with Scotland, who had the best record of the second-placed teams. Italy were one of eight runners-up who were forced into a series of play-offs. They eventually edged into the finals by getting past Russia. A 1–1 draw in the snow of Moscow was followed up with a narrow 1–0 victory in Naples and Italy were there – just.

For Glenn Hoddle there was the satisfaction that he had qualified for a major tournament at the first time of asking. Although Graham Taylor had managed a similar feat, qualifying for the European Championships in Sweden in 1992, the feeling persisted that Hoddle's feat could mark a turning point in England's international fortunes. Hoddle's method was more reminiscent of Alf Ramsey, who, while not having to qualify for the 1966 World Cup, turned England into world beaters after they had ignominiously crashed out of the 1962 World Cup in Chile. Ramsey's turning point had come after beating Spain in an away match in 1965 with the then revolutionary 4–4–2 formation. It was unlikely that Hoddle would stick rigidly to any one inflexible system like Ramsey, but he had built a squad which appeared to share the disciplined approach of the 1966 winners.

At home, the whole of England basked in the glory of an Italian job well done. Speaking before the game, Hoddle had insisted on injecting a note of realism, saying, 'I think the squad has grown [since the previous year] but we are by no means anywhere near the finished article. You never have the finished article in football anyway. What you try to do is to strive to get there.' With some pundits deciding that England could go 'all the way' after the Roman experience, Hoddle put matters into perspective when he confirmed that, 'We are learning. The hard work starts now.'

The hard work for the FA was also just starting. Its lobbying for England to be seeded in the group stage of the finals was rebuffed by FIFA but England did benefit from an amnesty on yellow cards collected in the qualifying competition. This enabled Sol Campbell to be available for selection for the first game in France. Which team that game would be against was about to be determined, as FIFA's very own game-show host stepped out from the shadows to spin the wheel of fortune.

CHAPTER FOUR

Carry On World Cup

THE SECRETARY GENERAL of the Fédération Internationale de Football Association (FIFA), Mr Joseph 'Sepp' Blatter, despite being one of nature's bureaucrats, is no stranger to public occasions. Not all of them, however, have gone smoothly. At the Stade-Vélodrome in Marseille on 4 December 1997, Blatter was ringmeister of the World Cup draw for the thirty-two qualifying countries. The first of a galaxy of football luminaries to assist the Secretary General was Franz Beckenbauer and, naturally, Blatter welcomed him in their native German. The moment the cursory greeting was completed, however, Blatter launched into a series of instructions – in high-speed French. When he was finished, the multilingual Secretary General asked Beckenbauer if he had understood. A startled Beckenbauer, who obviously had not kept up with Blatter's linguistic gymnastics, looked like a rabbit caught in a headlight beam. 'Non,' he blurted out to Blatter and over a billion television viewers in 170 countries. Carry On World Cup had begun.

In the best showbusiness tradition, Sepp Blatter ploughed on regardless, as if nothing untoward had occurred. Perhaps he had long harboured secret desires to be a game-show presenter. More likely, he had summoned up the reserves of decorum learned the hard way – from bitter experience at the hands of Hollywood's finest when the previous World Cup draw was made in Las Vegas for USA 94. On that occasion, FIFA made the mistake of inviting a number of 'A list' celebrities who had no particular connection with football. Among them was the actor and comedian, Robin Williams. Throughout the proceedings Williams insisted on referring to the Secretary General as 'Mr Bladder'.

This embarrassment was merely continuing the tradition of other less than perfect World Cup draws. For instance, for Spain 1982, the same system was used as for the Spanish Lottery, with balls buzzing around in wire cages. Unfortunately, the contraption broke down and the balls had to be prised out by hand. This led to the adoption of a simpler method, not the black velvet bag so beloved of the FA for so many years, but a number of what can only be described as giant salad bowls, with the balls picked out by hand. For Italia 90, the *Guardian*'s David Lacey recalled that 'Sophia Loren was persuaded to fondle the little footballs as only she could and the rest was straight out of a Fellini film.' This was a reference to a smoke machine, which was deployed to add an air of fantasy but went haywire and enveloped the hall with smog.

The Italians, though, hit the right note by closing the 1990 tournament with the first 'Three Tenors' concert (Pavarotti, Domingo and Carreras), which was encored in Los Angeles in 1994. The French organizing committee picked up on this cultural theme for the initial World Cup draw in 1996, when the participants were divided into groups for the qualifying tournament. The French held the draw in the Louvre, making an extravagant statement in the process. France 98 was envisaged as an epoch-making event, bringing together sport and art in a marriage of popular and high culture. The French love a big event, particularly if they can show off their cultural wares to a foreign audience.

Until the French got involved, World Cup draws, while televised around the world, were small, intimate affairs, only enlivened by borrowed glamour from guest celebrities and the perennial gaffes. This traditional approach was opposed for France 98 by a man whose exploits had made him a national hero, Michel Platini. The proceedings should, said Platini, 'involve supporters of football. Previously this type of event was always reserved for a few hundred VIPs.' What lent weight to Platini's view was the fact that he had been recruited to the French World Cup Organizing Committee as co-President and was, most unusually for a former player, in a position of some power. Once Platini's opinion gained widespread support, the decision was taken to hold the draw in a stadium. From there, the agenda grew and it was decided that the draw would be built around a gala match, played mainly for schoolchildren, between Europe and the Rest of the World, with one player from every qualifying nation taking part.

The choice of Marseille was in part conditioned by climatic considerations. Being the most southerly big city in France it stood the best chance of having reasonable weather in December. However, in the days leading up to the ceremony, the Mistral started to blow and temperatures dropped to freezing-point. Luckily, the wind abated on the appointed day, but it remained cold enough to force many of the participants to don winter coats, which detracted somewhat from the intended festive spirit.

Never mind, Sepp Blatter was there to run the show. Blatter arrived on stage wearing a face microphone of the kind usually reserved for the likes of Madonna, which enables performers to sing and dance at the same time, hardly a necessary activity for the Secretary General of FIFA. Blatter's entrance provoked a cacophony of noise from the assembled French crowd, which was only transformed into applause when the city of Marseille was mentioned. The World Cup trophy itself was delivered on to the stage by the head of the Brazilian Football Federation, Ricardo Teixeira, who ceremoniously handed it over to his French counterpart, Claude Simonet. The symbolism of this ritual involving holders and hosts was lost on the live audience, however. They took the opportunity roundly to boo Simonet because of the decision of the French federation to relegate the local club, Olympique Marseille, from France's top division. FIFA had insisted on this action following the bribery and debt scandals which had plagued both the club and its ex-President, Bernard Tapie, since they won the Champions' Cup in 1992. Blatter too suffered the crowd's opprobrium when he asked for 'a little bit of attention so you can follow the draw'. It was as well that the administrators soon gave way on stage to the entertainers. These included the African singer, Youssou N'Dour, and the Belgian chanteuse, Axelle Red, who performed the France 98 official theme song, 'Les Cours des Grands' (The Playground for Grown-Ups).

In 170 countries across the globe 'Les Cours des Grands' seamlessly segued into a commercial break dominated by FIFA's official suppliers, partners and sponsors. The global economic transaction – worth billions of dollars – that the World Cup has become, swung into operation. In France, the host broadcaster, TF1, not only carried advertisements paid for by FIFA's favoured corporations, it also sold the rights to sponsor its World Cup broadcasts to three companies, Mastercard, Crédit Agricole and Manpower. It was a cornucopia of sport-driven commercial activity, even though the draw was just an aperitif for the upcoming summer extravaganza.

When Sepp Blatter returned to the stage, he was helped out by famous players, past and present. Many of them were French and there was one member of the USA's World Cup-winning women's team, Mia Hamm. Like Blatter, they were all fitted with face-mikes, which were superfluous to say the least since all they were required to utter was *oui* and *merci*. When they had completed their tasks (selecting balls from the salad bowls and handing them to Blatter) they were chased off the stage by Footix, a garish red, blue and yellow bird-like mascot. Footix drew criticism from a number of quarters and indeed was damned by Michel Platini's faint praise. 'On the short-list [of designs] we had five cocks and a frog. For an animal, it's not bad,' he explained. Worse, Footix was not the only mascot. The French team, suffering from a bad case of commercial overkill, had its own, a sad duck-like creature called Jules, named after Jules Rimet, the founding father of the World Cup. Rimet's family not unnaturally thought his memory was being tainted by its association with the Donald Duck-in-a-beret character. Platini said, 'I don't think it is normal that there is a second mascot when the organizing committee already has one.' The row was put into perspective by Monaco's young star, Thierry Henry, who said: 'I don't give a damn about the mascot. For all I care, it could have been a penguin dressed up as a drag queen.'

The draw itself was a relatively straightforward affair, despite Sepp Blatter's attempts to complicate it by announcing that teams would be drawn 'horizontally and vertically'; in plain English, according to seeding. As Blatter read out each country, the representative player who had taken part in the earlier Europe v Rest of the

World match was led on to the stage. (When Scotland were drawn, Darren Jackson's name was announced but Gordon Durie emerged, having replaced Jackson a couple of days previously. During the game, he had been called Ian Durie, presumably because the public address announcer was a Blockhead.) The fuss over the allocation of the eight groups should not divert anyone from the real deal. The cost of the show in Marseille, some £2 million, was earned back many times over through commercial revenue from worldwide television transmissions.

England came out of the draw in good shape, despite being unseeded. They could be forgiven for thinking their luck was in when they were placed in the same group as Romania, Colombia and Tunisia. With typical understatement, Glenn Hoddle said: 'All in all it could have been a lot worse and we're not too disappointed.' What he didn't say was that for one moment it looked as if it was going to be a lot better. England could have been drawn with Germany and two no-hopers. As it was they had three difficult opponents to face. Even if France 98 were the biggest finals ever, at least there would be no complicated mathematical formula for ascertaining the best third-placed teams as only the first two in each group would progress (the system will, perhaps, prove to be a precursor for the Champions' League). Ladbrokes installed England as joint third favourites to win the World Cup at 7–1, along with Germany and Italy. Brazil were made favourites at 3–1, while France's odds were 6–1. The poor Scots (at 100–1) drew the short straw again. They were placed with Brazil, Norway and Morocco but at least had the consolation of knowing they would play the holders in the tournament's opening showcase match.

The day before the draw, a nostalgic Sepp Blatter

waxed lyrical over his role in the ritual. Having officiated at twenty-five such events since he cut his teeth in the 1979 Youth World Cup, he was perhaps entitled to elevate its importance in the scheme of things. 'The draw is my job and my responsibility,' he crooned, 'I've given the draws a festival atmosphere. You have to admit it is more pleasant . . .' The sixty-two-year-old Secretary General also admitted his love of performing and recalled his student theatrical days, which might explain the tacky presentation with face-mikes. 'Comedy suited me better than tragedy,' he said. What he preferred not to recall, however, was his presidency of the international society in favour of women wearing suspenders, dismissing it as a 'jape' and a result of his linguistic abilities. But once a suspender man, always a suspender man.

Sepp Blatter joined FIFA in 1975 and became Secretary General in 1981. By 1994, Blatter felt that the ageing FIFA President, João Havelange, then seventy-eight, was ready to relinquish his position and he, Blatter, was the natural successor. However, Havelange had no such intention and while Blatter was the consummate bureaucrat, in order to become President, he would have to fight an election. And in that murky, political world, there are few better operators than João Havelange. Havelange had become head of FIFA in 1974, when he conducted a brilliant campaign to oust the incumbent, Sir Stanley Rous, who was outmanoeuvred at every turn. Havelange had since ensured that come each successive election, he was returned unopposed. Havelange publicly rebuked the Secretary General after Blatter, encouraged by UEFA, had flirted with the idea of standing for the office Havelange was determined to hold on to for at least another four years. João Havelange and no other would determine the timing of his departure and probably the name of his successor too. As the President himself declared, 'For twenty-four years I have worked night and day for football. The greatest difficulty is not in arriving but to know when to leave.' The difference this time was that Havelange had announced his decision to retire after France 98, so someone had to succeed him.

In the run-up to the finals, another potential successor to Havelange emerged, in the ample shape of Lennart Johansson, President of UEFA, who had been forced to watch from the sidelines as Havelange tried to whittle away UEFA's power within FIFA in favour of South America, Africa and Asia. Johansson's candidacy in 1998 annoyed Havelange even more than Blatter's had in 1994. This was probably because Johansson's manifesto promised to democratize FIFA. 'I would like to see FIFA play by their own statutes,' Johansson exclaimed. 'I would like to delegate responsibility and encourage people to develop themselves. I would involve the confederation presidents more.' No doubt Havelange saw this as criticism of his more autocratic regime. On a personal level, Havelange blamed Johansson for forcing through the joint hosting of the 2002 World Cup. Havelange had favoured the candidacy of Japan over South Korea but felt that he had to go along with the European proposal for sharing, against his better judgement, 'as a president mustn't lose'.

As President of UEFA for the last seven years, Johansson has ensured that the European governing body was not usurped by the big clubs, which have sought an increasing share of what has become a multi-million pound industry. But if the Champions' League is the result of moving with the times, UEFA's response to Jean Marc Bosman's appeal for freedom of contract was Canute-like. Having lost an embarrassing and costly court case, Johansson still hopes that the European Union will treat football as a special case. This naivety makes this essentially amiable, sixty-eight-year old grandfather an unlikely choice to head up what is, in effect, a multi-national corporation that is often embroiled in sensitive political issues. As if to prove the point, Johansson's jokey manner landed him in hot water when, in an astonishing interview reported in the Swedish newspaper, *Aftonbladet*, in November 1996, he was quoted as saying (about an argument he had been having with Havelange over the prospective hosts for the 2006 World Cup), 'When I got to South Africa the whole room was full of blackies and it's fucking dark when they sit down all together. What's more, it's no fucking fun when they're angry.' His apology (even though there may have been a misinterpretation) coupled with his undeniable and wholehearted record of support for African football, enabled him not only to continue his campaign, but apparently to retain support from the African states, who gave him the benefit of the doubt. Despite this support, Havelange did not want Johansson at any price, and in the absence of any other declared candidate he executed a perfect volte-face and endorsed Blatter for the post. 'If my friend wins I will shake his hand, if he loses I will weep,' Havelange declared.

For Sepp Blatter, however, it was a case of once bitten, twice shy. His first reaction was to distance himself from any thoughts of running for the highest office. 'It's thoughtful [of Havelange to recommend me],' mused Blatter. 'I can take from that a confirmation of my worth, but leave me where I am . . . Confucius said "Never mind the title, it's the power that counts." ' Blatter was referring to the relative positions of President and Secretary General. The President, while honorary in name, has one of the most powerful positions in world sport. However, it is the Secretary General who takes day-to-day charge of FIFA's affairs. Havelange had the vision and shaped the policies, Blatter made sure they were carried out. 'I myself like to be involved in daily problems, that's what enthrals me,' he said.

FIFA has come in for criticism over the years for its autocratic tendencies. It recoils in horror at the idea of clubs or federations using the courts to settle disputes, preferring its own internal arbitration. After the scandal of the Marseille bribery case, FIFA actually incorporated a rule change which sought to abolish any right of litigation. This desire to be omnipotent – a sovereign super-state – extends to many areas. For instance, FIFA wanted to bend the rules of football itself to win over the American public and attract the major US television networks. Prior to USA 94 it promoted the use of bigger goals, kick-ins instead of throw-ins and four quarters to replace two halves. A worldwide outcry forced the abandonment of these extraneous stunts but FIFA has carried on pushing for other changes, switching the emphasis to internal reforms, such as stricter application of existing laws. 'The World Cup is the shop window,' Blatter stressed. 'If you can get the referees to apply the laws of the game strictly in it, referees and players at lower levels will accept that is the way to do it.'

In the World Cup, unlike the major leagues around the world, there would at least be, if this policy was maintained, consistency of interpretation. No longer would the last defender be able to bring down an attacker and escape a red card. No longer would television commentators be able to make the comment that 'if he hadn't already been booked, he would have got a yellow card for that one'. Referees would be forcefully reminded to give the attacking side the benefit of the doubt, especially in dubious off-side situations. All this meant that belatedly, FIFA appeared to be exercising its power in the right direction in an attempt to make the game more attractive.

Moreover, it cannot be denied that FIFA has made a better fist of running its sport than many other governing bodies. Football has never suffered from the boycotts and financial losses that blighted successive Olympic Games, nor the systematic, nation-based drug abuse that has bedevilled many Olympic sports like swimming and athletics (Diego Maradona and Willie Johnstone notwithstanding). Political problems were solved without rancour. For instance, both Taiwan and China were accommodated by the World Cup long before they ever were by the Olympics or even the United Nations. The potential for disruption because of the situation in the Middle East was handled by the simple expedient of putting Israel in the European federation and the Arab states in Asia. South Africa was expelled from the World Cup during the major part of the apartheid era and re-admitted as the Rainbow Nation, qualifying for the finals at the first time of asking.

This is not to say that FIFA gets everything right, far from it. FIFA's view of itself as a catalyst for change on the world stage has to be questioned after several dubious decisions made during Havelange's presidency: the award of the 1978 World Cup to Argentina when the country was in the grip of a military dictatorship, and to Mexico in 1986 when personal relationships between Havelange and the television magnate Guillermo Canedo appeared to be the determining factor, and an ill-timed bridge-building visit to Nigeria at the time of the world's horror at the execution of nine dissidents. The wish to arrange a match between Israel and Palestine in New York, the site of the United Nations – 'There, where politics, diplomacy and financial influence have failed, I believe that football could succeed' – as the last gift of Havelange's reign, must have made the former Secretary of State Henry Kissinger recall his thoughts after failing to land the 86 World Cup on behalf of the USA: that the politics of FIFA made him nostalgic for the Middle East.

For the future, the decision to award the 2002 tournament to Japan and South Korea may test FIFA's ingenuity, as not only will there be co-hosts, with different languages, customs and football traditions, but there will also be increasing pressure to accommodate a hostile third party – North Korea – in some capacity.

Many have accused FIFA of selling out to commercial interests. Kick-off times of World Cup matches to suit television schedules and the proliferation in the number of games as the countries involved in the finals rose from sixteen to twenty-four in 1982, then to thirty-two in 1998, have been the most dubious innovations. But FIFA has to operate in the modern world and it did secure television coverage for free-to-air networks, at least until 2002 (although long-term contracts entered into during the 1980s seriously undervalued the income from the sale of television rights). Furthermore, the growth in the number of World Cup participants reflects the rise in standards and the upsurge in popularity of the game worldwide. The new international tournaments based on age limits have taken the game to the youth of the under-developed world and FIFA has done more than any national association to promote women's football. In addition, sponsors have entered the World Cup on FIFA's terms, with no sell-out to a title sponsor. Instead, a limited number of 'partners' have been put in place. FIFA has also managed to build long-term partnerships with companies such as Coca-Cola and JVC, although it has allowed the Under-20s to compete for the Coca-Cola Cup and the Under-17s for the JVC Cup. However, these are pragmatic concessions in mutually beneficial relationships as the two corporations in question underwrote

Havelange's grand plan outlined as long ago as 1974; the need to take football to every territory. In a word, globalization.

Perhaps the most significant development within FIFA is the creation of a task force to examine ways of improving the game. Task Force 2000 was initiated by Sepp Blatter following widespread concern over the quality of play in Italia 90. A key member of the Task Force is Michel Platini, whose clout derives more from being co-President of France 98 than his position in the pantheon of all-time great players. Unlike his English counterparts, who were either totally ignored (Bobby Moore) or belatedly employed as 'ambassadors' (Bobby Charlton, Geoff Hurst), Platini has real power and he seems determined to use it. Platini initially advocated a ban on tackling, citing the case of his friend, Marco Van Basten, perhaps the finest player of his generation, whose career was ended prematurely because of injuries sustained in bad tackles. However, as Platini surely knows, players have always been at risk of career-threatening injuries and always will be, because football has to remain a contact sport. His suggestion was unsurprisingly rejected by the Task Force but they did agree to focus on the worst types of tackles. Thus Platini succeeded in rekindling the old debate over the tackle from behind, which FIFA has since vigorously taken up. This may well have been Platini's real intention. If so, he looks as adept around the committee table as he was on the pitch.

Platini has argued firmly against the implementation of artificial devices to make football superficially more entertaining. 'We must not make the goals bigger [or] play with nine men,' he said. 'We must not mess around with the game whether it pleases us or not. Football has its tradition ... I am absolutely for the golden goal [the first goal in extra-time winning the match]. Why?

Because the philosophy of football is to score goals and I prefer to finish a game with a goal scored, rather than with a penalty missed.' Referring to the Germans' golden goal which won the final of Euro 96, he says, 'If the goal had been scored two minutes before the end of normal time, everyone would have said that's OK; two minutes after, why should anyone expect something different?'

Platini appears to have convinced Sepp Blatter that 'the game's problems are not much to do with the laws as they are the mentality ... It is vital to use the laws to change attitudes, not the game and that is what we [the Task Force] have done. We have created an environment in which players can express themselves.' The Task Force's brief was to speed up the game and encourage more attacking play. To this end proposals were put forward to build on the new back-pass rule, limiting the time goalkeepers can retain possession of the ball to six seconds, and extend the period of normal time by up to ten minutes to offset time lost by injuries or time-wasting. In addition, multiple balls were used in the Under- 17 Championship so that when the match ball went out of play a replacement was immediately to hand. As a means of extending the time the ball is in play this small change, which has also been used in the UEFA Cup, could prove to be one of FIFA's better experiments.

One of Platini's supreme assets as a player was his sense of anticipation, his ability to see the move ahead. Nowadays he is still thinking ahead, sometimes to the consternation of his colleagues. He is, for instance, a supporter of the use of video replays as an aid for referees. While this idea produces forceful and perhaps merited opposition, Platini puts forward a cogent argument in favour of such a change. 'Has the foul been committed in the penalty area, has the ball crossed the goal line, has the goal been scored by hand?' These were the questions he asked when advancing his view of the circumstances in which video should be employed. 'At a certain moment the referee must make his decision. There is so much at stake – not necessarily just financially – but the passion of people throughout the world. People will say there is corruption, that sort of thing [as they can see if the wrong decision has been made]. It is necessary to deal with these small problems. That's why I'm for the [use of] video.' Although FIFA has so far shown little willingness to go down this particular road, Platini gives the impression that he believes change in this direction is inevitable. When asked if FIFA had agreed to incorporate video replays for the World Cup, he replied, 'Not this one.' If Sepp Blatter continues to call the shots, it will never take place. 'Can you imagine,' Blatter asked, 'what would happen on the field of play if you are not sure if it is inside or outside the penalty box and then you refer to somebody and then he comes back? This game is based on human error; of the player, the coach, sometimes even the media, but also the referee, because this creates the emotion, this creates the passion. If the game became scientific and there were no more errors, there would be no more emotion, no more passion.' Yet despite their disagreements, Platini and Blatter have been able to work together to put forward a cohesive strategy for the Task Force and Platini has not forced issues which he was unlikely to win.

FIFA's problem with technology is that any rule changes have to be applicable just as much to Atletico Neasden as Atletico Madrid. Hence the difficulty of introducing such simple and obvious innovations to the professional game as an independent timekeeper, the referee increasingly having his work cut out to control the game without being the sole arbiter of time as well. Moreover, there seems to be a fear that any reliance on hardware will be the thin end of the wedge. According to FIFA's Director of Communications, Keith Cooper, 'There is a strong feeling that once the technologists get a foot in the door they will never take it out again.' Nevertheless, Platini's revolutionary ideals will not be easily dismissed.

Now in his forties, Michel Platini's media-friendly persona – he is the antithesis of the traditional continental smoothie, with an unruly mop of hair and the top button of his shirt invariably undone – makes him the most accessible of sporting icons, yet he has not lost his sense of his working class upbringing. He opened the new national stadium (Stade de France), constructed for the World Cup and beyond, with a match involving the workers who built it. Somewhat unconcerned with the material side of the World Cup, his hope for France 98 was that the occasion 'resembles what football is: *sympa* [engaging] the game, the emotions, the goals, the players. Those are the important things. That people come and learn what a beautiful country France is, that they are welcomed. *Une belle fête* [a wonderful gala] and the fans of football will participate in this festival, that's what interests me.' Eric Cantona, who has little time for administrators, was disappointed by Platini's decision to join their ranks. He thought it better to fight the good fight through the International Players Union. He can be reassured, though, that his mentor has not sold out. Recalling his World Cup experience, Platini asked: 'Who remembers the organizing committees of 1982 and 1986? It is the goals that are remembered.' Platini also has another answer. 'If Cantona can go into the cinema [for a new career],' he said, 'why can't I go into football administration? In a country like France when you want to organize the World Cup you need it fronted by a personality because there isn't the tradition or history that there is in England. I was the first big personality to be able to do this.'

As for the future, Platini initially would look no further than his World Cup assignment. Significantly, though, his last official duty would be to organize the conference to elect João Havelange's successor. Havelange dismissed the suggestion that Platini might stage-manage the situation to procure the top job for himself. In typical Havelange style, he said: 'If Platini presents himself [as a candidate], then football should be pleased, just as it should be pleased with the candidacy of Mr Johansson.' Platini put his own opinion with some candour, which suggested more than an academic interest in the future direction of FIFA. 'At FIFA it's a political world,' he said. 'The world of football has just about had enough of not being taken into consideration. The loss of contact with what is going on is too big. That's what Pele thinks. That's what football people think. There is no relationship between the people at FIFA and the footballer.'

As if to prove Platini's point, João Havelange banned Pele from taking part in the Marseille draw because of Pele's position in the battle for control of Brazilian football. The Brazilian game is revered around the world by football fans. The country is without doubt the premier football nation and the Brazilian team draws crowds wherever it plays. This pre-eminence is not reflected in its domestic organization, however, which has for many years been a ramshackle affair. The national championship is incomprehensible to most outside observers; there are voluminous state championships and players are forced to play an inordinate number of games. The absence of commercial acumen co-exists alongside stories of corruption, nepotism and power battles among the political and social elite that runs the show. In 1993 Pele questioned the actions of the head of the Brazilian

Football Federation (CBF) over some major television deals. The head of the federation was Ricardo Teixeira, who also happened to be João Havelange's son-in-law. Havelange intervened in the ensuing dispute by dropping Pele from the 1994 World Cup draw in Las Vegas, to much public dismay.

Having made his point, Havelange later explained: 'If you have children and one of them misbehaves, you give them a smack. That is what happened with Pele but now it's all forgotten.' Havelange may have forgotten but Pele certainly had not. In a rare display of populism, the Brazilian government made Pele the Minister for Sport. Pele then promoted legislation to reform the archaic structure of Brazilian professional football, which involved curbing the power of the CBF and allowing litigation where necessary to settle disputes. Making it possible for the courts to intervene is, of course, now a heinous crime in FIFA's book. Havelange therefore banned Pele once again from taking part in an official World Cup ceremony. For Las Vegas, read Marseille. The matter was complicated by the fact that Pele also works for Mastercard, a key World Cup sponsor. Had it not been for the intervention of Michel Platini, who insisted on Pele's presence, the great Brazilian might have ended up commentating on the draw for his employers from his hotel room. This victory showed Platini's growing influence in FIFA's corridors of power. The exception that even governments will make for the exceptional is illustrated by the fact that the Brazilian administration found a way to grant Pele leave of absence from his ministerial duties for the duration of the World Cup. It decided to allow him to resign for a month, after which he would be reinstated. This unusual procedure was designed to allow Pele to attend to his commercial obligations to Mastercard.

FIFA, of course, was dancing to a different tune under the regime of João Havelange. Back at its Zurich headquarters, autocracy was still alive and kicking. The faction holding the line against criticism was personified by Sepp Blatter, who was not about to alienate Havelange as Lennart Johansson had done. In a eulogy to Havelange, delivered in the FIFA magazine, Blatter was once again the performer. Writing about the sound financial base of FIFA, he commented: 'FIFA succeeded in achieving this aim [while enhancing the game and its stature in society] when it had far less means at its disposal, so there is no reason why this policy of continual improvement should not apply also in the future. That policy is a vital part of João Havelange's legacy to our sport, for which we can only say thank you.'

The fact is that all top-level football has generated huge income streams over the last twenty years. National federations, particularly in Europe, along with the big clubs and UEFA, have all benefited. The success of the commercial revolution can only be judged on its results, not on the mere fact that it has taken place. And anyway, the money generated by football should be seen in context. It pales into insignificance when compared to the American gridiron game, which is run by the National Football League (NFL). The NFL reached agreement with US television networks in January 1998 for a new, eight-year TV deal worth $17.6 billion – over $2 billion a year. For football, crowing about increases in revenue is not enough. It is how the money is spent that is the most important question of all. The way money does or does not reach down to the roots of the game today will determine the shape of football's tomorrows.

CHAPTER FIVE

Young at Heart

WHEN DAVID BECKHAM scored the first goal in the FA Cup tie against Chelsea at Stamford Bridge in January 1998, he stopped, leaned towards the Chelsea fans behind the goal and raised both hands to his ears, as if to say 'I can't hear you now'. In these days of extravagant celebrations, Beckham's ear-cupping might not have seemed unusual. However, in this case it signified far more than a triumphalist pose. It was a deliberate response to the lewd chants that Beckham is habitually forced to endure wherever he plays. Even at Old Trafford, the away support makes sure there is no respite. Worse, they are often not directed at Beckham himself but at his fiancée, Victoria Adams, one of the Spice Girls.

The Hollywood image and the glamour attached to modern footballers, their astronomical wages and attendant lifestyle, probably leave most fans thinking they are fair game. Stewards and even the police stand idly by when obscenities are expressed en masse in this way. That is bad enough, but some fans have become such hypocrites that they complain when players react to their provocation. Both Ian Wright and Mark Bosnich, among others, have felt the long arm of the law after exhibiting what was essentially silly behaviour towards supporters, yet players are supposed to put up with the foul mouths among the crowd without complaint.

Berating opposition players has long been a speciality of the tribal support of British football clubs. In the past it was, in the main, kept in check by the fact that most footballers were rooted in the same communities as the supporters themselves and even a star player was viewed by the fans as one of their own. This meant that there was a line of decorum the crowd was reluctant to cross. In days gone by, abuse was confined to what would now seem gentle and anodyne, like the suggestion that Bobby Moore was weighed down by his wallet. However, the emergence of black footballers in the 1970s heralded a more disturbing trend. No insult was too base to hurl at opponents. Although there were years of indifference, the authorities, through anti-racist campaigns, eventually managed, with no little help from fanzines and the civilizing effect of all-seat stadia, to make some progress in limiting such behaviour, which even to the prejudiced now appeared absurd when his own team was liberally sprinkled with black stars. But a more personalized form of verbal abuse has now become prevalent. The poisonous atmosphere can be fuelled by those who claim moral authority, such as the *Daily Mirror*, whose anti-German invective at the time of England's semi-final match against Germany in Euro 96 was followed by disturbances across the country after England lost.

That the bad behaviour has been fostered to a large extent by the tabloid press and its voracious appetite for cheap rabble-rousing and scandal should surprise no one. On the one hand the papers present the new breed of professional footballer as if they were writing a spread in *Hello!* magazine, complete with lifestyle pictures and gushing commentary. On the other, transgressions, feet of clay and less-than-perfect private lives are sought out with diligence.

It is into this milieu that young footballers are now thrust. Those at Manchester United have also to contend with more vehement reactions from opposing fans than players of most other teams. All clubs have a local rival whom the fans love to hate, but just as Kevin Keegan's Newcastle was supposedly every fan's second favourite team, so Manchester United have donned the mantle of the most loathed for many people. This cannot be explained simply by United's recent success. The all-conquering Liverpool side of the 1970s and 1980s never drew such antagonistic attention, neither did the previous great Manchester United side of the 1960s. That team was as glamorous as its modern counterpart, and George Best left David Beckham far behind in the celebrity girlfriend stakes without producing any reaction other than regret from opposing fans that they didn't have a comparable star. These days, free-market forces have given a harder edge to competitiveness, which has been further distorted by media hype. This, and a perceived arrogance endemic at Old Trafford, has helped turn Manchester United into the recipient of that most potent of brews – fear, envy and loathing in equal measure.

United is undoubtedly a singular institution. The postwar rise under the guidance of Matt Busby, taking in triumph and tragedy and culminating in the triumvirate of Best, Law and Charlton and the European Cup victory in 1968, has bestowed on the club an epic, almost mythic status. Perhaps it is the widely held belief among opposing fans that United feel they have a divine right to success, that they are graceless winners and poor losers that has polarized opinions and created resentments. Drawing strength from such criticism, United are instilled with a sense of self-sufficiency, their opponents dismissed as suffering from irrational envy; they are ABUs (anyone but United).

Of modern successful football teams in England, only Arsenal and Manchester United have been drawn predominantly from a group of youth-team players who have grown up together. The Arsenal title-winning side of 1990/91 sometimes contained as many as eleven home-produced players out of a thirteen-man squad. Some of them succumbed to the resultant pressures, of which Tony Adams's prison sentence for drunk driving and Paul Merson's problems with drugs and gambling are only the most high-profile examples. Perhaps the Arsenal experience was heeded by Alex Ferguson, as it was certainly the case that Ferguson protected his brood from too much media intrusion during their rise to prominence. While this policy prevented individual casualties of the type that was seen at Highbury, it imbued an insularity that could account for the feeling that United get petulant and aggressive when things are not going their way and attempt to intimidate referees through constant questioning of decisions.

As the Chelsea fans were to find out, the self-contained can find strength in the malevolence of others. Perhaps David Beckham and company were particularly hyped up by the fact that they were playing the London glamour team that was seeking to depose them, or then again maybe it was because this was the FA Cup and a showpiece match selected by Sky television (and probably everyone else) as the tie of the round. Whatever it was, when added to the usual tirade of Beckham-baiting, United became unstoppable and the Chelsea team paid the price of its supporters' excesses. The ex-United forward, Mark Hughes, hinted at the aloofness which pervades the United mentality. During the warm-up he greeted his old comrade, Ryan Giggs, saying, 'All the best, Giggsy.' Hughes's friendly gesture, however, went completely unacknowledged.

At the time of the Chelsea game, United were leading the Premiership by a healthy five points, another title well within their sights. The Champions' League was in abeyance for the winter so there was little to cloud the horizon. Having put out understrength teams for the Coca-Cola Cup, it was just conceivable that Alex Ferguson would downgrade the FA Cup as well. However, United were facing the Cup holders, expensively assembled by Ruud Gullit. In the battle of egos which ensued, one man's self-belief was no match for the collective self-discipline of the United team and Chelsea were, quite simply, humiliated, and on their own ground at that.

After twenty-two minutes of skirmishing, Andy Cole centred from the byline, Teddy Sheringham headed it on and Beckham, cruising effortlessly and unmarked from the blindside, sidefooted into the goal from six yards. It was the cue for the Beckham celebration, and the harbinger of Chelsea's total destruction. Five minutes later Sheringham illegally pulled Dan Petrescu out of the wall at a United free-kick, but out of sight of the referee, Beckham curled a shot through the resulting gap and United were in command at 2–0. Thereafter, the insults aimed at Beckham and his love life were muted. By the seventy-fifth minute United were 5–0 up. Through a combination of United easing up and Chelsea seeking to redeem some pride, the Londoners pulled three goals back by the final whistle. 'We got sloppy towards the end and that took a bit of the shine off a very good performance,' was how Denis Irwin described the last fifteen minutes. The 5–3 scoreline, however, could not hide the fact that the young but now experienced United team had once again shown the value of the years of growing up together under a stern but paternal regime.

Apart from Beckham, there were four other products of the Manchester United youth system playing that day: Gary Neville, Paul Scholes, Nicky Butt and Ryan Giggs, all of them internationals. Their sudden emergence as a force to be reckoned with in the early 1990s surprised everyone. They had eclipsed bought-in talent and old favourites alike. And in a team which was liberally sprinkled with stardust, it was undoubtedly David Beckham who was the man of the moment both on and off the pitch.

Beckham, born and raised in east London but always ambitious to play for Manchester United, came to headline prominence with a goal against Wimbledon on the first day of the 1996/97 season, struck from his own half. By that season's end he was an England regular, had been voted the Professional Footballers Association Young Player of the Year and had won a championship medal. The start of the 1997/98 campaign saw Beckham facing the kind of situation with which many youngsters who make a big initial impact have to deal. Most young players learn to adjust to the rigours of the professional game in relative obscurity, which helps them accommodate the learning process. The physical and mental demands of the modern game make such handling even more important if burn-out and unfulfilled expectations are to be avoided. The temptation to overplay a gifted youngster, which might happen at a smaller club, could be resisted at United. There were so many of them that Alex Ferguson could afford to bring them on gradually. So when Beckham exhibited signs of tiredness at the end of the 1996/97 season and appeared somewhat jaded during England's participation in the summer Tournoi de France, Ferguson was able to take remedial action by leaving him at home when the club toured the Far East, pre-season, and opted to put him on the bench at the beginning of the 1997/98 campaign.

While the tabloids misread the situation, thinking that the player was out of favour, Ferguson took some pains to point out that his actions were designed to enable Beckham to learn to pace himself. It was also a measure of Beckham's progress that in a squad that allowed any one of the youth brigade to be omitted without detriment to the overall team plan he was seen by many as indispensable. It was not long before Ferguson recalled his most promising star and Beckham played in all United's Champions' League games, doing enough to convince Glenn Hoddle to use him in every one of England's World Cup qualifiers, clearly demonstrating that the player's phenomenal first season was not a one-off but a prelude to even greater fame and fortune.

Following Italia 90 and the inception of the Premier League and its alliance with Sky, English football underwent a dramatic resurgence. Even when the crowds flooded back to the game after the Second World War, and again after England's World Cup win in 1966, the most high-profile footballers were generally, with one or two notable exceptions like George Best and Terry Venables, only concerned with one career – football. In the 1990s world of marketing there is an irresistible number of money-making opportunities on offer. Thus David Beckham has become involved in a plethora of side deals which spring from his prowess as a footballer, his youth, his good looks and his association with the world of pop music. To supplement a renegotiated five-year playing contract which put him in the same salary bracket as his manager, there was the obligatory link with a boot manufacturer, in Beckham's case a £3.5 million, seven-year deal with Adidas, and an advertising contract as the 1990s Brylcreem Boy worth another £1 million.

In keeping with the transition of football's image from a working-class game to one which has more in common with Cool Britannia fashion, the Brylcreem contract was not just a testimonial appearance like the Glenn Hoddle Shredded Wheat commercials. Beckham is used in the same way as an Estée Lauder girl; that is to say, a special person who is seen as a role model for a generation, an aspirational spokesperson for the brand. Notwithstanding the 1970s adverts for Brut featuring Kevin Keegan and Henry Cooper, in recent times it would have been astonishing to think that a male personal grooming product would use a footballer, albeit a good-looking one popular with young girls as well as young boys, rather than, say, an actor, pop star or male model. Yet the day after England's dramatic draw in Rome, full-page colour advertisements appeared in the popular press saying: 'England BRYLiant, Italy CREEMed'.

The campaign as a whole is built around Beckham as a contemporary icon who can rejuvenate a product many thought consigned to history. Interestingly, Brylcreem was one of the first products to build a campaign around a sports star when Dennis Compton advertised it in the 1950s. Then, the objective was simply to trade on the endorsement of an outstanding sportsman (England cricketer and Arsenal footballer) to modernize the appeal of a product which had few competitors in post-war Britain but was identified with the Establishment and the Royal Air Force, whose slick-haired pilots were the original Brylcreem Boys. Forty years on, it was the same strategy but with a different treatment. The Beckham campaign used the very 1990s association of footballers with independence, fashion, free spending and youth in what may be the last attempt to resuscitate the product.

Along with the celebrity, of course, comes the goldfish bowl. At the age of twenty-two, coping with the downside can be difficult and for a time, not surprisingly, Beckham's self-control was called into question. A series of bad tackles committed in the Champions' League against Feyenoord upset the Dutch side and led to a sour atmosphere in the second game in Rotterdam, resulting in a career-threatening foul on Denis Irwin. Then a public spat with Frank Leboeuf of Chelsea blew up after Beckham called Leboeuf 'Big Ears' in the Cup tie at Stamford Bridge, displaying an obsession, hopefully temporary in nature, with hearing faculties. There followed a confrontation in the tunnel and Beckham went on Sky television and said Leboeuf was a 'little baby'.

The wonder isn't that Beckham was reduced to childish and tetchy responses but that he continued to play outstandingly for club and country. Probably no one, certainly not in recent years, has had to take so much stick so often from opposition fans. With other players, the chant of 'reject' occasionally gives way to Judas when a former favourite returns to his previous home. Paul Ince at West Ham is a good example of such vendettas, but Beckham, and to a lesser extent, David Ginola, are special cases, and the antagonism against them is born of an irrational and rampant envy. This is particularly true among young men. Both Beckham and Ginola share a supreme footballing talent and good looks that encourage admiring females, and have crossed the dividing line between footballer and pop star via the catwalk and the television commercial. In Beckham's case there is his girlfriend and his team to deride as well.

Fortunately for Beckham, he is surrounded by colleagues who came up through the ranks with him and he has the guiding hands of Alex Ferguson and

Glenn Hoddle to help him. He may not be an intellectual but he knows where he is going. Enjoyment of the material rewards – from BMW Sports to Porsche Carrera and Jaguar XK8 – has not upset his priorities. Speaking at the launch of his new Adidas deal, he made it plain that his football career came first, when he said, 'I do actually practise, you know, nearly every day with my free-kicks, and you know I've not got it to perfection. I'm probably a long way to getting it to every one where I hit the target and score, but that's the level I want to get to and hopefully I will do.' (On the morning of the Champions' League home game against Juventus, Beckham spent half an hour after training finished hitting free-kicks.) Although he shares with Paul Gascoigne an unease with the English language, and is sometimes guilty of petulance on the pitch, he is more likely to fulfil his ambitions to succeed Gascoigne in England's central midfield than to emulate Gazza's propensity for self-destruction.

David Beckham is, of course, only one of a group of young stars at Manchester United, all of whom are on lucrative long-term contracts. Despite the undoubted expense of setting up and maintaining a quality youth programme, they have also spared United from a reliance on the transfer market. It remains to be seen whether this tempts United into an over-dependence on the production line in the future. In addition, if the next batch of players is blocked by the arrival of big names from outside, or the longevity of the present bunch, United may have to release some of them, to the benefit of other clubs. At nineteen, John Curtis has already been capped by England at Under-21 level, but for how long can he realistically be expected to bide his time as a reserve?

Successful youth policies do not happen by accident.

They require vision from at least one person in a position of power. At Arsenal, it is Vice-Chairman, David Dein, who fulfils this role. Dein is an enthusiastic spectator at youth games and pays as much attention to them as he does to the senior squad, often attending a youth match and a first team game on the same day. This gives the boys themselves a feeling that they are valued. All of this fosters the kind of spirit that cannot be bought. 'What you know about all of my players,' said Alex Ferguson, 'is that they have the temperament. You can develop a player to high technical excellence and to high physical strength. But you don't know about temperament till they are on the pitch. All my young players have it.'

Even with the necessary commitment, success is inevitably a long haul. The class of 1989 was the first group of Fergie's Fledglings of whom much was expected. Most were eventually released, having failed to achieve what many fans thought they were capable of when they first saw them. Only one, Mark Bosnich, who was lost through work permit problems, has been a conspicuous success at the highest level, as Aston Villa's and Australia's goalkeeper. Shaun Goater, who did well at Rotherham and Bristol City and Russell Beardsmore at Bournemouth, have become lower division stalwarts but Lee Martin, Mark Robins and Darren Ferguson have been unable to sustain consistent performances, despite transfers to major clubs.

It took another three years before the policy really bore fruit. For the 1993/94 season, an unusually large number of the previous season's youth team were signed as pros, eight in all, including David Beckham, Gary Neville, Nicky Butt, Paul Scholes and Keith Gillespie. Mark Hughes later mused on the impact that the youngsters were beginning to make. 'The first time we became aware of them was when Mr Ferguson told us he'd got a group of about fifteen lads, all of whom would be given professional contracts,' he said. 'That was unheard of, so as soon as we were told that we sat up and took notice.' The following season a Coca-Cola Cup tie against Port Vale heralded their arrival on the first-team stage. There were many complaints that night that the fans who had paid good money to see the United stars had been short-changed by Ferguson playing a group of young unknowns. The selection was interpreted as a slight to the competition. Little did the critics realize what they were witnessing. As the group began to appear in more games that season, Alex Ferguson decided to make the move that facilitated United's current pre-eminence. The backbone of the Championship team was sold, three of the club's most influential players, Paul Ince, Mark Hughes and Andrei Kanchelskis, moved out as Ferguson backed his judgement of the youngsters' potential. It was a remarkable and bold gamble. It also moved Alan Hansen to proclaim on the BBC's *Match Of The Day*, that 'You never win anything with kids.' Hansen was more than once made to eat those words as United's young team, inspired by Eric Cantona, went on to win a second double.

No matter how much effort is expended on a youth programme, it cannot thrive unless the boys who are attracted to it in the first place are of sufficient quality. Many of the current United players might in the past have gravitated to Manchester City, a club which had stronger links to the local grassroots. The man who trans-formed the situation was Brian Kidd. Kidd was himself a teenage prodigy, scoring twice in United's European Cup win in 1968, when he was only nineteen. He was discarded by Tommy Docherty and went on to play for Arsenal, Manchester City, Everton and Bolton Wanderers before returning to Old Trafford as Youth Development

Officer. Being aware of the pitfalls and, in his own words, 'how hard it is to play for United', Kidd was ideally placed to persuade parents to let him have charge of their sons. There can be no doubt that Kidd possessed an eye for talent and was prepared to put his judgement and conviction to the test. 'I first spotted [Paul Scholes] playing in a little five-a-side, locally,' he said, 'and I never had any doubt that he'd make it.' These qualities were allied to a work ethic that ensured he was not shy of knocking on doors. Indeed, it was this personal touch, along with support from Alex Ferguson, that was responsible for Ryan Giggs leaving Maine Road for Old Trafford.

Like his rivals in the North West, Kidd was aware of the phenomenal record of a local youth side, Boundary Park Juniors, which provided the first rung of the football education ladder for gifted under-sixteens. Of the Boundary Park squad which won the Lancashire Youth Cup in 1989/90, twelve signed for professional clubs, half of them, including Gary Neville, Nicky Butt and Paul Scholes, for United. Paul Buckley, the former Chairman of Boundary Park Juniors, had no doubt where the credit for the signings lay. 'United have Brian Kidd to thank for that because he was the one who was out in all weather, snow and rain, watching the boys,' he recalled.

Once at Old Trafford, the youngsters benefited from a number of factors: an enlightened approach by the senior management; the rare chance to be part of several exceptional talents emerging together; and Kidd's move up the coaching hierarchy to replace Archie Knox as Ferguson's assistant. This provided 'a lovely continuity,' as Kidd put it. 'I was able to bring the lads all the way through.' Taken at face value, Kidd's comment seems to play down the role of Eric Harrison, whose coaching ability moulded the Beckham group at a formative stage and brought the club a trophy, the FA Youth Cup. However, it should rather be viewed as a paternal sentiment which is extant throughout the club from top to bottom. The 'lads' may now be England internationals but Kidd remains ever watchful for any faltering in their dedication to the cause. 'The attitude of the young players has never been a problem and won't be,' he said. 'We keep reminding them that work has got them where they are, and that if they stop there's always somebody else ready to come in. If we felt anyone was getting big-time, me and the gaffer would soon take care of it.'

It has not always been a story of unblemished behaviour, though. In January 1996 United was twice found guilty by the FA of poaching boys from other clubs and was ordered to return Matthew Wicks to Arsenal. There was also a fine of £20,000 and an order of compensation to Oldham, which might eventually amount to £100,000, in the case of David Brown. Nor have the allegations gone away and United was one of four clubs under investigation in 1998 for similar alleged offences.

These murky waters have come about because the youth system in England was never properly organized, but grew piecemeal like the rest of football's administration. Traditionally, boys still at school came under the jurisdiction of the English Schools Football Association (ESFA), a separate body from the FA but affiliated to it and holding a seat on the FA Council, the decision-making body. The ESFA, run by teachers who gave their time free to coach children of school age, regarded football as one of those useful and desirable extra-curricular activities but saw it as subordinate to the main goal of attaining the best possible education. This brought the ESFA into conflict with the professional game, which was denied the amount of access to the boys it required to turn out professional players. The ESFA ensured that the time any boy could spend with a professional club was strictly limited. The ESFA also controlled international teams at Under-15 and Under-18 levels. These age groups were designed to fit in with exam commitments but were out of step with the age groupings instituted by FIFA when international youth competitions were introduced. This led to the extraordinary situation whereby England had no representatives in the early FIFA youth tournaments.

In the late 1980s the tensions between the ESFA and the clubs, fought mainly within the confines of the FA Council and thus out of the public eye, came to a head. The ESFA reluctantly agreed to the establishment of a National School at Lilleshall, which was supposed to select a handful of the best fourteen-year-olds who would attend the school as full-time boarders for two years. In return for the cooperation of the ESFA, the FA called off its attacks on the schools organization, attacks which had seen the ESFA gradually squeezed of funds. The FA also agreed to continue to support schoolboy internationals, which provided the ESFA with its main source of income. It was a compromise that could not last, however. Clubs were still not getting the access they required and they continued to agitate for change.

England's poor performances in the international arena, both by clubs or the national team, along with the revolution that produced the Premier League, brought pressure to bear for further reform. At the same time, political changes in the education system left fewer teachers willing to give up their free time for unpaid activities. The ESFA, nominally independent but always in thrall to FA patronage, agreed to compromise again and the system was altered once more, this time radically.

Howard Wilkinson, the FA's new Technical Director, was to prepare and oversee the new system. As in every other area of the game, it was the clubs that were the ultimate beneficiaries. Having broken the old Football League and outmanoeuvred the FA when the Premier League was formed, the clubs now got their way with the youth system. By agreeing to set up local centres of excellence and academies which would provide an educational element, the clubs convinced everyone that their policy was for the good of all. Steve Heighway, who is in charge of youth football at Liverpool says, 'We really make it clear to everyone that the children are having an education in football but not a preparation for professional football. It's only at sixteen that there is a likelihood they will be retained for professional football.' It would be nice to believe that all clubs are as candid. The new system allows boys to go to clubs from the age of eight, where the plan is to put the emphasis on technique at the expense of match play. This, according to the clubs and the FA, will help them increase the number of talented players coming through.

The National School at Lilleshall will be superseded by the Academies based at Premier League clubs. The Academies are to play a key role in Howard Wilkinson's plan, the Charter for Quality, under which Wilkinson will appoint coaches at various levels, including Under-15, the traditional preserve of schools football, thus allowing the FA to operate an Under-15 team for the first time.

The England coach fully endorses the new system. 'I didn't discover there was a better way,' he said, 'until I was twenty-eight and went to Monaco. Now we've got young boys of eight and nine working with the clubs, getting the right grounding. And that generation's technique – their first touch, receiving the ball and tactical awareness – is going to be so much better.' While few would disagree with Glenn Hoddle's sentiments, the fact remains that it was not just the youth system that was different.

The results of the years of isolation from Europe following the Heysel disaster hit the English game harder than most people realize, to the extent that its effects are still being felt. The Europe England returned to was not the same Europe as before. Coaching and development had undergone a scientific revolution. Nutrition, alcohol intake, optimum training regimes and a host of other new approaches had been developed and widely applied by the continentals to go with their traditional emphasis on technique. The great unspoken in all this is that if the system of youth coaching has to change, then coaching higher up must also change so that continuity is maintained. You can't simply abandon the new way when a boy signs as a professional. Of course, clubs in England are slowly modifying their practices, but the change is uneven, uncoordinated and unregulated by the FA. And it still makes the newspapers when a club requires its players to train in the afternoon.

Alex Ferguson, speaking at the inaugural FA Coaches Conference in October 1997, paid tribute to the legacy Eric Cantona left to United. 'When Cantona first came to the club we used to finish training at midday. On his first day he came up to me and said, could he have two players to practise with. I shouted to Eric Harrison [then the youth coach] and asked for two players. He said, "What for?" I replied, "To practise with, you stupid bugger." The jungle drums began to beat and soon everyone was dying to join in. Players are striving to get to the top and practice makes the player. Eric had a million faults but that's the biggest thing he did for the club.'

Forty years ago, Sir Walter Winterbottom urged that technique be prioritized in the coaching method. Successive coaching gurus after Winterbottom put match activity at the centre of their methods and this reached its zenith in the gospel of Charles Hughes, the supreme advocate of 'direct play'. Now, Howard Wilkinson's plan seems set to allow the wheel finally to turn full circle.

To show it has learned the lesson, the FA is going to upgrade its coaching qualifications. This begs the central question of the Wilkinson Charter. Can the coaches coach? And what evidence is there to give confidence that the organizations which are to run the system – the FA and the clubs – will live up to the hype? At the top level, the majority of Premier League coaches would be unable to hold down a similar job in Germany. Even Glenn Hoddle possesses only the FA Preliminary Award, which is below the equivalent UEFA 'B' Certificate and would not allow him to coach a German youth team. (However, as motivational skills, man-management and tactics are as important at this level as coaching, their own rules did not prevent the Germans from appointing the 'unqualified' Franz Beckenbauer to the post of National Coach.)

As so often is the case nowadays, it all comes down to money. Barcelona spends over £3 million annually on youth development. There is a full-time director, doctors, physiotherapists, dietitians and twelve qualified coaches. All this for a group of twenty boys, at a club which has also to operate at the top end of the transfer market to fulfil expectations. The Italian club Parma is sponsored by the food company Parmalat, which has encouraged and supported its youth programme. This sponsor's money has been spent in a way which the club believes will achieve the finest youth set-up possible. It also fits into similar Parmalat schemes in other countries, including Brazil. The desirability of the new system will not change the fact that most clubs' youth policies will be found wanting once they know the price-tag of competing with the likes of Barcelona and Parma.

In the meantime, the free-for-all goes on. We can marvel at the fact that Manchester United have produced such a spectacular crop of youngsters and that they have all come through at the same time. England fans can perhaps also look forward to the better performances that the contribution of these players promises. Whether anything has been done to mitigate the feeling that it is now ambitious club owners and opportunistic players and agents who really rule the roost remains to be seen.

CHAPTER SIX

Too Much Monkey Business

THE EUROPEAN COURT of Justice in Strasbourg is not the place where anyone would expect football's important issues to come under scrutiny. But in January 1995 that august body delivered a seismic shock to the old game, one which overnight affected every area, from the finances of clubs to the number of overseas talents that fans can watch every week, from the sale of players to the ability of UEFA and national associations to legislate as they please.

The judgement is commonly known as the Bosman Ruling, after the plaintiff in the case, a little-known Belgian player, Jean-Marc Bosman. Through the ruling that bears his name, Bosman was destined to become as famous and influential as any footballer who ever played the game. The key decision of the court was that professional sports clubs and their governing bodies, such as leagues and associations, are commercial entities and thus are subject to EU law, just like any company or business. As far as players were concerned, this made a massive difference in two main areas. First, it paved the way for Article 48 of the Treaty of Rome, guaranteeing free movement of goods, services, people and employment, to be applied to football, so the various national restrictions on overseas players in member countries could be deemed illegal. Second, it ensured that players could no longer be held on restrictive contracts – true freedom of contract had to apply, just as in any other business.

Until Bosman, clubs were unwilling to treat players as a business would normally treat its employees. In no other industry was compensation – the transfer fee – payable once a contract was at an end. Worse, within the more reactionary federations – Belgium and Scotland, for instance – a player could be forced to accept a wage cut and his club could refuse to play him until its evaluation of his worth was met by another club. In England, at least, a player was free to move on payment of a transfer fee, settled in cases of dispute by an independent tribunal. The rules were different across Europe, but some element of the basic precept of selective freedom of contract applied in most countries, albeit with restrictions. English clubs had been dragged kicking and screaming out of a feudal system a generation earlier, again through the courts, before restrictions were lifted on players' maximum wages and the right to transfer. But still no one challenged the basis of the transfer fee and its counterpart, the ability of a club to retain a player, until Bosman. Totally unprepared for the decision of the European Court, UEFA was thrown into chaos, and attempted to defend the existing archaic structure. Meanwhile, predictions abounded that any change would produce dire consequences for the game.

Clubs in England did not rush to praise the decision for delivering them from a situation that had put them at a severe disadvantage compared to their continental counterparts. The Bosman ruling put an end to UEFA regulations which meant that, for European games, Scots,

Welsh and Irish had to be counted as foreigners. Since 1991, the permitted number of non-nationals was restricted to three with an extra two 'assimilated foreigners' allowed, which removed a traditional strength of English clubs. On one famous occasion, the restriction led Alex Ferguson to leave out Peter Schmeichel for a Champions' League match against Barcelona and United were trounced 4–0. The sweeping away of the constraints allowed English clubs the chance to become a force within Europe once again, although to listen to most of the reaction within England, the only result of the Bosman ruling would be anarchy. Alan Sugar, Chairman of Spurs, was the most trenchant in his views and commented: 'Bosman could turn out to be the biggest single disaster for football in the last twenty or thirty years. We have seen an increase in players demanding higher salaries and people prepared to pay them. But the wrong mathematical calculations are being made and the effects in the longer term are going to include the bankruptcy of some of the bigger clubs.'

Initially, football thought it could get away with applying the Bosman ruling only to transfers between different countries but it soon became clear that each country would also have to change its domestic arrangements. England's rule revision, introduced for the 1998/99 season, is based on the French system, where transfer fees are still payable to the club with whom the player signed his first professional contract, but only up to the age of twenty-four. In such a case the fee will be seen as compensation for the time and expense of bringing the player through the ranks. However, this dubious compromise is unlikely to survive any challenge in the courts.

Suddenly, with no limit on the number of overseas players, and all players in an improved bargaining position, wages at the top level started to soar. In England, wages had already been on an upward spiral since the influx of money that occurred when the Premier League began. Now a new importance had to be attached either to renewing the contract or selling the player before the contract ran out. In addition, longer contracts became a priority. But it was not only players that benefited. The new situation, with clubs panicking, was tailor-made to unleash another destabilizing force, empowered agents.

For years, football clubs controlled wages with an iron hand and even today they can still refuse to pay more than they think prudent. They can invoke that old standby, 'wage structure', in their defence, as Martin Edwards did when justifying the non-signing of overseas stars like Gabriel Batistuta. Unfortunately, consistency is not one of football's most notable virtues and from the formation of the Premiership, with its associated commercial income, clubs have been prepared to up the ante in terms of players' wages at every turn. When rich sugar daddies like Jack Walker at Blackburn Rovers or Steve Gibson at Middlesbrough put vast amounts of wealth into luring star players to hitherto unfashionable clubs, players, through the negotiating skills of their agents, quickly jumped on the bandwagon. And once supply and demand were allowed to operate freely in the international market after the Bosman ruling, players' wages really started to go through the roof.

It is an oft-stated opinion that footballers' wages are now far too high, to the point of obscenity. It has therefore been suggested that a salary cap be brought into the English game. Salary caps work well enough in the USA because club owners and players are partners and share in the growth of their sport. However, the size of their home market, with little competition from other countries, means that players have the opportunity to exploit their status through commercial deals which far exceed their basic salaries and dwarf any similar possibilities in any other territory. Hence there can be more of a willingness to compromise. In the USA, some sports that did not traditionally embrace the wage cap have suffered disputes that have ended in strike action, as has happened in baseball in recent years. Most of the time, from the sports' point of view, controlling wages prevents owners of big-city teams buying success, which inhibits the creation of a dynastic league within a league. Moreover, if a ceiling is put on a club's total wage bill, it does not prevent discretionary payments to individuals but can act as a brake on what would be spent on basic salaries overall.

However, in a career which is effectively over by the time a player reaches his mid-thirties, there is a need to maximize income over a relatively short period. Moreover, if the money doesn't go to players, where will it go? It is a fair bet that it would not go into holding down ticket prices, as these too are governed by market forces, and most Premiership clubs have more fans wanting to watch games than they have seats in their stadia, a classic scenario for a price-hike no matter what the wage level may be. In addition, if players in Italy and Spain can make far more money than they can in England, then it will be impossible to tempt foreign (or even English) stars to ply their trade in the Premier League, which would soon become a second-rate competition.

Thus a salary cap, while superficially attractive to chairmen who cannot control themselves, would not work unless it was Europe-wide and it is unlikely that other countries would be interested in such an arrangement. It might even be contrary to European law. And anyway, some European giants like Milan are less concerned with the balance sheet than the trophies in the cabinet. Some, and Barcelona is the most notable example, even put principle before revenue. Barcelona has refused all offers of shirt sponsorship, believing a commercial endorsement would besmirch the famous red and blue striped shirt, which is regarded as a symbol of the Catalan nation. Yet Barcelona will spend whatever it takes to achieve success on the field.

If wage caps won't work, then the gap between rich and poor will forever widen and the league within a league will become even further entrenched than it is already. While there has always been a gap in English football, it has never been as marked as it is in many other European countries, where there tend to be two or three massive clubs who always dominate. In order to avoid this and keep overall wage costs at manageable levels, a strictly enforced 'transfer window' could be applied. This would mean that clubs have to have their playing staffs in place at the start of the season as no transfers would be allowed during the campaign, apart from a short period of, say, two weeks, when the window would open. Wealthy clubs should not be able to offset deficiencies by panic-buying in mid-season. A ban on purchases outside the window would force clubs to place more emphasis on planning and youth development. This is a suggestion that might work well, but again only if Europe-wide agreement can be reached and providing there is a contingency for exceptional circumstances, such as the French idea whereby a club can apply for a 'joker' if it is devastated by injuries. In addition to aiding the creation of a level playing field, a transfer window of this sort could curb the opportunities for agents to make waves and slow down the inexorable rise in spending at the top end of the market.

With high prices in too small stadia, and the interests of fans seemingly lower in priority than corporate clients and sponsors, clubs have come in for much criticism. However, they have managed, with media support, to deflect some of the blame on to a convenient scapegoat – agents. But agents are accepted as the norm in showbusiness or publishing, for instance, without causing any controversy. Nowhere have they been portrayed as the demons they have become in sport, especially football.

In reality, the case for a good agent speaks for itself. Sometimes, a client will make the point better than anyone. Frederic Dobraje, a former French first division player, is now an agent with many clients who have been with him for years. One of them, the Montpellier goalkeeper Bruno Martini, who has played for the national team, put it this way: 'Frederic Dobraje is the man who allows me to sleep soundly and maintain a calm approach to my job because he looks after my affairs and as a result I have only to look after myself.' For Martini, who is certainly not unique, serenity and security at a cost of less than ten per cent of earnings doesn't seem such a bad deal.

As the money coming into football snowballed, agents came in to get the best deal for their clients, and therefore for themselves. Initially, the agent had no loyalty to a club, only to the player he represented and himself. If a player is worth more than his current club is paying, or willing to pay, then it is a good agent's job to agitate for a move. It happens all the time in other walks of life. In television, ITV might offer more money for a star who made his name on the BBC, for example. When it comes to football, however, agents, players and even managers are 'greedy', while chairmen and shareholders are simply getting a return on their investment. Desperate to stay in the Premiership, chairmen have fallen over themselves to pay ever more money in players' transfers and wages (over £100 million on overseas players alone).

They have broken FA rules to do so. Expediency and fear have led to a culture which gave rise to the murky world of the bung, which is symptomatic of the appalling business practices that have long characterized the game, with the FA, as ever, totally powerless or unwilling to intervene effectively.

While the wages received by players in England fall somewhat short of the gold mountains reported in the media, actual income is often difficult to discern, the more so because of bonus payments which are doled out for success, for so-called 'loyalty' and even for the avoidance of relegation. For example, Steve McManaman, writing in *The Times*, said: 'There is a public fascination with players' wages but the figures quoted in some of the more imaginative newspapers are well over the top. Players just laugh when they read this stuff because it is mere speculation, but it can be difficult when supporters start believing it.'

What can be said is that costs have escalated for superstars and journeymen alike, with knock-on effects on ticket prices and merchandising operations to fund it all. In the Premiership, the search for success (Manchester United, Chelsea) and the avoidance of failure (Coventry, Southampton) have put a premium on even a modicum of talent. This has led to more foreign imports and a decrease in transfers between the Premiership and the Football League. The money generated by this activity in the past helped keep many small clubs afloat. Now, a Football League club receives more in television money, which amounts to a paltry £250,000 a season on average, than it does in transfer fees. Gerry Boon, the head of the football department at accountants Deloitte & Touche put forward the view that 'Money that previously supported smaller English clubs is now backing Italian football.' Arsenal's manager, Arsène Wenger, puts the case slightly differently and with a neat sense of irony considering he has signed five French players. 'Foreign players,' he declared, 'are a threat in rich countries like Italy and England because young [home-grown] players have no real chance to play. But in France, for example, it is good because the exodus [over thirty French players, including most of the national squad ply their trade abroad] gives young people a chance.'

Paradoxically, the end of the 1997/98 season was the first occasion when a plethora of out-of-contract players became available. One leading agent anticipated that 'there are going to be a lot of players out of contract at the end of this season. Clubs are calling the shots at this level – players may be grateful to sign a week-to-week [contract].' This is a process that will be repeated in coming years and will lead to two distinct levels of players. Those at the top will be able to profit even more from their scarcity value and take in wages what was previously paid out in transfer fees. For squad players downwards, life will be much harder as costs propel clubs in the lower divisions to work with smaller squads and even some Premier League clubs will be forced to rely more on youth development than they do at present. In addition, clubs have begun to put pressure on players they wish to retain but who are coming towards the end of their contracts. Shaka Hislop, who refused a new contract at Newcastle, was dropped from the team, even though his contract was still in force, something which would be unthinkable in any other business. Phil Smith, one of England's leading agents, who with his brother, Jon, runs the First Artists company, remarked on this trend. 'This is the first year [1998] that clubs will see for the first time that they are losing out and they are not taking it lying down and they are fighting back,' he said. 'Now, the morals have gone out of the window. [They say] "You, the player, have got rights you didn't have before and we are not necessarily going to treat you in the same way." '

On the continent, the practicalities of coming to terms with player power is more often mitigated by long-term planning. FIFA permits a player to sign for another club in the last six months of his contract, whether he is moving domestically or overseas. The Premiership has refused to apply this ruling to its own competition for fear that it might lead to a conflict of interest, which could have a direct bearing on promotion and relegation issues. However, this leaves the way open for overseas clubs to sign the best English-based players.

Towards the end of the 1997/98 season, two players who had interested Alex Ferguson announced transfer deals. Danish international Brian Laudrup, reaching the end of his contract with Glasgow Rangers, decided to accept an offer from Chelsea. Surprisingly, it seemed United did not even bother to compete for his signature. As a free agent, Laudrup wanted, and received, a massive signing-on payment approaching the level of the transfer fee Rangers would have received before Bosman.

In addition to Laudrup, Marcelo Salas was transferred from River Plate of Buenos Aires to Lazio of Rome for a transfer fee of £13.5 million (countries outside the European Union are not subject to the Bosman ruling). Salas had made his name with Universidad of Chile before his 1996 transfer to River Plate and he scored many of the goals which took Chile to the 1998 World Cup finals.

In Salas's case it is not clear whether the financial deal was the stumbling block, or whether Alex Ferguson lost interest once Andy Cole started to score a few goals. David Mellor, on his radio programme, reckoned that he had been told by someone in the know that Ferguson thought the acquisition of a major world star like Salas would upset the balance of personalities within his squad. Against that, Ferguson personally went to South America to watch Salas, an unlikely trip for someone who felt he could not risk upsetting his existing employees. Ferguson was at the head of a queue of clubs seeking to purchase Salas but he failed to make any contact with the player's agent, Gustavo Mascardi, and Salas will only deal through Mascardi. On the other hand, it seems that while the plc gave Ferguson the go-ahead to sign Salas – a fee of £12 million was sanctioned – it would probably have led to the release of Cole. Cole's contract was in the process of being renewed and the board felt that two exorbitantly paid strikers would be a luxury they were not prepared to tolerate. In effect, Ferguson was asked to choose between them. In the event, with Cole, according to Martin Edwards, 'scoring goals for fun', Ferguson stuck with his most expensive purchase.

Later, reflecting on why Salas didn't go to Old Trafford, Ferguson said simply, 'Sometimes these things just pass you by and there's nothing you can do.' Despite Martin Edwards's conclusion – 'It was the manager's choice not to go for Salas' – there was always the impression that when it came down to it, Italy or Spain were the preferred destinations of the player.

Whatever the reason for Salas turning to Rome instead of Manchester, United fans could be forgiven for thinking that their club did not possess the mindset to compete with the best, or even the second best, as Lazio, however well it has performed over the years, has never been among Italy's elite clubs. So Laudrup and Salas were lost and United's fans have since questioned the club's ambition. This is a charge that cannot be levelled against the Lazio directors, who already had three front-rank internationals, Mancini, Boksic and Casiraghi competing for two striking roles. After Salas scored both goals for Chile in a 2–0 victory against England in front of a near-capacity crowd at Wembley (one a stunning volley, the other a penalty he won himself), Alex Ferguson was left to ruminate on the fact that, as Paul Wilson put it in the *Observer*, 'Manchester United's loss is Lazio's gain. Although there is nothing to say a fit Cole [he was a late withdrawal] could not have chipped in with a couple of goals for England, they just wouldn't have been as spectacular, and they wouldn't have left defenders questioning their technique instead of [merely] their speed and anticipation.'

English clubs in the main don't have the contacts to attract the top South Americans and are prevented from developing them at the insistence of the PFA (the players' union) and by the government's refusal to grant work permits to non-EU players unless they are current internationals. Aimed at protecting the home market this regulation in effect handicaps English clubs as gifted young Africans, for example, are picked up early and developed by clubs such as Ajax who are not restricted in this way.

None of this has prevented club chairmen heaping blame upon players or agents. Brian Richardson, Chairman of Coventry City, referred to 'financial diarrhoea', Alan Sugar of Spurs to 'the prune factor', by which they meant that money coming into the game was going straight out again to players and their agents. Richardson went so far as to suggest that players are 'getting very close to blackmail'. Yet it was Richardson who upped the stakes for smaller clubs when he spent heavily on players in an effort to retain Coventry's Premiership status – 68 per cent of Coventry's income goes on wages – and then offered Dion Dublin a reported £16,000 a week to sign a new contract, even though spending on transfers and wages put the club into debt to the tune of over £10 million. And Richardson anticipates spending even more in the future. When asked where he drew the line on spending, he replied, 'Well, you draw the line first and foremost that you have to stay in the Premier League. I think we've all taken certain gambles to try and ensure that.' As for Sugar, having been one of the most vociferous opponents of player power and overseas imports, he, having failed to convince anyone to endorse his views, admitted spending £2 million more than he should have done on Les Ferdinand (who cost £6 million from Newcastle), and when the spectre of relegation threatened was prepared to countenance an unheard of contractual clause that guaranteed Jürgen Klinsmann selection in the first team no matter what his form or the opinion of his manager.

At the other end of the table, at Arsenal as much as Manchester United, success will not be bought at any price. The Arsenal Vice-Chairman, David Dein, said of this philosophy, 'We wish to be the most successful team, domestically and in Europe. We are working towards it. It is a fiercely competitive industry.' But despite spending over £15 million a year on players' wages – over 50 per cent of turnover – Arsenal will refuse, according to Dein, to do anything 'reckless' which might 'endanger the heritage of the club'. In practical terms, Dein puts it this way: 'Would we buy Ronaldo for £30 million? Highly unlikely. Would we pay him £3 million a year? Highly unlikely.' With the single exception of Alan Shearer's transfer from Blackburn Rovers to Newcastle United for £15 million, English clubs have been unwilling to match the excesses of Italy and Spain. Nonetheless, spending by Premier League clubs on transfers in 1997 was not far short of £90 million.

The shadowy world of the football transfer hit the headlines when Alan Sugar, during his 1993 court battle with Terry Venables, drew attention to the practice of unauthorized payments – bungs. As a result, the Premier League set up a three-man committee of enquiry, comprising Premier League Chief Executive Rick Parry, Robert Reid QC and Steve Coppell, then head of the League Managers Association. George Graham, who had been named in a *Mail On Sunday* article, admitted taking an 'unsolicited gift' from the Norwegian agent Rune Hauge, money that the committee felt was linked to transfers to Graham's club, Arsenal. Graham was subsequently banned by the FA for a year.

In 1997, the Premier League committee, after four years of investigation, delivered a 300-page report to the FA. A grand total of three individuals were charged, two of whom are no longer in the game. Brian Clough and Ronnie Fenton, who were manager and assistant at Nottingham Forest, and Steve Burtenshaw, who worked under George Graham at Arsenal, were found to have a case to answer. Clough and Fenton are both retired and no longer fall under the jurisdiction of the FA, while the case against Burtenshaw, who is now a scout at Queens Park Rangers, rumbles on. In addition, Clough and Fenton's club, Nottingham Forest, was also charged, although it is now under new ownership so most of the individuals involved with the club at the time of the alleged misdemeanours have left the game as well.

Cynics say this is all very convenient for the FA. One or two are named, the justice of it all lost in the argument over who actually gets to carry the can apart from George Graham. So little is done to address the widespread rule-breaking that has gone on and perhaps continues to do so. The FA, meanwhile, complains that it is extremely difficult to obtain cast-iron evidence of wrongdoing. The FA's argument would hold more force if it had done anything to change its rules and regulations over the years to bring itself into the real world. In theory, as the supreme authority, the FA has all the power it needs to enforce total financial disclosure from its member clubs and leagues but it has never been proactive in this area.

In a belated move to find a way forward, the FA asked a former Commissioner of the Metropolitan Police, Sir John Smith, to review how it should deal with financial irregularities. In his report, entitled *Football – Its Values, Finances and Reputation*, Sir John first dealt with the existing opinions within the professional game. 'Certainly,' he said, 'there is a generally held view that there is not too much wrong with football ... it's a well-ordered game which is properly regulated ... If there's not much wrong with it then why seek to fix it by establishing these mechanisms which will be costly and perhaps intrusive and perhaps damage your opportunity to develop the game?' But he went on to describe the inability of the FA 'to ensure compliance with its rules and [that] for a variety of reasons [it] doesn't have that ability.' To Sir John, this was an obstacle to be overcome. 'If football is to progress ... then it is absolutely essential that it ensures that it has an obvious integrity, that it has the sort of financial probity that all good businesses must have.' Sir John further observed that the FA needs to give itself powers to investigate, and a permanent police force to root out wrongdoing at clubs. Graham Kelly, the FA's Chief Executive, retorted that: 'The FA has always said we are not a police force. There has to be some form of policing. There has been a gradual awareness that we cannot rely on old rules and procedures.' Any change in these rules and procedures, however, requires a 75 per cent majority in a vote of the FA Council. Sir John shouldn't hold his breath.

There was no such hesitancy on the part of the FA's superior body, FIFA, which decided to act after a number of unsavoury transfer allegations were exposed by the media. The most important move was the decision to force agents to pay a bond of 200,000 Swiss Francs (£80,000) for a licence, without which they were not allowed to operate. Once a licence was obtained, the agent could only be paid by one party in any deal. However, clubs continue to deal with unlicensed agents when it suits them. Thus, those agents that cooperate with FIFA often lose out to more unscrupulous elements or, conversely, those with professional qualifications. Lawyers, for instance, cannot be excluded from acting for their clients in any capacity and are not required to obtain a licence.

There are contradictions at every turn. The PFA needs only one licence between its three personnel who work in this area, whereas the Smith brothers of First Artists have to have one licence each. Agents still act for any number of parties to a transaction: the buying club; the selling club; the player. This state of affairs exasperates Jon Smith of First Artists, who commented that: 'The licensing system doesn't work, full stop. The next sentence should be, "How do we make it work?" But there is no next sentence because FIFA doesn't want a discussion about it.' It certainly appears that there are double standards. As a result of his involvement in the George Graham affair, Rune Hauge was banned from acting as an agent for two years. But by working with a licensed partner it was soon business as usual, with over $1 million in commissions raked in. Now licensed, Hauge still draws players to him because of his record of always getting them a good deal, usually at the expense of their clubs.

To be fair, there is little any governing body can do with agents other than 'hitting clubs and players [who employ an unlicensed agent] in their pockets', which was how Andreas Herren of FIFA put it. 'It discourages them,' he continued, 'from going to these people.' For using an unlicensed agent and signing an agreement with Real Madrid while still under contract to Monaco, French star Thierry Henry and the Spanish club were fined SFr100,000 (£40,000).

However, the fines are small beer compared to the money that can be earned by everyone involved in a superstar transfer or a post-Bosman 'free' signing of a star player; commissions of $750,000 are by no means unusual. This is too much in all senses for David Dein, who feels that 'obscene amounts of money are being taken out of the game by agents'. He recalled that Ronaldo was being offered around Europe at $36 million but was told that Arsenal would have to come up with $40 million as the player's four agents expected $1 million each. Dein supports a Premier League proposal which will attempt to introduce 'a proper code of conduct to undress the transaction'. If it is accepted, all parties in a transfer will have to sign a document to verify the role of the agent. 'I want,' said Dein, 'to know where the money goes.'

At the top end of the market, clubs not only put up with agents, they regard them as indispensable. Dennis Roach, having earned the sobriquet 'Cockroach' from Brian Clough and with the endearing habit of calling those he considers lesser mortals, 'boy', is nonetheless used again and again because of his wide range of contacts and associates, a network which extends across the world. Unusually, but usefully for an agent, Roach is also recognized as a good judge of a player. In the old, pre-licence days, Roach admitted to the 'bungs' enquiry that 'you tended to get your commission where you could'. He found the players often resented paying him directly and were only reassured when he told them he was getting his share from the club. As the turnover of superstars has grown, Roach has gravitated to fulfilling the needs of clubs. He has, for instance, supplied Glasgow Rangers with a veritable conveyor belt of foreign players. Clubs have put their faith in him and even clubs which have felt themselves at the wrong end of one of his deals turn to him again and again.

Often there are people Roach would rather avoid. His secretary is instructed to tell callers that he is not in the office even when he is, until the status – friend or foe – of the caller has been established. If her absence compels Roach to answer the phone himself, he often pretends to be the secretary, putting on a false accent which can sound like anything from Margaret Rutherford to Paul Robeson.

He has, though, remained totally committed to one player, or rather, one ex-player. Roach is both agent and friend to Glenn Hoddle. 'When he was a player, Hoddle trusted Roach and that trust was reciprocated. Roach often put Hoddle's concerns at the top of his priorities, which may not have always been appreciated by other involved parties. The two met at Heathrow airport in 1987, Hoddle thinking he was going to sign for Paris St Germain, after leaving Tottenham for a long-cherished move to Europe. However, at the last minute, Roach got them on a flight to Nice and Hoddle joined Monaco. Hoddle, a great believer in destiny, was reassured as Monaco appeared in many ways to conform to a premonition he had had. On a more mundane note, it turned out to be the right choice: a glorious autumn to his playing career, an appreciation of the arts of coaching and management from Arsène Wenger, and equanimity off the field. Many years later, Roach was discussing an extension to Hoddle's managerial contract with Ken Bates of Chelsea, while at the same time negotiating with the FA for Hoddle to succeed Terry Venables as England coach. Right up to the very day Hoddle signed for England, Roach was, according to Bates, talking to Chelsea about Hoddle's role at Stamford Bridge.

Some of the more traditional managers, and Alex Ferguson comes into this category, find it difficult to come to terms with the maverick power of men like Dennis Roach. Roach feels that Ferguson holds him responsible for getting Mark Hughes to pledge himself to Barcelona in the middle of the season in 1988, thereby destabilizing the player and scuppering United's championship challenge. Whether or not this was the case, it has not stopped United using Roach since, indeed he organizes most of the club's overseas tours, but then he is a friend of Martin Edwards.

Five years ago Roach 'retired' to Bournemouth but is now busier than ever, because, as he says, 'clubs are desperate for world-class players'. David Dein concurs. 'There is too much money chasing too few stars,' he said. Scarcity at one end is putting a premium on youthful discoveries at the other. Arsène Wenger remembers that in 1990 he was the only senior coach at the World Youth Championships. 'Now,' he says, 'there are over fifty scouts at any youth tournament.' The problem, he feels, is 'the speed at which players get the money. No problem at twenty-seven but when they are rich before they play . . .'

When it comes to bungs, exploding salaries and the high prices fans pay for tickets, it is obvious that the present system is full of inconsistencies, does not have public confidence and is characterized by secrecy and under-the-table practices. Whenever fans complain about prices, chairmen tell them that if they want the best players, if they want their clubs to win trophies, these prices are necessary to generate the required income. This is also why, it is explained, so much space in stadia has to be devoted to corporate hospitality and so much effort put into maximizing merchandising profits.

Of course, the clubs have to do this because the Premiership is the only game in town. So long as Sky continues to hype its investment, players and agents will be the foremost beneficiaries of 'New Football'. Fans will have to pay for the extravagances of their clubs, and television – paymaster and ringmaster – will tell everyone what they should have whether they like it or not.

CHAPTER SEVEN

The Worst of Times?

Aᴼᴴᴿ ᴛʜᴇ ʙʟɪꜱᴛᴇʀɪɴɢ performance against Chelsea in the FA Cup, which appeared at the time to be a defining moment of the season, Manchester United seemed to shudder to a halt. The young players were unable to maintain the necessary consistency while the squad suddenly appeared to lack substance. It wasn't long before United exited the Cup, in a replay against Barnsley, and the team's league form stuttered badly, only fourteen points coming from ten games – hardly championship form. By the middle of March, a mere two months after the victory at Stamford Bridge, United still led the Premiership, but Arsenal had put together an unbeaten run and were now only six points behind with three games in hand.

The knockout stages of the Champions' League now assumed an even greater importance as domestic dominance waned. Having finished top of their group, United were in good shape to reach the final. In the draw for the quarter-finals, they were paired against Monaco, assumed by most pundits to be the weakest team left. The first leg in Monte Carlo, a turgid affair, ended in a 0–0 draw. Perhaps if United had pushed Monaco harder they might have put themselves in a better position.

Eight Monaco players were on one yellow card so a more committed attacking display by United could have resulted in some key opposition players missing for the return. Rob Hughes of *The Times* commented that Alex Ferguson was 'the only man I know who went to Monte Carlo, didn't gamble and came back broke'. Others were more inclined to defend Ferguson's tactics. 'Suggestions that Ferguson betrayed his instincts, the strengths of his squad and the traditions of the club by adapting the philosophy of the end justifying the means are too silly to warrant rebuttal,' was the opinion of Hugh McIlvanney of the *Sunday Times*, who helped Ferguson with his autobiography. It was left to another manager – and one with plenty of European experience, Roy Hodgson of Blackburn Rovers – to sound the alarm. 'You tend to think,' he said, 'that a draw will be a good result over there and we'll beat them back at our place. But if you do not score that away goal, you are in a very difficult position if you concede one.' Even the United players were disappointed at not making more of a game of it in Monaco but were reassured by their manager's conviction that the 0–0 draw was a good result.

United's poor Premiership form had culminated in a 1–0 home defeat by Arsenal on the Saturday before the second leg. If that wasn't enough, by the Wednesday, several key players – Peter Schmeichel, Gary Pallister and Ryan Giggs – were out injured, and others – including Paul Scholes and Gary Neville – were not fully fit. It was ironic that Ferguson found himself in the position he had hoped to avoid by fielding below-strength teams in the Coca-Cola Cup. The intensity of the matches in England had left him depleted and he had to approach the most important match of the season under the handicap of missing players. No matter, the consensus was that Monaco were not that good, having lost a number of the team which had won the French championship the previous season. They had also experienced a few injuries themselves and were off the pace in their bid to retain their title.

The match ended 1–1 and United were out on the away goals rule. The Manchester fans were stunned as early as five minutes into the game when David Trezeguet unleashed an astonishing drive which gave Monaco a 1–0 lead. Trezeguet had been missing from the first leg but showed the kind of striking class that Alex Ferguson, for all his skill at bringing through young players, had failed to find in his own youth system. Trezeguet, only twenty years old, had already scored fifteen goals in twenty-three games in 1997/98 and was a full French international. From then on, United were chasing the game and unlike in the match against Juventus, the players were unable to turn the tide, even after equalizing in the second half through Solskjaer. Despite the excuses that United were below strength, the truth was that the movement and organization of the Monaco players were superior to United's. Without Giggs there was no width in United's attacks and as a result their midfield play lacked subtlety and penetration. The lions of autumn had become the lambs of spring. The failure to build a squad with enough world-class players to challenge the best was now revealed for all to see. *The Times* summed up the response of the media when it ran the headline: 'United Pay Price For False Economy'.

Elimination by Monaco, while Juventus, who had only managed to make the knockout stage through a last-gasp win against United and results elsewhere going their way, looked set for a third consecutive final, brought a terrible sense of anticlimax. Moreover, Monaco were merely the latest in a long list – Dortmund, Volgograd, Gothenburg, Galatasaray, Torpedo Moscow, Atletico

Madrid – of 'smaller' clubs who had put paid to United's European hopes since the Rotterdam triumph against Barcelona in the Cup Winners' Cup final of 1991. Of course, bad luck played a part but the will was also lacking. Teddy Sheringham's woeful performance at Old Trafford, for instance, reminded United fans why they are suspicious of 'cockney' players and underlined just how much Eric Cantona is missed. Yet 'Dieu', during his English sojourn, never truly punched his weight in European games. Despite having won the Cup Winners' Cup with two different clubs, will a similar epitaph have to be written for Alex Ferguson?

The manager's post-match analysis was certainly cogent but begged the question of why the team had been allowed to stagnate. 'We need strengthening, no question of that,' was his verdict. 'After we lost Keane with the injury early in the season, Scholes and Butt did really well immediately and that allowed me to think we could get through the season. They were playing so well but, when it came to it, we had to patch up the team without Keane and Scholes. We had lost the central midfield and with no Giggs the balance was not right.' The truth was that other teams which had reached the quarter-finals, notably Juventus, Real Madrid and Borussia Dortmund, had gone into the transfer market for reinforcements, while United not only dithered over strengthening the squad, they weakened it with the sale to Benfica of Karel Poborsky, a wide player who could have filled in for the missing Ryan Giggs. The transfer activity – or lack of it – shows only too well which are the really ambitious clubs of Europe. Barcelona, for instance, knocked out of the Champions' League in the group stage, nevertheless bought Winston Bogarde from Milan in order to try to secure first place in the Spanish Primera Liga, having already laid out tens of millions at the start of the season.

It was now apparent that it had been a mistake to rely on the existing squad. While United have developed some excellent young prospects, they have signally failed to supplement them with experienced, quality players of the front rank. Although linked with the likes of Batistuta, Salas, Nadal and Babbel, their interest was not pursued to a conclusion. Hindsight, of course, is a wonderful faculty, but one expert, George Best, had seen the writing on the wall. Before the Monaco game he prophesied: 'He [Ferguson] lacks a central striker and a central defender of world class in this team. It will not win the European Cup this year.'

Juventus, following coach Lippi's dictum that more work would lead to improved performances, notched up an exceptional 4–1 victory in their quarter-final away leg against Dinamo Kiev. The Ukrainians' coach, Valery Lobanovsky, gave fulsome praise to the man he viewed as the most potent his team had to face – Zinedine Zidane. Zidane, according to Lobanovsky, 'undertook everything that should be expected of a star of the millennium, firstly for his team and afterwards for himself. He is not a player who only thinks of money.'

The other clubs which added to their squads for the quarter-finals of the Champions' League won through to the semi-finals, with the new acquisitions making significant contributions. Another factor they had in common was that they all fielded at least one world-class striker. While United played Solskjaer out of position, Real Madrid, despite being over £50 million in debt as a result of refusing to trim their sails, spent £8 million on the Brazilian, Savio, and the Frenchman, Christian Karembeu, and left Davor Suker, the Croatian star of Euro 96, on the bench, so spoilt for choice were they up front with Fernando Morientes and Raul.

There can be no doubt that Alex Ferguson had

misjudged the situation and, either through conservatism or overconfidence, had been unwilling to take a risk on real stars. He preferred to shop in Norway rather than Brazil. Moreover, in the week following United's exit from Europe, he preferred not to shop at all, since no reinforcements were brought in before the English transfer deadline to help in the struggle to retain the Premiership title; a case of once bitten, twice bitten.

Success in European competitions is not merely a matter of short-term decision making. Clubs like Juventus and Real Madrid have vast numbers of supporters who demand success as of right, just like Manchester United. But the difference is that the tradition of real world stars is stronger at the continental clubs, fed by massive and relentless challenges at home from equally grand rivals (Real–Barcelona; Juventus–Internazionale), and by their historic roles in the European pantheon of glory, all of which leaves United in their shadow. For all the United fans' belief in a divine right to success at home, Europe is a hope, a dream, rather than a specific objective. There is no planned strategy. At Old Trafford, the board does not take into account any possible Cup successes when setting the club's budget. Progress in the Champions' League, therefore, is regarded as a bonus. While this may, at first sight, appear prudent, it takes no account of the old adage that you have to speculate to accumulate. United were fortunate that the UEFA system allows the English champions a bye into the group stage and thus a guaranteed income of £5 million. But reaching the semi-finals could double your money. So it might produce a better return if a calculated risk were taken and United became a big-time buyer.

As a business, Manchester United does not have to win the Champions' League to be successful. On the

130

morning of the Monaco match United's share price was
down by four pence, anticipating somewhat the possibility of defeat. After the game, the shares dropped a further
three pence, wiping a notional £26 million off the club's
total valuation. However, this is a small amount when
seen in the context of the capitalization of £500 million. In
the half-year accounts, which covered the six months up
to 31 January 1998 and which were announced two
weeks later, rises in wages and transfer costs led to a
drop in pre-tax profits of 24 per cent on the same period
the previous year, down to £15 million. It was still good
business, though, putting United, literally, in a league of
its own.

Even with the extra costs, it was surprising that the
inexorable rise in merchandising sales did not make up
the shortfall. The half-year figure was down 11 per cent
to £15.6 million. 'There is nothing to suggest to us that
the replica market is slowing down,' said Peter Kenyon,
United's Deputy Chief Executive. Rather, he implied that
it is a reflection of the cyclical nature of replica shirt sales,
which always fall off during the second year of a kit's
life. Edward Freedman, the former merchandising chief
at United and therefore a man who should know better
than most how much store to put on shirt-selling cycles,
has another explanation. He feels sales have peaked. 'The
ceiling has been reached,' he commented. Although
Freedman may be too modest to say so, it might also be
the case that the regime which replaced him is not as
adept at maximizing merchandising income as he was.

A price increase, according to Freedman, is not the
answer to declining sales. Commenting on rumours that
the 1998/99 shirt would cost £40 plus, Freedman said:
'Kits have become a fashion item and now a lot of products have come on to the market to vie for that £40.' With
expenditure planned for a hotel and a training centre,

of the opinion that the next step should be
ls 'serious brand development'. That,
is for further serious investment. Unlike
ports brands like Nike, United eschews the
deployment of the weapons of mass communication, not
spending a penny on promoting itself to its loyal audience of millions. By allowing an ill-informed or
prejudiced media to do its job, is it any wonder that the
motives of the plc are questioned, particularly over the
number of kit changes and the lack of transfer activity?

The Champions' League, like all major football competitions these days, is underwritten by television and the
vast revenue that comes with it. The 1997/98 season's
biggest UK audience for a football match was 10.3
million, for the first leg of the quarter-final against
Monaco. Had United won, this figure would have
increased for the semi-final and final, making the
Champions' League the most popular sports programme
among British television viewers. However, absolute
numbers are not always the most important factor in the
modern world of televised sport. When Sky gambled on
paying over £200 million for the rights to the Premier
League in 1992, over a million subscribers were added
almost overnight. The deal, mutually beneficial both to
the infant league and to the satellite station, enabled Sky
to leave its previous troubles behind with the immediate
and unexpected success of the alliance.

Rights fees are no longer based just on audiences of
millions but on revenues generated by far fewer people
being prepared to pay for niche subscription channels
and pay-per-view events. Hence, with over six million
homes signed up, Sky now outspends ITV by a ratio of
five to one. According to Kevin Morton, the Managing
Director of media buying company Equinox, Sky 'are to
be admired in the way they have turned a disastrous

product that advertisers, a decade ago, didn't want to be associated with, into something that is the jewel in the crown of every beer, car, [and] mobile phone marketing man's dream. It was only when Sky discovered what a beautiful thing you could do with football in terms of marketing that ITV realized what missed opportunities there had been.'

Now, every commercial channel wants football because of its ability to attract and hold a valuable audience for advertisers and sponsors. It is also fashionable. That is why Channel 5, having started off by declaring it did not intend to broadcast much sport, soon saw the error of its ways and bought the rights to Arsenal, Chelsea and Aston Villa matches in Europe and is a contender for England's away games. With ITV, Channel 4 and Sky holding the rights to almost everything else, the poor old BBC is left with the crumbs of edited highlights and the odd live match.

It is the same story across Europe where the major leagues – Italy, Germany, Spain and France – have spearheaded the latest developments in televised football by embracing new delivery systems. As a consequence, the introduction of cable, satellite, subscription and pay-per-view have all helped to fuel an astronomical rise in rights fees. In England, the last year of the old ITV contract, 1991/92, brought in £18 million. By 1996/97, the last year of the original Sky deal, fees had risen to £90 million, comprising £40 million due under the agreement and a bonus of £50 million for sealing a new undertaking which came into force a year afterwards. In the first year of the second Sky contract, 1997/98, fees went up to a staggering £135 million, accruing to £693 million over the course of the four-year BSkyB/BBC agreement. From being the paupers of Europe, the Premiership now has one of the highest television incomes of all.

With such escalation it is little wonder that club chairmen have behaved like schoolboys in a sweet shop with too much pocket money. But it doesn't stop there. The next great surge in income will come with the introduction of digital television. This will be led by Sky in the UK and the number of available stations will, through this futuristic new delivery system, dwarf the thirty-odd channels currently available. The expansion will enable Sky to move away from the current meagre pay-per-view fare, which consists of a few big events such as world championship boxing and films, to a regular menu of pay-per-view sport, with Premiership football at the top of the bill.

In this volatile market, the big question is whether Rupert Murdoch can repeat the success he achieved with satellite. In France, Italy and Spain it is football that has, so far, driven pay-per-view services but it is, as they say, 'early doors'. The greatest penetration is, at present, in France but it has been helped through subsidies to subscribers who trade up from analogue to digital systems. Nor should it be forgotten that in most European countries many of the best domestic fixtures are already contracted to existing television services. The question is whether a second, more personalized tier, will have the popularity to attract a big enough audience outside of the major clubs to make it worthwhile.

In France there are already two pay-per-view services. The cable and satellite network, Canal Plus, developed the prototype system on the back of its domestic football coverage. The main French terrestrial channel, TF1, broadcasts one live match from each Champions' League programme. With two French teams in the 1997/98 competition, TPS, its pay-per-view satellite service, screened the other match. In addition, all other Champions' League games are made available on an à la carte basis. As TF1 was committed to giving the two French clubs' equal exposure, there were occasions when Monaco was shown on free-to-home television, while Paris St Germain, the bigger attraction, and all other Champions' League games, were available on pay-per-view.

This type of service is a forerunner of what might happen with the Premiership. A twenty-club Premier League offers ten games per week. If two of these are reserved, as now, for Sky's subscription service, that leaves a possible eight matches that could be available on pay-per-view, some 320 games in a full season. However, the continental experience shows that it is the top clubs which generate the biggest pay-per-view income. So existing agreements on the distribution of spoils within the Premiership – 50 per cent in equal shares, the remaining divided between facility fees and a sliding scale based on final positions in the table – could go by the board. In Italy, there is understandable frustration at Juventus, Milan and Internazionale, which are together responsible for 60 per cent of pay-per-view revenue but receive only 20 per cent of the total. Obviously, the clubs feel they could greatly increase their income if they could sell their rights individually. They might well achieve their wish when the existing television contract ends in 1999. So could their English counterparts.

At present the Office of Fair Trading is investigating whether or not the sale of rights by clubs banding together (the Premier League) is breaking the law by acting as a cartel, thereby forcing the consumer to pay more for televised football than would be the case in a truly free market. And the alternative to the Premier League selling rights is their individual sale by each club. In anticipation of a changing legislative environment, some clubs have already begun to create their own television channels. But until either the OFT decides the Sky contract is anti-competitive or the contract is terminated, these fledgling services can offer little in the way of live games and can show no Premiership action at all.

Nevertheless, Manchester United, in association with Granada Television and Sky, has announced plans to start its own television channel. The respected commentator, Raymond Snoddy, Media Editor of *The Times*, wrote in the magazine, *Marketing*: 'These channels are founded on the hope, if not the assumption, that they can one day become serious ppv [pay-per-view] channels charging large amounts of money, and everyone is taking them seriously just in case. They will have only one obvious thing in common. They will all be total crap.' While Snoddy is probably correct, the fact that they may be crap will not stop fans from wanting to see them. The various clubcall telephone services, for instance, are hardly the most brilliantly produced artistic endeavours, but football fans are insatiable consumers of information about their own clubs and will pay to find it. Two calls a week on a clubcall line can cost in excess of £5. This shows that quality of production comes a poor second to the chance of getting an inside track when it comes to a supporter's decision on spending.

Rick Parry, the former Chief Executive of the Premier League, now fulfilling a similar role at Liverpool, warned against clubs forming their own services. 'The bigger clubs can't just do their own thing,' he said. 'They are attractive only because they are top of the Premier League . . . The Premier League is the product. You can't just discount a series of matches. The competition sells the rights.' When Parry made his comments, he was immediately attacked by Chris Akers, Chairman of the Leeds Sporting plc which owns Leeds United. 'Rick Parry,' claimed Akers, 'has to protect the Sky contract which he negotiated. I am just trying to get the best deal for our club. The problem for Parry is that lots of clubs have gone public and have a different agenda to his.' This may well be true but if Manchester United is allowed to negotiate for its home Premiership matches, it will, according to economist Bill Gerard of Leeds University, 'grow larger and larger and it will become ever more difficult for the smaller ones to compete'. Dr Gerard argues for safeguards to be put in place along the same lines as American anti-trust laws, which ensure free competition in most areas but allow sports to operate a cartel system when selling television rights. 'Football is unique in that it takes more than one single business to produce the product. Unlike any other industry there's nothing to be gained if the top club forces all the other clubs out of business. The clubs need one another to produce leagues. In economic language football is a joint product. You need the businesses to cooperate.'

If the Office of Fair Trading rules that the Sky deal is unlawful, football in England will be blown apart. In an attempt to strengthen its hand, Sky is pushing for the immediate introduction of pay-per-view before the digital system comes on stream, even if it can only be effected by further weakening the Saturday football programme. With a financial killing on the horizon – annual pay-per-view income estimates have ranged from £280 million to an absurd one billion plus – it is unlikely that the chairmen will be able to resist. After all, as players' wages continue to rise faster than income, a new source of revenue will eagerly be seized upon.

Indeed it was surprising that the Premier League rejected Sky's proposal to switch four Saturday fixtures to Sunday. The chairmen were opposed to underwriting Sky's marketing plans for digital television because the

Saturday league programme would be decimated and the number of viewers would be minimal.

Nevertheless, circumstances may conspire to enable pay-per-view to emerge early in the 1998/99 season. Clubs in the UEFA and Cup Winners' Cups can, unlike those in the Champions' League, negotiate their own television rights. With half a dozen clubs involved there are not enough slots for all of their matches to be accommodated on the existing UK networks. The situation would then be ripe for Sky to provide a pay-per-view opportunity. If Manchester United fail to qualify for the Champions' League, a successful UEFA Cup run would provide pay-per-view earnings from fans prepared to pay up to £10 per match, producing an income far in excess of revenue generated from even so prodigious a source as the Champions' League.

When the current Sky contract runs out, the balance of power will have shifted away from television companies to the Premier League. Sky may well face serious competition in all areas, not only from existing networks but from new players, such as British Digital Broadcasting (which will operate the terrestrial digital service), the Mirror Group's television arm and the two biggest cable operators, CWC and Telewest. The Premier League will have a number of options; it could establish its own channel, share its product among several operators, or institute a joint venture with one or more of the networks. What it does not have to do is put all its eggs into one basket over which it has no control.

There is no doubt that Sky has brought a new dimension to football coverage, both in terms of quantity and quality. Even today, Sky uses more cameras to televise a match than the traditional broadcasters. However, the hype can be counter-productive and even does football a disservice sometimes. The promotional campaign for the start of the 1997/98 season was a case in point. It was based on a strident, patronizing message proclaimed by the actor, Sean Bean, and climaxed with the slogan, 'We know how you feel . . . We feel the same way.' If this were true, Sky would never schedule a game at 11.15am on a Saturday morning between a team from Manchester and one from London, as it did for the crucial Manchester United–Arsenal match in 1997/98. Arsenal vice-chairman David Dein reluctantly accepts the situation, even if he doesn't like it. 'If you are going to take that money to improve the welfare of the game and the entertainment value for the fans,' he said, 'something has got to give. The other side want their pound of flesh. If you take the money, you've got to dance and we are dancing all over the place.'

Paradoxically, Arsenal, although a long-time opponent of Sky, initially supporting ITV's bid for Premiership coverage, has faithfully carried out its responsibilities to Sky. Elsewhere in the Premiership, the Sky outside broadcast unit is often received like a leper. Sky receives a similar lack of assistance from fixtures compilers. Knowing their preferred encounters, like Manchester United–Arsenal, Sky asked for them to be kept away from European weeks. The unobliging response was largely responsible for the Saturday morning timing of that match. In fact, Sky could insist on their Sunday afternoon slot, which would severely handicap the preparation for the midweek European ties. However, this doesn't excuse the heavy-handed approach to its presentation.

In fact, Sky's view of football is characterized by images of joy and despair, painted faces, replica shirts, excessively loud music and endless, often witless pundits (Andy Gray excepted), who have yet to witness a poor game on the channel. This has nothing to do with fan culture as represented by such developments as fanzines and independent supporters' organizations. Nor does it connect with anybody old enough to have seen George Best or who experienced the game's troubles of the 1970s and 1980s.

Sky would have us believe that it invented football. Perhaps in a sense it did. Everything has to fit around the Premiership. After Sky first took over, the Premiership became the only competition that mattered. As successive years saw the accumulation of rights to England home internationals, the FA and Coca-Cola Cups, the Scottish League and Cup and the Football League, competitions previously marginalized by television have worked their way back on to the bill as supporting acts.

The former Chief Executive of Sky, Sam Chisholm, told the incredulous Premier League chairmen, when he first met them: 'When we play, everybody wins.' Some years later, from a position of strength, he commented that 'what the general public want is raw live sport. That is the last great theatre of life and Sky is delivering it.' But Chisholm didn't say that Sky is delivering it only to a minority, a minority which is willing and able to pay handsomely for it. To Sky, football does not exist beyond its subscription frontiers. A Sky Sports viewer could be forgiven for thinking that the Champions' League and the World Cup do not exist.

The great danger is that football may have become a hostage to a boom and bust culture. What happens if the 'New Fans' lose interest and the ratings drop? There will then be no access to Manchester United and Arsenal for kids who have been attracted to them by television rather than their local clubs. They could disappear from the ranks of football supporters altogether, the potential parochial magnet for their affections having long since lost any relevance. There could well be a backlash from people force-fed on football as the epitome of popular culture, and corporate customers – the arrivistes – will depart.

While no one can blame football for cashing in while it can, especially after the dark days of the hooligan era, in typical fashion there has been no planned contingency, no sound infrastructure to be left behind. Instead, everybody wants to jump on the short-term gravy train. With France 98 about to open its money-making doors, the stampede to get a piece of the action would be renewed. Thus the message continued to be that money talks, and this time to a worldwide audience of billions.

CHAPTER EIGHT

A Numbers Game (Part One)

THE STAKE-OUT AT the warehouse lasted for two weeks. It had been instigated amid great secrecy at the beginning of May after an informer had given the authorities a tip-off. By the middle of the month the undercover officers felt they had enough evidence to bring the operation to a conclusion. The ensuing raid netted no stolen goods, no illicit narcotics, nor any smuggled contraband. What the officers found was 3,000 footballs.

If that sounds like a modern version of the Keystone Kops it should be mentioned that they weren't any old footballs. They were cheaply produced imitations of Mitre's official England World Cup football, which, according to the investigators, were about to be distributed to shops around the country and sold to an unsuspecting public as the real thing.

The agency which conducted the operation was not some SWAT team from Scotland Yard, nor was it the SAS, but the innocuous-sounding Office of Trading Standards. Its purpose is to put a stop to what is described as a rising tide of false claims and outright rip-offs perpetuated on an ever-growing number of consumers. It wasn't, though, investigators from the capital or some other crime-ridden metropolis who carried out the raid. It was,

al office in sleepy Devon, where the balls
d after they were manufactured in India
nto the UK.
s designed to take advantage of the surge
all official World Cup merchandise in the
run-up to the tournament. According to the chairman of
Devon's Community Safety Committee, Keith Baldry,
such activities cost UK companies £1 billion a year.

It is a measure of the success of the commercialization
of the World Cup that unscrupulous elements seek to
involve themselves in it. Normally, manufacturing a fake
football would hardly be worth the candle. But a ball
associated with the World Cup has obviously crossed
some kind of threshold in order to become of interest to
the criminal fraternity. The numbers must be high
indeed.

The World Cup has itself become a 'numbers racket'
and the numbers get bigger with every tournament.
Most people expected USA 94 to reach the apex of
commercialism; after all, everyone knows that in
America, sport and Mammon are, to all intents and
purposes, synonymous. The onward march of commercialism, however, is inexorable and the Organizing
Committee for France 98 used it to create, with FIFA, the
biggest World Cup yet.

The World Cup has become a global industry. It offers
three levels of involvement to both national and international businesses, which pay handsomely for the
privilege. For 1998, the highest level accommodated
twelve companies, each paying up to £20 million for the
right to be called Official Sponsors. The list of names
sounds like a roll call of the world's most visible corporations: Adidas, Budweiser (Anheuser-Busch), Canon,
Coca-Cola, Fuji, Gillette, JVC, Mastercard, McDonald's,
Opel (General Motors), Philips and Snickers (Mars). For

their £20 million they get the right to display the World Cup logo on their products, they are allowed to use their association with the tournament in their promotions, they can put their names on advertising boards at World Cup grounds (except for Budweiser, which has to sell on its board rights as beer falls foul of French anti-alcohol and tobacco laws prohibiting these product categories being linked with sport), and they receive tickets and hospitality for matches. The money from this source goes directly to FIFA, producing a cool £200 million for its coffers.

For the companies, the money they spend on sponsorship of the World Cup is just the beginning. There are competitions and special promotions on products and packaging, with tickets and other World Cup memorabilia as prizes. These efforts are supported by massive advertising campaigns. Coca-Cola, for example, was scheduled to spend over £100 million on advertising and promotions, exploiting its official status to the full in an attempt to swamp its competitors.

Below the top tier of sponsorship there are two other categories called Official Suppliers and Official Products/Services. In the main they comprise companies which trade in equipment or services needed to keep the show on the road, such as communications (France Telecom) and travel (Air France and Opel). There are nearly thirty companies in these categories and they bring in £100 million, much of which goes to the French Organizing Committee.

Unsurprisingly, France 98, like USA 94, was expected to turn in a handy profit. That it makes economic sense for the sponsors can be seen in the fact that most of those in the top echelon are repeat customers. Only Adidas and Budweiser, which upgraded from supplier to sponsor in 1998, are first timers.

However, to get full value for their sponsorship dollar, their World Cup involvement has to be integrated into their marketing plans. This is why Coca-Cola spends five times as much on supporting its World Cup sponsorship as it does on the sponsorship itself. To back up its global advertising campaign (Eat Football, Sleep Football [in France, Live Football], Drink Coca-Cola), which positions Coke as the drink of the fans, the trophy (or at least a perfect replica) was taken on a world tour to provide countless photo opportunities for both clients and kids. Coca-Cola, in fact, ran their biggest promotion ever, targeted at the under-twenty-fives. The company took over 1,500 children to the finals to act as flag carriers and ball boys and girls, thereby strengthening the Coke brand within stadia. Perimeter boards were only allowed to display a registered trademark but Coke had the foresight to register 'Drink Coca-Cola', and so were the only company able to convey an advertising message alongside its logo.

With the sale of alcohol restricted and advice from the organizers to drink in order to combat the effects of the heat, Coca-Cola anticipated that more than half of the fans would take up the message of their advertising board.

Coca-Cola believes that the World Cup is so important to its successful marketing that it is the only sponsor that has already signed up for 2002 and 2006. The company knows that if it relinquished its position, Pepsi would be in like a shot. Their precious investment has to be protected by fighting off attempts by their competitors to muscle in on their territory. As media strategist Graham Bednash put it, 'All advertisers using football imagery are now sponsors. Whether they are official or not is of no interest to consumers.' To the football authorities and their commercial partners, this 'ambush marketing' is the spectre at the feast.

Ambush marketing has become a key weapon in what can only be described as a sales war. It is exemplified by two companies, Adidas and Nike, which have been slugging it out toe-to-toe for some time. Both identified France 98 as a key battleground.

At the Atlanta Olympics in 1996, Nike created its own hospitality and promotional village, making a great show of its presence. It ran an extensive poster campaign, with sites in close proximity to the main venues. The posters featured many star athletes under contract to Nike. Those same athletes displayed their Nike affiliations whenever possible. The most visible was the double Olympic gold medal-winner, Michael Johnson, who took to the track in his gold Nike shoes. However, the company was not an Olympic sponsor and had paid nothing for its association with the games. The Nike village was not part of the official Olympic village and its contracts with athletes were all-year-round deals that had nothing to do with the Olympics as such. So successful was the ruse, a survey concluded that a majority of the public – over 70 per cent – incorrectly believed Nike was actually an Olympic sponsor.

Nike did this because it could not allow its main rival, Adidas, to exploit without hindrance its status as the Olympics' official sponsor in the sports goods category. Since each product category is exclusive, once Adidas was in, there was no room for Nike. With Adidas in the same position for the World Cup, and Nike's US sales down 11 per cent on the back of a downturn in the American sports goods market, Nike decided on a similar ambush strategy for France 98.

Nike, unable to gain a foothold in the world's two biggest sporting events, has taken to sponsoring some top-flight national football teams, including Italy, Nigeria, Holland and Brazil, and stars like Ronaldo and

Paolo Maldini. It is an indication of the importance the company now places on targeting football, since at USA 94 no major country played in Nike colours. Moreover, Nike's backing of Brazil goes much further than has previously been attempted with a national team by any company. Nike holds television and marketing rights for a minimum of five Brazilian international matches a year. For this, and the right to supply the kit, sell the replicas and have the endorsement of the world champions until 2006, the company contracted to pay the Brazilian federation £250 million. Of course, the Brazilian players are the most popular in the world, filling stadia and attracting large television audiences wherever they go. Nike, not unnaturally, exploits its rights to the full, using the Brazilian team as missionaries to open up sales in new territories, such as South Africa and the Middle East. Nike posted a fourth quarter loss of $68 million in 1998, so it is imperative the company finds new markets. This means more travelling and more matches for the already overplayed Brazilians and prioritizes commerce over preparation for major tournaments. This, according to no less an authority than Pele, is to the detriment of the team's chances of retaining the World Cup.

The first shots in the battle of France 98 came when Nike produced its memorable television commercial featuring the Brazilian team playing football in an airport against the background of the familiar samba tune, 'Mas Que Nade'. To make the film, the authorities agreed to close Rio de Janeiro airport for twelve hours, a testament to the power of football in Brazil and the 'true marriage' that is claimed between Nike and the federation. Not content with disrupting air traffic at one of the world's busiest airports, Nike also hired the action director John Woo, fresh from his hit *Face/Off*, to make the film. The obvious pleasure of the players as they go through their repertoire of skills gave Nike a more human face, a major departure from the aggressive tone of previous advertisements featuring Ian Wright and Eric Cantona. It provided a solid and attractive platform from which to launch further commercials, one of which featured a new generation of stars, including Ariel Ortega, Hernan Crespo and Ibrahim Ba, having a kickabout on a beach. Its schemes, however, do not come cheap. Nike was set to spend half of its annual marketing budget around the World Cup.

Nike is breaking no rules in its bid to ambush Adidas. It is merely taking full advantage of the multifarious commercial opportunities that exist around the world to become involved in football. To those whose job it is to promote the official business of the World Cup, however, actions like those of Nike are against the spirit of the game. Glen Kirton, former Head of External Affairs at the FA and Director of Euro 96, who now works at ISL, the marketing company once owned by Adidas, said that Adidas's management was concerned at Nike's promotions because they 'risk having people believe that there are certain companies associated with the event who have no right to be associated [with it]'. Unfortunately for Adidas, the fact is that football long ago sold out to commercial interests and those who live by the sword, die by the sword. Nike's opportunism would not be possible if, for instance, the Brazilian game was run as expertly as the NFL in America. In the meantime, it is up to Adidas and other ambushed companies to fight their corner.

Adidas, of course, has a long history of association with FIFA. João Havelange's original plans back in the 1970s for the enlargement of the World Cup were bankrolled by Horst Dassler, the German founder of Adidas who died in 1987. In return for its support,

Adidas received supplier status (it still provides clothing for officials and the match balls) and, through ISL, gained control of selling the World Cup marketing rights, the same rights that now produce such vast fortunes for FIFA. When ISL secured an extension of its World Cup marketing rights to cover the tournaments in 2002 and 2006, there were noises from other outfits, notably Mark McCormack's IMG and UEFA's Champions' League partners, TEAM, that there was no fair bidding process in place. Their complaints were summarily dismissed by FIFA.

When Adidas was taken over in 1990 by the French politician and owner of Olympique Marseille, Bernard Tapie, the company was far ahead of any of its rivals as far as the World Cup was concerned. On the eve of the 1990 final between West Germany and Argentina, Tapie jubilantly claimed: 'Whoever wins tomorrow, Adidas wins. We supply both teams and the official kits and the ball. The only thing we don't provide is the referee's whistle.' If the same circumstances applied again, the likes of Nike will be there, spoiling away. So high have the stakes become, the days of absolute hegemony for one company have gone for ever.

With Nike making the running, Adidas was forced to respond in kind with campaigns of its own, featuring national teams like France, Germany and Argentina, and stars like David Beckham, Alessandro Del Piero and Zinedine Zidane. Adidas used these assets to promote a new football boot in its Predator range, launched to coincide with France 98. With its stars striking moody poses against a sombre and gothic background, Adidas tried to convey that theirs was a brand that took its sport seriously and regarded football as no laughing matter.

Mindful of Nike's Olympic village in Atlanta, Adidas got its retaliation in first by setting up its own World Cup village under the Eiffel Tower in Paris to advertise and promote its official status. A company spokesman declared: 'We are going to ambush their ambush.'

More important than who comes out on top in the war between the sports goods manufacturers is the vast amount of money the global brands are prepared to commit to the World Cup. That neither can afford to ignore the tournament and both are prepared to go to extraordinary lengths to gain an edge shows how vital the World Cup has become to commercial interests.

The organizers of the tournament itself realized that they too could get in on the act. Thus for France 98, World Cup merchandising was taken to levels of hype that would impress even Sky Television.

In this world of 'New Football', people involved in the game's merchandising operations have promoted the idea that supporters should be treated as customers rather than fans. By this they mean that the level of customer care expected in normal business should apply to football. That it has not been the case in the past is due to the fact that football supporters are not customers in the true sense, and are, in fact, fans. The difference is crucial. Fans are not promiscuous, unlike customers. Even if a customer is generally loyal to a particular product or service, that loyalty will not prevent the occasional dalliance if there is better value to be had elsewhere. Not only that, if a customer is dissatisfied, a permanent separation can be on the cards.

For fans there are no such possibilities. A Spurs fan knows that at present there is a better product a couple of miles up the road but it would still be inconceivable to contemplate a change of allegiance. Even relegation cannot erode this kind of brand loyalty. And it is the strength of this emotional bond that has provided the basis for football's merchandising revolution.

In these days of lower ground capacities and high prices a fan may not be able to go to a game but identity with the cause can still be proclaimed by buying the merchandise. Clubs are the fans' main focus of attention but for four weeks in the summer of 1998, the national team, appearing in the greatest sporting event the world has ever seen, moved temporarily to the top of the bill. This meant that fans of different clubs could share in the common experience. Rivalry, which rules for the other forty-eight weeks of the year, could suddenly become camaraderie, or perhaps, with England's followers' record, conspiracy. Whatever the case, there is no better way to advertise membership of the brotherhood than to buy the merchandise.

The very success of the World Cup as a four-week sporting spectacle presents a problem when it comes to merchandising. As the finals arrive only once every four years, there is very little time to create brand awareness and only a relatively short sales period. A club shirt, for instance, has a life expectancy of two years and its potential buyers have built their loyalty over a lifetime. World Cup products start from scratch. To create a stream of high-profile products across continents at speed is no easy matter.

When the garish, bird-like Footix cavorted on stage with Sepp Blatter et al in Marseille the previous December, it seemed a comical idea for a mascot. But Footix is now an instantly recognizable symbol and contains considerable appeal to the youth market, the MTV generation, which considered it 'cool' – at least for as long as was necessary for the licensees to make a killing.

France 98 merchandise was produced using Footix as the stamp of authenticity. Another giant corporation, this time Sony, supervised the licensing on FIFA's behalf.

Every time Footix appeared on any merchandise, Sony took a cut of between 10 and 15 per cent of the cost price. Crucially, among the approved products – and there were over 400 of them – many were of superior quality and imagination compared to the usual wares sold in club shops. For instance, the designer, Louis Vuitton, produced a limited-edition football in a leather holder priced at almost £300 (the English World Cup merchandisers preferred to promote their own class act – a Union Jack bra). As if to prove the point, on Sky News a special presentation of France 98 merchandise was given, not by the football or business staff but by the station's fashion correspondent, Karen Kay, who pointed out that 'footballers are the new icons for teenagers – this year's poster for girls' bedrooms is Michael Owen'.

Everything, however, must contribute to the numbers game. The 200-odd companies licensed to manufacture France 98 products will, according to reliable estimates, generate £800 million in sales worldwide, with at least £50 million coming from the UK.

The journey through the World Cup numbers game staggers the imagination at every turn, except one. Those deals that were designed (merchandising) or revamped (sponsorship packages) especially for France 98, showed big increases in revenues over anything previously witnessed. Surprisingly, the one area where France 98 was subject to a woeful deal came from the sale of television rights.

The ringmaster and paymaster of British football, Sky Television, had its relentless march through the British sports calendar momentarily halted for the four weeks of France 98. Moreover, during the hiatus it would, for once, have to take a back seat while the BBC, in what may prove to be a last hurrah, again assumed a lead role, along with ITV. The two traditional networks would

share the screening of the World Cup, while Sky had
nothing except talking heads discussing the action on a
phone-in.

It was just like old times. However, lest it be thought
that ITV and the BBC had begun to take on Sky at its own
game, it should be pointed out that they did not acquire
the rights by their own negotiating skills but through
their membership of the European Broadcasting Union
(EBU), a cosy protectionists' club of European 'public
service' broadcasters that was formed in the 1950s, osten-
sibly to cooperate in Europe-wide ventures but actually
to establish a cartel that could freeze out other, newer,
services. Even now, Sky cannot gain entry.

The EBU acquired the European television rights for
the World Cup finals over a decade ago – ancient history
in television terms – in a renewal deal which was to last
for three tournaments: Italia 90, USA 94 and France 98.
Since rights fees have shot up in the intervening period,
it is not surprising that ITV and BBC (and broadcasters
from the other European countries) are paying far less
than they would have to cough up if the bidding had
taken place in today's market. In fact, the difference is
massive. ITV and the BBC each paid £1.8 million for the
whole tournament (potentially, sixty-four matches each).
This is less than Sky pays for one Premiership game,
which comes in at around £2.5 million. Furthermore,
because nobody had heard of the Internet ten years ago,
there was no provision made for distribution on the
World Wide Web and France 98 appeared to have missed
a trick by having no live audio commentary or pictures.
This let in a plethora of unofficial Web sites which could
thrive because the official sites had nothing exclusive
with which to tempt potential hits.

Television income for France 98 is therefore a fraction
of its true value. However, the deal at least ensured that

the majority of the world's population could watch this World Cup on the small screen. They should make the most of it. Sepp Blatter said this was the last time there would be a 'World Cup of the poor' and, sure enough, rights for 2002 and 2006 have already been sold to the German media group, Kirch, and the ever-present ISL, for £1.4 billion. This is the classic scenario for the World Cup finals to be removed from free-to-air television and screened on subscription and/or pay-per-view channels. By 2002, the digital revolution will truly be underway and a radical shake-up is definitely in store.

A worst-case but possible scenario would be where only the opening match, the semi-finals and the final were reserved for the great traditional networks like the BBC. All the other games would then be up for grabs by pay television. However, a directive of the European Union, known as 'Television Without Frontiers', empowers member states to legislate for a number of sporting occasions of importance to a particular country – called 'listed events' – to be prohibited from exclusive sale to subscription or pay-per-view services. If legislation is widespread and has teeth, it may open the way for the EBU to get involved again, although it would have to break the bank to have any realistic chance of renewing its rights.

Whether the sponsors who are paying such vast sums will be happy if they lose the billions of viewers that free-to-air television brings is another matter. Until now, FIFA has insisted that the World Cup must be shown to the widest possible audience. However, by excluding pay channels from the outset, terrestrial networks have been encouraged to bid low, since the big money generally comes from the likes of Sky. According to Jean Paul de la Fuente, ISL's Head of Media, France 98 was 'the bargain of the decade'. The networks, he insists, 'are making ten to fifteen times what they are paying in rights'. The message seems to be that things will be different next time and fans should enjoy it while they can. De la Fuente is not impressed by the 'listed events' argument either, calling any such system a 'market distortion ... based on the idea that football is a basic need like water or gas – but it isn't. It is a market-driven business.'

Meanwhile, Sepp Blatter was busy muddying the waters when he warned: 'FIFA is in control of the distribution policy of television rights and in no way would national laws be jeopardized. Pay-per-view is totally excluded ... but could be possible if there is 60 per cent penetration.' However, it is not primarily low-penetration figures that national politicians and fans object to but the fact that they are forced to pay for the service, not once, but twice, first through either taxation or advertising costs on the goods they buy, then again if they have to pay a subscription charge.

Apart from television, then, the numbers kept on rising as France 98 got closer. This didn't mean that there was a lack of controversy, however. Far from it. In fact the issue which provoked the most acrimony of all was one that should have been plain sailing: the sale of match tickets.

CHAPTER NINE

A Numbers Game (Part Two)

THE *DAILY STAR* GOT STRAIGHT to the point. 'Up Yer Jacksee', its headline screamed. Of course the *Star* was picking up where the *Mirror* had left off two years before when it greeted England's Euro 96 semi-final against Germany with the infamous headline: 'Achtung Surrender. For You Fritz The Euro 96 Championship Is Over'. But while the *Mirror* drew opprobrium from all sides for its xenophobia, the *Star*'s ill-considered words were soon supported by an outbreak of righteous indignation, which more or less echoed the paper's sentiments: the French Organizing Committee (CFO) for the World Cup was somehow deliberately discriminating against the rest of the world in general and the British in particular over the allocation of match tickets.

Ticketing had never before been such a controversial issue for a World Cup. For France 98, similar percentage allocations were initially made as for previous tournaments. FIFA and the CFO ordained that 12 per cent of the tickets would be set aside for sponsors and suppliers, 8 per cent would go to official tour operators and 20 per cent would be allocated to the thirty-two competing nations. In fact the competing nations saw an increase of 5 per cent over USA 94 but, as it turned out, the increase did nothing to satisfy the huge demand, particularly within Europe. The allocations meant that less than 10 per cent of any specific stadium capacity was going to be available to fans of the competing countries. In any case, the percentage increase over USA 94 was academic, since there were one million fewer tickets than were available for the matches in the USA, where seating capacities were much larger.

After the allocations, 1.5 million tickets were left in the hands of the CFO. Planning for the sale of these tickets began in 1994 with no protests or opposition. Although the demand from France's near neighbours in Europe was likely to be high, qualification would not be decided for another three years so no one knew exactly which countries would require tickets.

Perhaps everyone was lulled into a false sense of security by some strange goings on at Euro 96 in England. A similar percentage allocation of tickets to competing nations was made as for France 98 yet some games were sparsely attended. This happened because unfancied nations progressed at the expense of some traditionally well-supported countries, which led to a flood of tickets being released on to the black market from disenchanted Dutch and Italian fans, for which there was no great demand from the insular English. There certainly didn't appear to be any problem with availability and no complaints were forthcoming from other countries.

That was not the only anomaly of Euro 96. The country which was at the forefront of the commercial revolution in football hardly managed to produce any profit from the tournament, nor was there a significant boost to tourism or other spin-offs. The thrust of England's marketing seemed to be: 'Come and see these lovely new football grounds we've built.' There were a number of extraneous events but they were locally based and did nothing for the country as a whole. Even the slogan 'Football's Coming Home' was popularized through an independent recording. The song, 'Three Lions', was taken up by the fans, but it was never the official song and the FA only took it on board once they were forced to by its popularity and after their own musical effort – a funereal dirge sung by Mick Hucknall – had sunk without trace.

The French, on the other hand, were determined to make the most of the commercial possibilities. They also had another important objective. Unlike England, they decided to integrate the World Cup into the mainstream of French cultural life; to raise the tournament's sights so that it would advertise not just football but also the glory of France. The French President himself instigated the campaign to secure the World Cup. When the Stade de France opened in January Jacques Chirac reaffirmed the importance he placed on the World Cup, saying, 'It is down to us [the French] to do whatever is necessary so that this event marks the history of our country and not just its sporting history.'

To this end, the CFO limited the number of tickets they were prepared to sell to foreigners and reserved the greater proportion for their own citizens. The French wanted to put on a 'big show' to impress the watching world, certainly, but also for their own people. And they wanted to avoid the pictures of half-empty stadia evident at Euro 96. They regarded their decisions on ticketing as legitimate for a host nation and despite the protestations from England, the FA based its own bid for the 2006 World Cup on the same principle.

Once the qualifying countries were known, the allocation brought immediate condemnation from France's neighbours, notably Germany, Holland and Belgium, but the most vociferous critics by far were the English.

The FA, in response to the violent and abusive behaviour by English fans abroad over many years, had encouraged supporters to join a travel club under its control. By doing this they tried to ensure that the only way English fans could obtain tickets for games overseas was through membership of the club. Over the years the travel club grew to over 30,000 members, despite the £15 plus joining fee. Many would not go to particular games, so the demand was easily satisfied. Unfortunately, no one had considered what would happen should England qualify for France, when nearly all travel club members would want to go to England's matches. The allocation would not be anywhere near the numbers needed but little was done to prepare members for the inevitable disappointment. To compound matters, in order to bolster the campaign to stop the ticketless travelling, the FA had, over the years, fostered the belief that they could supply demand through the travel club. 'Become a member and get a ticket' was an important message which FA propaganda was designed to convey. So when England's initial allocation turned out to be a meagre 9,000 tickets for the three group games, it was greeted with outrage and a disturbing outburst of anti-French sentiment from the media and the authorities alike.

Urgent meetings were held, the press fulminated, lots of important people went to see other important people. But whichever way you dissected it, the demand could not be met. However, anybody in England could buy a World Cup ticket if they were prepared to pay the enormous sums demanded by tour operators (for example, a one-day trip to watch England–Tunisia, travel and match ticket only, cost a minimum of almost £600), thus exposing membership of the travel club as practically useless in this instance. So while corporate entertainment was set to flourish, the ordinary fan effectively was being squeezed out.

As one of twelve recognized tour operators, the former England rugby international, Mike Burton, paid £500,000 for the right to sell his packages. No price restrictions were placed upon him and despite charging almost £3,000 for a one-day trip to Paris for the final, he received few complaints from his well-heeled target market. 'It's expensive, of course,' he said, 'but the once-in-a-lifetime occasion drives the price up.' Burton admitted that he would make 'some profit' from the deal. So too would a tour operator based in Los Angeles. Having realized how profitable World Cup ticket sales could be at USA 94, it secured 20,000 tickets for France 98, many of them bought from national federations, and experienced no trouble finding buyers prepared to pay as much as six times the face value.

It was not the exorbitant prices charged by tour operators, however, which concerned the World Cup's organizers. With less than 10 per cent of ticket sales accounting for over 50 per cent of revenue, the CFO felt they had struck the right balance between income and accessibility. Corporate sales were intended to hold down prices for the general public and indeed the official prices charged for tickets were not excessive. In explanation, Jacques Lambert, the CFO's Director General, emphasized the organizers' wish 'to have a popular World Cup at low prices'. However, Lambert accepted that the high-minded ideals had not altogether borne fruit. 'What has happened,' he claimed, 'has been the emergence of a parallel market [a black market in tickets], the politics of which have undermined our policy.'

It was the lower end of the black market that most concerned Isabelle Delaye, who was in charge of the ticketing operation. She was not particularly bothered about 'someone who can spend hundreds of pounds on a ticket'. Her main focus was on 'the tickets at £50 when there are thousands who can buy at this price', therefore encouraging many locals to capitalize on the black market.

In reality, the CFO's priority was to ensure that as many tickets as possible were sold. That meant selling first to the home market to avoid a repetition of Dutch, Italian or any other country's fans predominating to the extent that if their tickets were unused, stadia would have large swathes of unoccupied areas. Alongside the French market, sales to tour operators offered reassurance since their customers would turn up whoever was playing. It was a belt-and-braces approach which left supporters of the qualifying countries way down the list of priorities. There was no room for manoeuvre if demand was high. The consequence was that the organizers inevitably played safe and underestimated the demand. Jacques Lambert was honest enough to admit that they 'didn't imagine the excitement that exists around this World Cup. We didn't think it would be such a success, including overseas.'

Even if they wanted to, the French – who took the brunt of English criticism – and FIFA, could not alter the arrangements of a global mega-business less than six months before its showpiece event began. Michel Platini, in his role as Co-President of the CFO, put the case for the defence, saying, 'It's not so easy. When you [England] qualified it was November 1997, but we began the ticketing four years ago. For Brazil, for England, no problem if you come. But Mexico–Romania in Toulouse – who will buy the tickets?' Platini's colleague, Laurent Chetrit, added: 'Who has paid for all this [the $900 million it cost to build the Stade de France and the renovation of other venues]? The French taxpayer. That the French taxpayer should get more tickets is perfectly understandable.' The French also had to take into consideration the fact that only the domestic market could provide the amount of advance income necessary to fund the 'big show'. Unlike USA 94, which was organized by a private company, the profits making a few individuals extremely wealthy, any surplus going to France from the World Cup of 1998 would be divided between the state (on behalf of the taxpayer) and the French Football Federation.

All of this cut no ice in England. The only thing that mattered was the availability of more tickets. In fact, what was happening was a clash of cultures. For such close neighbours, it is amazing how England and France have diametrically opposed views of the world. The World Cup in France, unlike the European Championships in England, was an event beyond football. Despite fallacious English arguments that attendances in the French league are pitiful – with the opening of the redeveloped World Cup stadia, the end of the domestic season saw attendance records broken with over 56,000 for the visit of Paris St Germain to the Stade Vélodrome in Marseille and both clubs expected to have over 20,000 *abonnés* (season ticket holders) by August – the CFO's view was that their compatriots would attend in great numbers, precisely because what was being offered was not the everyday domestic fare. The first thought of the French was: 'How could the English not understand that?'

The divergence between the two countries applies to football as much as any other area of life. Football to the French is more than sport. It would be difficult to find any English philosopher acknowledging the existence of the game, let alone one who played it, like Albert Camus, who said: 'All that I know most surely about morality and the obligations of men, I learned playing football.' So how could the English possibly know about *l'esprit de jeu* (the spirit of the game)?

The French believe it was they who gave football to the world, just as they gave birth to the modern Olympics in 1896. It was the French who formed FIFA; it was the French who created the World Cup; it was the French who started European competitions. But who refused to take part in early World Cups? Who refused to join FIFA? Who refused to play in the first European Cup? The English, who will always have to be dragged kicking and screaming to the party like a naughty child. Once there, of course, they quite like it and want to eat all of the cake.

Matters did not end with any agreement to differ. To counter what they saw as the increased potential for trouble, the FA and the UK government mounted an ill-conceived advertising campaign to prevent those without tickets from going to France. They warned of dire consequences and insinuated that the French riot police would be waiting for them and spoiling for a fight. A leaflet was produced which stated: 'Any trouble-makers will face tough police methods and instant justice.' They then appealed to the supporters' better natures by telling them they could jeopardize England's bid for the 2006 World Cup.

All hell broke loose a few days after the launch of the advertising campaign. The French Minister for Tourism, Michelle Demessine, who was visiting London, publicly announced, to the dismay of the authorities, that the English were welcome in France during the World Cup whether they had tickets or not. At a stroke, she had totally undermined the whole British strategy. Mme Demessine was vilified by both the English media and politicians. One MP went so far as to suggest that a European war might ensue, causing David Lacey, in the *Guardian*, to wonder, 'who elects these characters? A.J.P.

Taylor's book, *The Origins of the Second World War*, is full of controversial arguments but nowhere does he suggest that Hitler invaded France in 1940 because the Germans did not get enough tickets for the World Cup there in 1938.' If the British government thought the tourism minister's views would be disowned by other French officials, they were sadly mistaken. In fact support for her was emphasized when plans were unveiled to install giant television screens in cities and resorts throughout France to show games to those without tickets.

Mme Demessine was offering a reiteration of what Michel Platini had said earlier. The World Cup was not just a football tournament, it was a festival to be shared by all. Can't get a ticket? Ergo aggro for the English; come and enjoy the occasion for the French. This World Cup was not going to be the preserve of football supporters alone, however important they might be. Football fans could discover the delights of the French way of doing things, while those who would not normally consider themselves football fans would, for once, get involved in the beautiful game. Those French who found themselves away from a television set, those foreign supporters without tickets, tourists and other visitors, all would be able to gather together in some of the most evocative public spaces in France, where they would be part of a unique experience.

The French had signalled their intentions from the start. Just as they had earlier broken with tradition by holding the original World Cup draw in the Louvre and the draw for the finals in a stadium, they conversely planned to hold an additional opening ceremony on the streets of Paris. The budget of £5 million would be spent, not just on the usual fireworks and folk dancing in a stadium, but on a huge artistic extravaganza, the focal points of which were to be four 'giants', each over twenty metres high. The giants would represent different peoples of the world and each would be at the head of one of four processions. After striding across the capital from their different directions, which would allow over a million people to watch their progress, they would converge on a model of the World Cup trophy, some eighty feet tall, in the Place de la Concorde, where 80,000 eager spectators would be waiting. 'I want to use Paris as a theatre,' said Jean-Pascal Levy-Trumet, the artistic designer of the spectacle. 'It will be a celebration of the people, by the people.'

While Levy-Trumet was rehearsing his giants in Paris, England raged. In an attempt to allay the confusion which all the publicity over tickets had caused, the Home Secretary, Jack Straw, went on David Mellor's radio phone-in show to answer supporters' questions. He displayed pride in the fact that he had managed to get England's allocation increased to 14,000, which would be sold to certain lucky travel club members. Anyone else would either have to purchase one of the expensive packages on offer from the tour operators, or stay at home.

Again and again, members of the public came on to the programme to say they did not have tickets but were still determined to go to France. Some explained how they often went abroad without tickets and no matter what the government or anyone else preached, they generally managed to get into games. One articulate caller declared that he was a law-abiding member of the public, he intended to take his holidays in France and while there would try to buy some match tickets. Since this was a perfectly reasonable and lawful activity, he asked if Mr Straw could give him any advice on how to avoid trouble and exhibit the correct behaviour.

In one of the most depressing points of this whole sorry saga, the Home Secretary had nothing to say to this

British citizen, other than, 'Don't go.' There would be no advice, no help, nothing to suggest any support for a UK national's right of lawful passage in a neighbouring European Union country.

At previous tournaments, the Football Supporters Association had set up 'embassies', which had been welcomed by fans and host countries alike. The 'embassies' provided a point of contact for supporters and dispensed invaluable information. The FA in its wisdom refused funds for 'embassies' to be set up in France. It looked for a while as if the service would be absent but fortunately Mastercard, one of the World Cup sponsors, stepped in and picked up the bill.

Meanwhile, the French put the last tranche of tickets, which had been held back – totalling 170,000 – on sale, having rejected an attempted intervention from the European Union's Competition Commissioner, Karel Van Miert, which came with the threat of a huge fine if the French favoured their home market rather than European Union countries as a whole. Van Miert was trying, even if it was at the last minute, to redress the balance of the allocation. He tried to do this because he had belatedly accepted the argument that selling the bulk of the tickets to French citizens was anti-competitive and therefore in breach of the Treaty of Rome.

Despite the French rebuff for Van Miert, when the sale took place it was believed the tickets would be available to anybody from any country as they were to be offered through a telephone service on a first-come, first-served basis. On the day, though, hardly any Britons were able to get through, due to the incredible demand, and if they did, they found there were no tickets remaining for England games. British Telecom announced that when the phone line opened, the national telecommunications system experienced its greatest demand ever.

It would be wrong to blame the FA and the government for being apprehensive about England's fans causing havoc abroad. After all, both the football and civil authorities had been severely criticized in the past for their failure to anticipate mayhem. However, all exhortations down the years have failed to prevent fans travelling without tickets. A repeat of this policy failure, which just about every English football supporter except those in the government expected, would mean that all the police expertise in the UK would have come to nought, no matter how much liaison there was between national police forces beforehand. It also seemed that little practical action was being taken to help enforce the message. Exclusion orders on known troublemakers had been stepped up, it was true; but to a grand total of sixty-three. The problem with the English approach, therefore, was that the government's policy would stop hardly anyone and the lack of any alternative plan (such as increasing the number of exclusion orders and having a visible police presence travelling with the fans) could lead to the warnings of trouble becoming a self-fulfilling prophecy.

Major public order problems have occurred in Dublin and Rome in recent times. Furthermore, the worst disorder knew no boundaries, it could occur inside or outside grounds, during, before or after games. When perpetrated inside a ground, it was clear that large numbers of English must have obtained tickets on the day. The authorities have always been loath to confront this harsh reality. It is the same poverty of analysis which dismissed hooligans as 'mindless' in the 1980s, even when it was obvious they were well organized. Indeed, many of the miscreants have good jobs and earn decent money. They are more, not less likely to pay the high prices being asked by tour operators and may even have infiltrated the FA's travel club. The only time they will be among the fans with no tickets is when they choose to be. If they didn't get tickets, or black market purchases were to invalidate segregation measures, the French public and authorities, having already been fingered by the tabloids, would be an easy scapegoat. The whole situation would be made worse if England played poorly. Even if they played well, they would lose at some point unless they were actually to win the trophy. The moment of loss has often signalled the escalation of English xenophobia and violence. They didn't need such calamities to cause trouble but they helped.

CHAPTER TEN

Even the Bad Times are Good

Back home, as Manchester United's season petered out in an anti-climax, the management of the club and the plc looked at what lessons could be learned as they geared themselves up to try once again to meet their own and their fans' aspirations.

If the Monaco result was bad for Manchester United, matters were about to get even worse. A healthy lead in the Premiership race had been whittled away by Arsenal and although United had led the Londoners by thirteen points in December, the advantage was lost and, with two games left, Arsenal had done enough to claim their first championship since 1991. When Arsenal went on to cruise to a 2–0 victory over Newcastle United in the Cup Final, thus pulling off the coveted double, the season had, for United, ended up a damp squib. The business of winning where it matters most to fans, on the field, had not been taken care of.

In retrospect, the denouement of the domestic season began just before the second Monaco encounter, when the Gunners beat United 1–0 at Old Trafford. The course of events was reminiscent of a game at St James's Park two years earlier, when United beat Newcastle with an

Eric Cantona goal in a victory which signalled Newcastle's squandering of a twelve-point lead to United, who went on to win the double.

The decline in United's fortunes was not simply the result of one game. The players put in some patchy home performances in the last third of the season, losing to Leicester City and drawing against Bolton Wanderers, for instance, which could not have been foreseen when United were destroying defences in the autumn.

There could be no complaints from Old Trafford and indeed there were none. There was no frustration like that experienced when the championship was lost to Blackburn Rovers on the last day of the season in 1995 and, if United had an image as graceless losers, that was certainly not the case this time. 'Truthfully though, we don't deserve to be champions,' admitted United fanzine *Red Issue* while Andy Mitten, editor of *United We Stand*, wrote: 'I've yet to meet a red who, although disappointed that we've lost the League, doesn't give credit to Arsenal for the manner in which they've performed this year.'

Among the obvious regrets, the turnaround in United's fortunes at least put paid to the tabloids' incessant stories about Alex Ferguson's supposed mastery of mind games with opposing managers. Kevin Keegan's famous 'I would love it if United lose' outburst on Sky was often cited as evidence of Ferguson's supreme skill in this regard though it was just as much a case of Keegan succumbing to stress. Then there was the time the previous season when Ferguson disparaged Arsène Wenger's knowledge of the demands of the Premiership, having come to England from Japan. The media gleefully suggested that the master had lost his touch and recalled how United had handed the title to Leeds in 1992.

The official line from Old Trafford was that injuries were the main reason for the failure in 1998. However,

Arsenal also had key players missing; Bergkamp and Wright were both out for lengthy periods.

The big question posed by United's post-Christmas collapse in 1998 was why, when the inevitable strains, pulls and assorted injuries struck, was Ferguson's cupboard so bare? The most common explanation was that the plc had frustrated the manager's attempts to add quality performers to his playing staff when he needed them most. Ferguson himself, however, at the time of the Monaco defeat, admitted that the positive way the young players had initially responded to the loss of Roy Keane had blinded him to the need to reinforce his squad.

Later, as he faced the fact that Arsenal were going to win the league, Ferguson, in an interview with Oliver Holt of *The Times*, questioned the board's priorities. 'The club has got to get to grips with what actually makes a winning club in Europe,' he mused. 'It has not approached that. It is not even anywhere near that. It is not a Barcelona, it is not an AC Milan, it is not a Juventus, it is not a Real Madrid . . . What may happen after I leave is that it will dawn on them that, when a new manager comes in, he may ask for £60 million to build a team to win in Europe . . . they will say, "I wish we had done that five years back down the road." There are big strides this club has got to take but when they will do it, I don't know.'

This criticism was somewhat borne out by Ferguson's boss, Martin Edwards, who, when commenting on Ferguson's observations, asked, 'Is there anything clever in being £50 million in debt and winning the European Cup?' However, the board's parsimony is only part of the story at best. Ferguson has vacillated on occasion. He has also endorsed the corporate line himself at times, and he has not exploited his apparently unassailable position to insist on the finance to sign the best.

In the interview with Holt, Ferguson came up with yet another explanation. There were, among his group of players, an unnamed few whose attitude was wrong. 'There has to be a bit of soul searching,' he said. 'There are one or two individuals where you have got to say, "Is the hunger the same?" It is very difficult to get it back and we will be making changes at the end of the season, changes in personnel ... People like myself and the staff and the supporters do not deserve to have it thrown away by the players like this, not after all the work that has been done here.'

Although the public condemnation was unusual, it was not the first time Ferguson had felt this way. After one particularly poor European performance, in the heat of the moment, he shocked the board by insisting that a number of top players be immediately off-loaded. They are still there.

The known facts are that there were some great performances in the first half of the season and some poor ones in the second. The poor period coincided with injuries to key players. In Europe and domestically, United's rivals responded to such problems by signing players or anticipated them by having adequate replacements. What is clear is that at United there was no strategy cast in stone to achieve a specific target. On the one hand, there was the emotional need to win the European Cup, which beguiled fans and media but which does not seem to have been a financial priority at board level; on the other the feeling persisted that the team was good enough to cruise in the league. When a Manchester bookmaker, Fred Done, actually paid out on United winning the title when they were well ahead but with some games to go, perhaps the players started to believe the publicity.

To take Ferguson at his word, once he knew he was not going to be able to purchase top-class players, then the chances of winning the European Cup were considerably reduced, yet he did not seem to be able to resist the pull of the competition and its place in United's history. A realistic target, however, would have been to try to do better than the previous season, when the team somehow qualified from the group stage of the Champions' League despite being unconvincing in most of their games and then produced a memorable display against Porto in the quarter-final before going out to Borussia Dortmund in the semi-final. But there was no agreement running through the club on a proper European objective nor any concomitant strategy to carry it out.

The lure of Europe conditioned United's approach to the Premiership. When they took their foot off the pedal, they could not put it back on. United's number-one priority should have been to retain their title. That way, direct entry to the group stage of the Champions' League is guaranteed and the supporters are satisfied. Year-on-year progress in Europe can sit comfortably with this. In United's case, the players made the mistake of thinking that they could coast through the league and still win it but when obstacles were thrown in their way the team could not rise to the challenge. 'Let someone else have it [the title],' said Bobby Charlton, making the best of his disappointment. 'We've won it four times in five years, it will be good for the game if someone else has it.' It would also, in the view of the manager, be a salutary lesson for his players. Yet Ferguson had advance warning of what might happen after the second Juventus encounter in Turin when the Italians could have been eliminated from the competition. Teddy Sheringham's post-match explanation that it was difficult to motivate himself when United had already qualified indicated the potential for complacency. (He was roundly rebuked by Peter Schmeichel, who felt that playing Juventus in the Champions' League at any time should be sufficient incentive.)

In the first half of this century, the domestic double – the league championship and the FA Cup won in the same season – was the holy grail of English football. Until 1961 the feat had not been accomplished this century. Once Spurs cracked it, other clubs – Arsenal, Liverpool, Manchester United – followed with increasing regularity. Another exploit, though, has been performed only three times in the same period and it was in United's power to equal it. The achievement in question is three championships in a row, which has only been managed by Huddersfield in the 1920s, Arsenal in the 1930s (both times, the manager was Herbert Chapman) and by Liverpool between 1981 and 1984. What a fantastic feat it would have been for Ferguson and United to emulate that. Even the great United team of the 1960s never came anywhere near it. Prioritizing that objective, at the same time that Rangers in Scotland were going for ten in a row to beat Celtic's nine, would have lit up the nation and given United an additional incentive and a total determination to win the Premiership again. Strangely, this chance for immortality was hardly mentioned by the board, the management, the players or the media.

So Ferguson and his depleted army fought on two fronts without ever being totally convincing on either. It was as if no one was thinking about what it would really take to succeed. Perhaps the domestic successes of recent years had blinded the club to the fact that every year the opposition would seek to improve so United had to work that bit harder to stay ahead.

Martin Edwards put forward the view that just about everyone in the country shared, saying, 'I don't think anyone would have believed you if you had looked at

Arsenal's fixture list and said they were going to get thirty points from those ten matches.' That may be so but it didn't negate the manager's challenge to his chairman to raise his sights and loosen the purse strings. In fact, there had been financial tensions between the two since Ferguson took over the job in 1986.

Alex Ferguson arrived at Old Trafford after the departure of Ron Atkinson. Atkinson's flamboyant style had flattered to deceive yet towards the end of his reign the board sanctioned a number of expensive purchases at a time when football's finances were in deep depression. Alan Brazil, Terry Gibson and John Sivebeck had arrived for a total of £2 million but failed to live up to expectations. So United were no nearer claiming the championship they craved and which had eluded the club since 1967. Having inherited a high wage bill from Atkinson, Ferguson soon found that United could not or would not always compete when it came to transfers. Ferguson's predicament was exemplified by the case of Paul Gascoigne, who might well have gone to United if the club had been in a position to mount a bid competitive with the offer from Spurs.

There were also times when Ferguson was forced to sell before he could buy and he never really had the resources to build a team as he would have wished. On the other hand, football was going through a rough patch and United were no longer the richest kids on the block. It was common knowledge that Martin Edwards would sell the club if he received an adequate offer. In the climate of uncertainty, Ferguson's own purchases were sometimes questionable. Were Mal Donaghy, Mike Phelan, Ralph Milne or Danny Wallace really United-class players? Despite this, when the clamour for Ferguson to be sacked reached a peak at the end of the 1980s, Martin Edwards stood by him and was rewarded with the Cup Final victory over Crystal Palace in 1990.

To Martin Edwards the firing issue did not arise. Recalling that period, he says, 'We were aware of how much work Alex was doing behind the scenes. We had just spent money on five players [Phelan, Webb, Ince, Wallace and Pallister] and we just felt we had to give him time for those players to bed in.' United needed someone with Ferguson's strength of character and who was not afraid of the scale of his task. Maybe, as Edwards suggested, it took longer than he expected to learn the nuances of the English game, but there was never any doubt that United had the right man.

The previous five years, during which time United had been in the wilderness, had seen English clubs banned from Europe as a result of the Heysel tragedy. Now, English clubs were back in the European fold and United went on to win the 1991 Cup Winners' Cup. With the victory in the final over Barcelona, capped with a memorable goal from Mark Hughes, United were once again in the top flight of British and European clubs and the corner was turned.

Now there was another, easier target for the fans' ire. It was Martin Edwards and the new business structure based around the plc which was holding the manager back.

The reasons for this lay in a series of events which led fans to question Edwards's commitment. In the mid-1980s Edwards had come close to selling United to Robert Maxwell, then in 1989 came the Michael Knighton fiasco. Edwards and Knighton had agreed a deal whereby Edwards sold his stake to Knighton for £10 million. Knighton had also agreed to provide a further £10 million to rebuild Old Trafford. The deal was announced amid great fanfare and was followed by the embarrassing scene at the first home game of the new season, when Knighton, decked out in full United kit, displayed his admittedly impressive ball skills to an astonished audience. However, Knighton was unable to realize his option on Edwards's shares amid a campaign led by Robert Maxwell, of all people, which discredited his financial viability. Knighton did, though, serve on United's board for a time and his innovative ideas might have served United well.

All the speculation over the possible sale of United contributed to the elevation of the club's value. Martin Edwards now decided that another possibility was open to him. Public flotations were no longer out of bounds, even Millwall had done it. Until United, however, the few flotations that had happened had all taken place when interest was due more to the expansion of the financial marketplace in the City of London than the intrinsic merits of football's potential for profits. Edwards realized that the flotation option would allow him to realize some of his assets – the shares he held in United – and let him maintain the lead position in the ownership and running of the club, which, of course, would benefit from a huge introduction of capital. Consequently, in 1991, United became a public company.

Once United was floated, it was not long before the breakaway Premier League would yet again push up the club's value to a level not even the most bullish could have envisaged and Martin Edwards became a very wealthy man.

Edwards had inherited shares in Manchester United from his father. Louis Edwards was introduced to the board by Matt Busby and soon set about applying the skills he had learned when expanding the family butcher business in a bid to take control of the club. When the task was successfully completed, Louis Edwards was chairman and majority shareholder, a position attained at less than the cost of United's most expensive player at the time, Denis Law, who was brought back from Italy for £115,000. When Louis died suddenly, soon after an exposé of his business methods on the Granada current affairs television programme, *World in Action*, Martin assumed control. The family business was soon sold to the Argyll food conglomerate and Martin was, in effect, no longer top dog. However, following lobbying from a number of chairmen, the FA relaxed its rule which prohibited paid directors and Martin Edwards became one of the first of a new breed when, in 1981, he joined the United payroll.

Initially, perhaps, his efforts seemed to be based more on his sense of duty to his father's memory than on a genuine enthusiasm for running a football club. His sporting inclination had been towards rugby rather than football and although he was steeped in the United tradition through his father's involvement (he was taken to his first game in 1952 and attended regularly from 1958), he was committed to playing the fifteen-a-side game for Wilmslow until injury forced him to give up playing.

Totally different from his extrovert, larger-than-life father, Martin Edwards lives unostentatiously in Wilmslow, on the outskirts of Manchester. He is a creature of habit, running every day and playing tennis twice a week. Mild in manner and neat in appearance, he is a rarity in football, a chief executive with no discernible ego who surrounds himself with men of substance.

Patrick Harverson, the sports business correspondent of the *Financial Times*, believes Edwards has 'done a very good job' for United in financial terms. 'It's difficult,' he said, 'to criticize someone who has overseen such success at the club. He deserves the most credit for sticking with Alex Ferguson at a time when perhaps others may have changed managers.' Someone who has worked with

Edwards said: 'The first impression is that h
across as someone a bit superficial and not wi
ways of football. But I think he plays up to this. He is
much more shrewd than people realize.' In a caveat,
though, the same observer speculated that 'he may not
be able to take United to the next level because of his
innate conservatism'.

As he sits in his office in the new Old Trafford, Edwards
admits that his father is often in his thoughts. Apart from
some landscape prints supplied by the interior designer,
the only personal adornment on the walls are the Premier
League Charter and a portrait of Louis. 'People say,' he
said, 'that if he could come back now and see everything
that's been achieved, the state of the ground, he would be
proud.' Against a wall in the L-shaped room is a bookcase
housing every volume that has ever been written about
Manchester United, even the ones criticizing him personally. There is also evidence of two heroes from his
boyhood: books about Muhammad Ali and Elvis Presley
CDs. In addition, the bookcase contains replicas of
trophies won by United since he became chairman.

Over the years, Edwards and his family have diluted
their shareholding and he now owns 14 per cent of
United, enough to be the single largest shareholder but
much less than his father had bequeathed and less than
the 40 per cent he had built up prior to flotation. The
series of sales brought in a considerable amount of cash.
The first was worth £6.5 million, although much of this
went to pay off the borrowings he took out in enlarging
his stake, with further offloads bringing in another £27
million. The sales also attracted voluminous criticism
suggesting that Edwards saw the club as a cash cow. In
his well-researched book, *The Football Business**, David

---

* Mainstream, 1998.

Conn indicts Edwards and his family for the money they, and others, made out of the success of United's flotation and the subsequent performance of its shares. 'United fostered a culture,' Conn wrote, 'which sees profit as the company's primary object; in which the profit end seems to justify the means, however tacky . . . The shareholders who bought their shares before football was a business, a means to make money, have got their cash out. Martin Edwards, Doug Ellis [chairman of Aston Villa], [Maurice] Watkins [United's legal counsel] . . . are men sitting on enormous personal fortunes created by football's boom.'

But as Conn himself admits, Manchester United's results since flotation have been spectacular, both on and off the pitch. Whatever success the team has enjoyed over and above other floated clubs cannot by itself explain the incredible growth in United's total value compared to that of their rivals, an almost tenfold increase since flotation, from £48 million to over £400 million. Newcastle United, despite maximizing their income, have seen their share price fall dramatically, as has virtually every other floated club. Yet most of them obtain substantial revenues from the Sky television deal and, just like United, are beneficiaries of the commercial revolution.

It is a belief in financial circles that a public company is incompatible with dynastic, especially family owner-ship. As financial journalists Lisa Buckingham and Pauline Springett pointed out in the *Guardian*, 'There have been few ruling families who have resisted the temptation to treat public companies as their personal fiefdoms.' Thus the trials and tribulations at Newcastle, with mass resignations from the board throughout the spring of 1998, can be directly traced to the inherent instability of a public company when a family retains too much control. The agenda of family directors is often different from the interests of the shareholders as a whole. For Manchester United to be the success it has become, it was absolutely necessary for Martin Edwards to avoid a situation where his family shareholding was so great it caused tensions with City investors and fund managers.

So while it is true to say that Edwards and his family enriched themselves considerably, they increased the worth of the company by decreasing their shareholding. Furthermore, over £90 million has been ploughed into the team, stadium and new training facilities, which is more than the total worth of most Premier League clubs. Much of this investment is viewed by financial institutions as the equivalent of research and development. It helps to establish a solid platform for future growth. If Martin Edwards had behaved like some medieval baron as some other chairmen do, then United's shares could have gone the way of other clubs' and the team might not have gone on to realize the deeds it has. Of course, the lack of any replica in the bookcase for 1997/98 rankled. Nevertheless, Edwards was prepared to accept that the prudent running of the company was of paramount concern, in his mind overriding even winning the European Cup.

'It's no use going out and busting the bank to win the European Cup,' he said. That, he went on, is 'what Real Madrid have done. It isn't necessarily the right thing for us. If we win the European Cup we've got to get there in our own way, from a position of financial strength, not just going out and spending a fortune.' This did not prevent United making what Edwards considers big offers during the summer of 1997. United were, in his words, 'heavily into the transfer market', during the close season. Edwards concluded by bemoaning the fact that 'none of these players [offers were made for Zidane,

Vieri, Laudrup, Thuram and Batistuta] could be purchased for £10 million', and he did not think 'many English clubs were offering £10 million per player, so that's how difficult it has become'.

All of this may well be true but Edwards's comparison is with other English clubs, whereas to the biggest club in Europe, £10 million is not a bank-breaking amount to pay for a player of true world class who would bring a new dimension to the team. And anyway, the English record – the £15 million Newcastle paid Blackburn for Alan Shearer – is half as much again as Edwards thought should be his cut-off point for Zidane, who had, by then, excelled in European competitions. Moreover, by confirming the 'either Cole or Salas' choice his manager faced, Edwards showed how the idea of squad-think, where a world-class striker is kept in reserve for the inevitable injuries, suspensions and loss of form, remains something of an alien concept at Old Trafford. This conservative strategy would have made more sense if Edwards's thinking on Europe was mirrored by a dedication to retaining the league on the part of the manager and players, but Ferguson was caught between the two, desperate to win in Europe but without the resources, yet lacking the focus to win the Premiership.

After failing to lift a trophy in 1998, United budgeted for two more players to be added to the squad for 1998/99, in addition to the Dutch defender, Jaap Stam, whose club, PSV Eindhoven did succumb to Edwards's magic number, and accepted his £10 million bid.

As for what shape any changes might take, Edwards said that he couldn't 'predict whether Ferguson will do it differently. He stands or falls by the results of his team so I don't think you can dictate. The only thing the chairman or CEO [Chief Executive Officer] can do is to analyse the things you are doing. The board of Manchester United

believe first and foremost that the thing you
to win your national league. You can never
win the European Cup even if you're in the fi
can go wrong on the day. I hope the lesso
learned from this season. Our theory is: we pick the
manager and he manages the club. If he does it, fine. If he
doesn't, you have to do something about it.'

Having said that, the manager has been given more
money than ever to spend. Both know full well that to
have an optimum business, it is necessary to achieve
some success with the team. The question is, will there be
a meeting of minds, a coming together of Messrs
Edwards and Ferguson to challenge Juventus and Real
Madrid? Or is the inherent risk, the personal and financial commitment, too great for the two men to
contemplate?

None of the doubts at United surfaced at Juventus. As
it turned out, the disappointment at the 3–2 defeat at Old
Trafford evaporated with the 1–0 victory over United in
Turin and the march to yet another Champions' League
final and Serie A title.

Yet it seems as if it is Juventus which should have the
problems, as they sell their star forwards each year, often
to the consternation of coach Marcello Lippi (a policy
called *vendere e vincere* – sell and win). With wages
running at over fifty per cent of turnover, transfer income
is a must and profits from this source amount to more
than £11 million. The fact that the policy is the brainchild
of an administrator, sports director Luciano Moggi,
nevertheless does not appear to produce the tensions it
would in England.

In an attempt to offset the high wage bill and limited
commercial scope, Juventus has at last capitalized on its
status as Italy's best supported club. Unlike English
clubs, it has moved in the direction of a comprehensive,

...tionwide educational policy – *Punto Juve*. Its aim is to serve each local community by establishing a school in every Italian province and is on a scale undreamt of elsewhere, even at Manchester United or Arsenal.

With their own way of doing things fully entrenched, Juventus just keep rolling along. Coach Lippi, who joined in 1994 after working his way through series 'C' and 'B' before making his mark at Napoli, has already delivered three scudettos and four European finals, including three Champions' League finals in succession. He may have more money to spend on players than United but he is not allowed to hang on to them. Although he is totally different from Alex Ferguson, with an outwardly calm and undemonstrative manner, Lippi similarly has the strength of character to cope with the high level of expectation. His greatest achievement is to deconstruct, then construct anew successful teams, and he does it on an annual basis.

With the league title a formality, attention at Juventus turned to the European Cup final against Real Madrid. Although the Italians learned their lesson from the previous year when they allowed Borussia Dortmund to dictate the tempo, they were let down, surprisingly, by Del Piero, who had an off night, and Inzaghi, who failed to convert his instinct for finding space in the penalty area into goals. Mijatovic showed them how it should be done and his single goal took the European Cup back to Madrid for the first time in thirty-two years. *Gazzetta dello Sport* said: 'The marvellous Juve, to which we are accustomed, failed to rise to the occasion.' But having won their twenty-fifth scudetto, Juventus were due, once again, to go straight into the group stage of the Champions' League, guaranteeing at least three home games and ensuring the bandwagon keeps going at the highest level.

The stakes, however, continue to rise. Clubs are still not satisfied and they continuously require more money to fund players' wages and transfers. For Juventus, the prospect of flotation appears increasingly attractive now that Italian regulations permit it. Lazio and Bologna have already taken steps in this direction and there are a host of other clubs waiting in the wings. At another level, the English National Investment Company (ENIC) has influential shares in a number of clubs, including Slavia Prague and Glasgow Rangers. And investments need a return on capital. This makes a European Super League almost inevitable. It will provide more big matches on a regular basis. Although the Champions' League is producing over £100 million for the clubs, there is a feeling that it is underperforming. The difficulty, of course, is finding more space in an already overcrowded calendar. The English and Spanish, with their twenty-club top divisions, will find any increase in fixtures difficult to manage. Arsenal manager Arsène Wenger concedes that he doesn't expect to win the Champions' League under the existing system.

A lack of action has led to pressure for a competition based on status rather than merit. For the second year running, Milan failed to qualify for Europe. With salaries accounting for more than 70 per cent of turnover, the club desperately needs a cash-rich showcase for its stars. Meanwhile, Jurgen Lenz of TEAM is desperately fighting to maintain the paramount status of the Champions' League. 'Just because you have the most spectacular players and pay the highest salaries,' he said, 'it means f-all.'

As Milan had shown, it's easy for clubs to blow money. Manchester United, however, one of the most successful money-making clubs, should undoubtedly qualify on merit, as well as financial power, in any Super League that emerges. But the jury is still out on how they would perform in regular competition with their continental peers.

For the time being, however, such matters were put on hold as UEFA, FIFA and national associations everywhere had their eyes fixed firmly on the World Cup and the expected riches and glory it would bring.

CHAPTER ELEVEN

Inside Fortress Hoddle

UNLIKE THE BIG clubs, the FA was slow to gain a foothold on the commercial bandwagon. Had those in charge exercised their 'special share' in the Premier League, which gives them approval over such matters as the name of the league and the criteria for membership, they would have been primary beneficiaries of the commercial revolution. As it is, they always seem to be playing catch-up.

This state of affairs goes back a long way and anything as entrenched as the amateur and patrician instincts which held sway at Lancaster Gate for so much of English football's history cannot easily be rooted out. There was a time a decade ago, for instance, when contracts were negotiated by the General Secretary and were unseen by anybody else, either inside or outside the organization.

This way of doing things was responsible for many of the FA's inept attempts at deal-making and over the years it cost football dear. The percentage of revenues going into the FA's pot from Wembley games, for example, has always been inequitable, the legacy of a twenty-year contract between the FA and the company controlling Wembley Stadium, which was signed in 1982.

The FA did not even have a commercial director until 1992. Under first Trevor Phillips, then the present incumbent, Phil Carling, commercial revenue has at last begun to flow. In 1996 he pulled in around £30 million, which was set to double in 1998, but even these figures are only a quarter of what is made by the Premier League. While broadcasting rights for the national team and the FA Cup have soared in the slipstream of the Premier League, sponsorship has been handicapped by the historic, ad hoc nature of the FA's contracts.

It was not surprising, then, when three weeks before France 98 an unseemly row broke out between the governing body and the England team. The FA wanted to upgrade its sponsorship packages, based on a post-World Cup 'Team England' programme. They aimed to offer ten sponsors total access to their operations, from the grassroots to the FA Cup and the national team. The plan also included use of the three lions logo and the players of the England squad. However, many England players have their own sponsorship contracts with companies which will not be part of the 'Team England' set-up.

Phil Carling put forward the FA view, which sounded perfectly reasonable except that it was stated at the same time that the row threatened to turn into a legal battle. 'We are questioning the morality of players taking money as a group [England] from a company and as an individual from a rival,' he said. Carling then indicated that an amicable solution could be found if a get-together could be organized with the players. However, Glenn Hoddle intervened and decreed that no such meeting would take place before the World Cup. So the England team set off for a pre-World Cup tournament in Morocco in the middle of a legal dispute with its own governing body.

Worse, the row overshadowed the ann
new kit deal with Umbro worth £40 m
years. Umbro hardly gained any publi
that it had beaten off a strong challenge fr
offered more money but attached string
stringent touring conditions along the lines of its
Brazilian deal.

Although the remuneration the England squad was to
receive might seem substantial, especially when players
so often talk about pride in putting on the England shirt
and doing it for love, not money, it pales into insignificance when compared to amounts paid to some other
European teams. French players were to earn around
£250,000 each if they reached the quarter-finals, and
more for going further. Apart from performance bonuses,
they have a collective deal with a kit supplier (under a
long-standing arrangement, Adidas supplies their boots
when they represent the national team at France 98,
whatever their personal deals) and take the lion's share
of team sponsorship revenues, which, at about £15
million, are much higher than the FA achieved.

At least the French fees bear some relationship to the
players' earnings outside the orbit of the national team.
For their English counterparts it could not be more different. The basic match fee, if a game is won, is £1,500. An
extra bonus was paid on qualification for the World Cup
and a number of extra money-earning incentives were
put in place for the World Cup squad. Half a million
pounds was earmarked for the players' pool with a
second tranche to come later, based on the performance
of the side in France. This came from the existing FA
sponsorship deal and was paid for, in the main, by five
companies: Green Flag (the team sponsor), Carlsberg,
Ariel (Procter and Gamble), Snickers (Mars) and Coca-
Cola. The money also included amounts received from

FOR LOVE OR MONEY

...al suppliers, such as British Petroleum, Sainsbury's
..d One-2-One, most of whom came on board after qualification.

Sainsbury's really went to town once the supermarket
chain had signed its deal with the FA. Unable to use the
official World Cup logo because its deal was with
England only, it nevertheless transformed its stores and
its products with its own, invented, World Cup decora-
tions and memorabilia. One of Sainsbury's smart moves
was to mint its own 'official' England World Cup medals.
Not only did this trade on the success of the present
team, it connected with the emotional pull of 1966 and all
that. It takes some effort to get children to urge their
parents to buy a particular vegetable, but that is exactly
what Sainsbury's achieved – buy Sainsbury's World Cup
carrots and get a free medal with every pack.

For the players, to see the FA getting huge sums from
sponsors because of what they do on the pitch naturally
encouraged them to seek a greater share of the game's
income from wherever they could get it. The problem
between the FA and the England players could have escalated into a situation which blighted the team's World
Cup chances. That it did not can be put down to a reluctance on the part of the FA to push the issue any further
with Glenn Hoddle and the plans were put on hold.

In his early twenties, Hoddle enjoyed the glamorous
lifestyle typical of a football star. His attitudes changed
profoundly when he discovered Christianity in 1986. His
beliefs developed over the years to the point where
Hoddle refers to himself as a spiritualist, firmly rejecting
the label of born-again Christian which has been thrust
upon him.

Most football managers are content with a belief
merely in their own ability. When results go against
them, disaster awaits. What faith can and does bring, and

the England coach is living proof of it, is an unshakeable belief in the rightness of the actions which faith dictates in an individual. In its positive, as opposed to bigoted mode, it can, as the cliché goes, move mountains. In the generally mad, and, according to some memorable court testimony by Alan Sugar and Terry Venables, amoral world of football management, such certainty, when driven by principles given from on high, can make a significant difference to the performance of someone in a job such as England coach. The downside to such faith is that it can make someone blind to reasonable arguments and opinions.

Hoddle has been influenced in his spiritual journey by the healer Eileen Drewery, who has herself moved from healing to cleansing. Whereas healing, or the laying on of hands, deals strictly with the physical (or occasionally mental) cause of any complaint, cleansing is akin to exorcism, in that it is concerned with the expulsion of demons from the human body. While healing is regarded as a force for good, cleansing has a much less positive image, with its overtones of occultism and fundamentalist fanaticism. When asked whether footballers could be excused bad behaviour by claiming to be possessed by demons, Eileen Drewery replied that this could not happen with her because she 'knows the difference [between culpability and possession] straight away'.

Hoddle talked of his beliefs during an interview on Radio Five Live, saying, 'This physical body is just an overcoat,' which will be shed for another upon death. 'Your spirit will go on to another life in a spirit dimension,' he continued. He thought of God, he said, as some kind of supreme film director and 'we're all playing a part'. Moreover, Hoddle believes profoundly in the power of prayer. Unlike many converts, Hoddle was magnanimous to other viewpoints, saying that everyone had their own way to the truth. He himself also felt there was something in the idea of destiny or predetermination. It is clear that Hoddle's faith is a peculiarly personal choice. There are elements of Buddhism and Hinduism (reincarnation), of conventional Christianity (the power of prayer) and even astrology (destiny). The overall pick-and-mix philosophy, with its deference to all the great religious leaders of the past, is typically New Age.

One salient effect of Hoddle's faith is that it has a practical application in the here and now. For Hoddle, his spiritual path is integral to the way he does his job and, in his own opinion, helps him perform it to the best of his ability.

This manifests itself in any number of ways. There is a calm authority about Hoddle which brooks no argument. This is born of what he often refers to as his 'inner belief', which is something he has looked to instil in his players. Then there is his use of astrology, playing to the supposed character traits of his sun sign, Scorpio. This, in his own view, makes him determined and single-minded. But astrologers will tell you that Scorpios can also be wilful, stubborn and secretive.

It must have been galling to hear the puzzlement of people like Platini, who said he should have had a hundred caps. It must also have been difficult for the new national coach not to take his sense of unfulfilled potential at the highest level as part of the baggage he brought with him to Lancaster Gate. Yet he was kidding himself if he didn't also plead *mea culpa*. At international level, Glenn Hoddle was an enigma, a world class player whose world class performances could be counted on the fingers of one hand. According to his England bosses, Hoddle just didn't have the personality to become an international playmaker.

This time, it would be different. Hoddle had the power. If he couldn't control destiny, at least he could nudge it in a direction of his choosing.

Taught the importance of earning the respect of his squad by Arsène Wenger at Monaco, Hoddle achieved it by example. He was the youngest ever England coach when appointed in 1996, aged thirty-nine and could still mix it with players who had grown up with his picture on their bedroom walls. Before a World Cup qualifier, the Moldovans thought they had done their homework on the English and were mystified as to how they could have missed the tall midfielder who was dominating their opponents' practice session.

At last, the FA had caught up with their rival federations. They had chosen a former world class player as their coach. Moreover, he looked the part and not just on the training pitch. With youthful good looks and a stylish dress sense, he was certainly the only England supremo who could carry off a press conference nattily attired in green suit and black suede shoes. Better not step on them: the convivial manner hides a firm resolve.

When Hoddle took over the England job following the departure of Terry Venables, he very deliberately let it be known that the achievement of Venables's team in reaching the semi-final of Euro 96 would not prevent him from ensuring that every aspect of running England would now be done his way.

In contrast to his predecessor, one of his first moves was to distance himself from the media. England having successfully negotiated the demands of qualifying, journalists were prepared to extend the honeymoon period. But as Hoddle, along with David Davies, began the attempt to manipulate them, a degree of resentment built up.

Hoddle's previous employer, Chelsea chairman Ken

Bates, suggested that while Hoddle would not lie, he wouldn't tell you the full story. The media termed this 'Hodwinking'. So when some poor results were produced during the run-up to the World Cup, particularly the loss against Chile and a 1–1 draw in Switzerland, and the media began some mild questioning of Hoddle's selection policies, it was no surprise when his attitude visibly hardened. 'I don't give two monkeys what anyone else thinks,' he said. 'I make my decisions and I go with them. Everyone's entitled to their view but at the end of the day the only view that counts is mine.'

In the run-up to the penultimate Wembley encounter before the World Cup, against Portugal in April (which England won convincingly, 3–0) media interest in Eileen Drewery's presence in the England camp intensified. To pre-empt the news emerging as a shock-horror scoop, Hoddle and Davies made a pre-emptive strike. Normally, when the squad is at Bisham Abbey, two players are provided to talk to reporters after training, one on each side of the room and both flanked by FA minders. When they have finished, Hoddle and Davies take up a more formal position on a raised platform and Hoddle talks about team matters. Before the Portugal game, this ritual was reversed and Hoddle appeared first. He casually dropped into his comments the fact that Eileen Drewery would be joining the set-up to work alongside the existing medical staff. Afterwards, the players took their turn. One of them was Ian Wright, who proceeded to give Mrs Drewery a glowing testimonial, calling her 'blessed'.

Despite the attempt to play it down, the story was headline news and reactions ranged from mirth to hostility (it was 'mumbo-jumbo' and the national team was now the 'barmy army'). A similar reaction greeted Arsène Wenger when he arrived from Japan with his strange, foreign ideas about such things as players' diet.

These insular attitudes were shaken when the likes of Fabrizio Ravenelli, who must know what he is doing since he won the European Cup with Juventus, felt that the treatment of injuries and training regimes in England were stuck in the dark ages, so he went back to Italy for medical advice.

Others saw a more sinister side to developments in the England camp. From somewhere within the squad came the eminently quotable phrase that playing for England was like 'joining the Moonies' and the jibe, it was suggested, was made by a 'Liverpool Lip'. Hoddle was livid at what he took to be a slur rather than a humorous aside and despatched Davies to track down the culprit. Whether Davies's sleuthing produced any accurate results is debatable but it certainly let all the players know that such comments were unacceptable. The *Daily Mail* then wrongly named Steve McManaman as the source. Hoddle would not let the matter rest, so much so that McManaman's solicitor was forced to enter the fray before a truce was called.

In his column in *The Times*, McManaman made clear he was not the guilty party and paid Eileen Drewery a tribute, calling her 'a lovely woman'. He went on to say, 'I would never criticize anyone or anything that could help a player when he was injured.'

The coach's over-the-top reaction to the 'Moonies' comment showed that, like all good jokes, it had obviously touched a raw nerve.

No one sought to put the inclusion of a healer in the same bracket as, for example, Bob Willis's use of hypnosis tapes when he was England's cricket captain. It was simply treated in isolation either as 'barmy' or perturbing, although, given footballers' penchants for collecting injuries, it would seem a most natural area for therapy of any kind.

There is surely nothing wrong with Hoddle suggesting to his squad that they might, if they wished, like to consider a visit to Eileen Drewery but the impression was created that there were brownie points to be earned; there was a sense that it was an obligation or duty rather than a voluntary option.

Media scepticism was fuelled by Mrs Drewery's comments that she had willed Ian Wright not to score a goal in the last minute of the Rome game (when Wright hit the post) because she was fearful of aggravating the crowd trouble. If this was treated with derision, the sale of her story to the *Sun* as part of a project to build a healing centre was seen as rank opportunism. Mrs Drewery's association with the England coach, it was said, was being used to help finance her plans. Moreover, her deal with the *Sun* had been negotiated by the ubiquitous Dennis Roach, Hoddle's agent. Glenn Hoddle and Eileen Drewery had been close friends for nearly twenty years. When Hoddle left his wife, he moved in with Eileen and her husband Phil, so when it became necessary it was natural that they should use the same agent.

The trouble with the New Age industry is that when one person gets some publicity, others suddenly appear with all sorts of angles of their own. But although one healer was welcomed by Hoddle, another, who claimed he could do amazing things for England, was not. Uri Geller, who had shot to fame with his spoon-bending and watch-stopping abilities, conducted a slanging match with Hoddle through the press after Geller claimed he was already part of the England set-up and Hoddle denied it. The row ended with Hoddle issuing a writ to prevent Geller from repeating his assertions that he and Hoddle had discussed how Geller might help. This was not Mr Geller's only intervention. He announced that he was literally going to bend the World Cup in England's favour. But before he could get his hands on it (it was touring England as part of the Coca-Cola promotion), FIFA, to the chagrin of the sponsor, was forced to diffuse the situation by revealing that the actual trophy was in a Swiss vault and the Coca-Cola version was a replica.

The dispute over Eileen Drewery's role begged the question: if there is room for practitioners of alternative arts, why was there no room for a fitness trainer? But of course, a fitness trainer would have been an independent specialist, and Hoddle gave every impression of being suspicious of people he couldn't control.

Chris Sutton, for instance, was frozen out of the squad because he refused to play for the 'B' side. Paul Gascoigne, on the other hand, was retained after his wife-beating became public knowledge. Hoddle said that the Sutton case was 'a football matter', whereas Gazza's was not. However, no attempt was made to show Sutton that he had gravely misjudged the situation and the player remained adamant that performing for the 'B' team was pointless. This was surely a case of Sutton proving immune to Hoddle's proselytizing. Sutton was not a true believer, if anything he was a heretic who had formed his own opinions. Gazza, by contrast, was a sinner but the coach thought he could be saved and it appeared that Gazza himself wanted a saviour. There is always room in the charmed circle for a sinner who repents, as Tony Adams and Paul Merson proved and as Rio Ferdinand was finding out. So for Gazza, there was the possibility of redemption if he paid heed to Hoddle's teaching but for Sutton, who was that most dangerous of creatures, a free thinker, there was none.

As the World Cup drew ever closer, speculation moved from esoteric matters to discussion of which players would make it into Hoddle's squad of twenty-two for France. Prior to naming the squad, there were three final friendlies for England to negotiate, for which Hoddle picked thirty players. His World Cup group would undoubtedly come from these but eight of them were destined for disappointment. The sense of let-down came early for Matt Le Tissier, who failed even to make the squad of thirty. He heard about his omission from the media. His reaction could have spoken for Chris Sutton as well as himself when he said: 'Before that "B" game we were told to try and use it as a stepping stone. I scored a hat-trick. What more could I have done? In retrospect it showed it was useless playing for them.'

On the face of it Le Tissier was just the kind of player Hoddle would have been prepared to accommodate. From his own experiences as an international player, when, despite his fifty-three caps, he never felt he was properly treated or utilized, Hoddle, it would be thought, would have appreciated someone with extravagant but inconsistently applied gifts. On the contrary, Le Tissier somehow failed to impress himself on Hoddle and only had two international starts, being substituted in the Wembley defeat against Italy. Le Tissier seemed to be treated in much the same way that Hoddle himself endured – and complained about – during his career. Hoddle did make the point that the margin between inclusion and exclusion was small, saying Le Tissier was 'this close' (holding up his thumb and forefinger) to being chosen.

Hoddle is obviously a sincere man but he appeared to shift the goal posts when it suited him. Rio Ferdinand could be taught a lesson, perhaps Dennis Wise was an expendable non-believer, and the 'young' Michael Owen had constantly to be reminded of the right path by dampening down enthusiasm for him.

Hoddle's remarks about Owen needing to get a sense of perspective and that he may not be a natural goal-scorer caused consternation. In fact the coach was making a well-intentioned, if clumsy attempt to alleviate pressure on himself from the media to pick Owen and let the Liverpool striker know that international football was different. It was reminiscent of Ron Greenwood, who dropped Hoddle after he had scored on his debut for England, saying that the player had to understand that there were disappointments in international football.

There were also some words for David Beckham. Beckham, according to Hoddle, was too prone to reacting to the opposition and the crowds that baited him. Hoddle compared Beckham to himself as a young player, saying he had to put up with similar treatment to that which Beckham has to face. The coach thought Beckham should do what he did – not react (although Hoddle was sent off twice in his career), but there was no understanding of the extent of the abuse levelled at Beckham. He just would not accept that Beckham's is a singular case.

Not only did Hoddle, like his contemporary at Arsenal, Liam Brady, transcend opposition fans' antipathy with his sublime skill, in the days when Hoddle played, fans were more interested in abusing each other rather than the players and no one, not even the emerging black players, ever had to endure the personal vilification which is directed at the United star. If Hoddle's understanding was wanting, he could not be faulted in his view that Beckham, in order to maximize his talents, had to learn to ignore the provocations. It was just that a more sympathetic approach might have paid dividends. Hoddle, however, was more concerned with picking his squad for France. In sight of the objective for which he had worked, he was going to have to be ruthless and practical in his decisions. Maybe Beckham was simply not a priority.

Back in September, at the Arsenal–Spurs derby, Alan Sugar was in the Highbury boardroom and was engaged in what might be described euphemistically as a conversation with the England coach. There ensued a foul-mouthed declamation from Sugar about a player who was a 'waste of space' and worse, had cost his club dear in terms of lost potential. This rant brought forth a comment of sweet reason – indeed there could have been two monologues taking place simultaneously, so far apart were they in tone. It was suggested that while Darren Anderton could be of no immediate benefit to Tottenham because of his appalling bad luck with injuries, his rehabilitation could begin if he were given permission to join up with the England squad in the pre-match preparations. The request was diligently pursued despite a blank refusal on the part of the Spurs chairman to deviate from his torrent of abuse.

Darren Anderton managed to get himself fit for Euro 96 and was promptly included in the team by Terry Venables. Following that competition he was beset by further injuries and had made only just over thirty appearances for his club in two seasons. Sometimes a player strikes a chord with a manager or coach. He doesn't have to be the most gifted but the manager can see him fulfilling a key role and the player is on the manager's wavelength. It appeared that Anderton was just such a player as far as Glenn Hoddle was concerned. During Anderton's convalescence there were regular telephone chats with Hoddle and visits to Eileen Drewery – so if he was fit, he was in.

There were, of course, some certainties for the squad. Of those who formed the backbone of Hoddle's team, it was Alan Shearer who stood out. 'Would I swap him for anyone?' Hoddle asked rhetorically. 'No, I don't think I would.' So when Shearer was accused of kicking Neil

Lennon of Leicester, Hoddle was perturbed in case his World Cup plans were jeopardized.

Since the referee failed to see the clash clearly, Shearer was not punished at the time and the media had a field day. The incident was replayed by Sky dozens of times and the FA was urged to take action. In a remarkable display of presumption, Hoddle publicly defended Shearer against charges laid by his own employers and suggested it could have all been an accident, as Shearer claimed. Perhaps the coach felt Shearer might withdraw from the World Cup if he wasn't exonerated, and certainly Shearer's 'nice-guy' image, which was in danger of being shattered, was an important part of his professional existence.

The hearing to consider the case was convened at the same time that Hoddle announced his squad of thirty. It was arranged at such speed and in such secrecy that even some members of the disciplinary committee were unaware of what was going on, believing it would be postponed until after the World Cup. At first it was announced merely that the charge of violent conduct was 'not proven' but within an hour this had been changed to a straight 'not guilty' verdict. Perhaps the 'not proven' outcome was not the complete vindication Shearer and Hoddle required, nor was there any precedent for it, so it was changed behind the scenes.

David Davies was left to explain to an amazed media exactly what had transpired while they were attending Hoddle's press conference. There was universal condemnation, exemplified by Bob Driscoll in the *Daily Mail*, who wrote: 'That those who engineered this insult to public intelligence appear so utterly impervious to the shame they have inflicted on English football only deepens the embarrassment felt by millions of us with the most basic sense of natural justice.' Hoddle, of course, couldn't give a monkey's. He couldn't afford to; there was a World Cup to win.

Once the Shearer business was taken care of, Hoddle could finally get down to choosing his squad for France. The unlucky Ian Wright was forced to pull out through injury, thus depriving Hoddle of one of his most faithful apostles and forceful personalities. Hoddle had said that he knew who twenty of his party of twenty-two would be but he didn't let on any more than that.

After a turgid goalless draw against Saudi Arabia at Wembley, the party flew off to La Manga, near Murcia in Spain, which was to be their base while taking part in a mini-tournament in Morocco. After further poor performances against Belgium (0–0) and Morocco (won by England 1–0), the final squad was all set to be announced at a press conference scheduled for the following Monday, 1 June. On the day before, Sunday 31 May, the news bulletins were dominated by the revelation that Geri Halliwell – Ginger Spice – had left the Spice Girls. Just before 6pm English time all that changed. At an impromptu press conference in Spain, Glenn Hoddle and David Davies announced to an astonished nation that Paul Gascoigne had not made the squad and would not be going to France. It was, said Hoddle, the simple fact that Gazza had not got himself fit enough for what was required at World Cup level.

The Gascoigne bombshell pushed all other stories off the agenda for days, such was the shock. Even those who agreed with Hoddle's decision – and there were plenty of them – could not quite believe it. It was the main item on Radio Four's flagship *PM* programme the following day. It took ten minutes for news of a reshuffle in the shadow Cabinet by Opposition leader, William Hague, to appear and over half an hour for the programme to feature news of an earthquake in Afghanistan. Later, BBC Two's

Newsnight programme also ran the Gascoigne news as its lead story and when the William Hague reshuffle came on, it was treated like the Gazza saga. Who was in and who was left out of Hague's twenty-two was the gist of its coverage, with pictures of Hague and Hoddle juxtaposed.

As the debate raged over whether Hoddle was right to leave Gazza at home, there was a large volume of support for the coach's decision. Many cited Gazza's poor performances in the final two games, even though the whole team had played poorly. Others referred to what Graham Taylor memorably termed Gazza's 'refuelling habits'. Those who disagreed with Hoddle's decision felt there was more to it, that there was a clash of personalities and Hoddle had allowed it to get the better of his judgement.

In fact, the reason was plain to see and was contained in Hoddle's comments over Gazza's lack of fitness. Gascoigne had been offered a place in the sun but he had failed to respond whole-heartedly and now the day of judgement had arrived. Gazza could have received all the benefits of salvation. All he had to do was get fit – again. But his lifestyle, his indulgent public paymasters and his stooges were too strong a pull for him to recognize the strength of Hoddle's intent. For the first time in his professional career, he was held to a standard he could not achieve and it cost him the chance of a final return to the stage of his greatest triumph, the World Cup.

The other omissions hardly merited mention. Hoddle had shown by dropping Gazza that he was the master of all he surveyed. He had also publicly declared his faith in his own judgement as a coach, no matter what the nation thought. It was now clear that Hoddle's was indeed the only opinion that counted.

Hoddle also sent Philip Neville home, saying he had lost form, but Teddy Sheringham stayed despite his poor showings. Gazza was gone because of doubts about his 'fitness', yet there was Anderton, who had hardly played all season, in the squad. But Anderton was manifestly desperate to play, while Gascoigne actually admitted to being drunk at La Manga.

An injury to Andy Hinchcliffe saw the left side of the team shorn of any cover for Graeme Le Saux, although Hoddle was adamant that he had enough resources in the squad to cover any contingency. Nicky Butt was probably just unlucky, while Rio Ferdinand would be going. He had presumably learned his lesson after his drunk-driving offence. Hoddle said that although Ferdinand might not get a game, he was being taken to gain experience. He might, said Hoddle, eventually turn out to be a great player at the back which would allow England to play the system Hoddle really wanted – with a sweeper.

Back in January when Manchester United followed up their victory over Juventus with the demolition of Chelsea in the FA Cup, Glenn Hoddle must have thanked his lucky stars that the majority of United's team was English. During the season eight of them featured in his squads but as United faltered so did many of its players' World Cup prospects. Injury-prone Gary Pallister was the first to go, quickly followed by Andy Cole. 'Sometimes you feel Andy needs to get four or five chances before he scores,' was Hoddle's opinion. However, the Carling Opta Index of performances in the Premier League showed that Cole's success ratio of goals scored to attempts was higher, at 16.4 per cent, than every other striker in the England squad. Nicky Butt and Phil Neville were sent home from La Manga, leaving Alex Ferguson to say that the omission of Neville was 'the most questionable decision Hoddle has made'. This left four United players in the squad: Teddy Sheringham, Paul Scholes, David Beckham and Gary Neville.

How this would affect morale remained to be seen. Franz Beckenbauer, recalling that he initially selected twenty-six players in 1986, described it as 'the biggest mistake I could have made. I was obliged to send four home. It's the worst management of a group you can do. It leads to personal problems and the team becomes diffi-cult to manage when it is much simpler to call up replacement players in the case of injuries. We lost in the final when I had been certain we had the best players in the world.' Four years later, Beckenbauer selected his twenty-two early, had no serious injuries and won the tournament.

For Hoddle, the die was now cast. There was no going back. The coach, for all his ways, had emerged as the dominant character he had promised to be. And with the FA forever displaying its tendency for ineptness, perhaps that is what England needed most of all, someone who, like Alf Ramsey, could not be contradicted. Whatever England did in France, it would be Glenn Hoddle who would either receive the plaudits or carry the can. Before that, a man who had ruled supreme for twenty-four years was about to leave the stage and the battle to replace him had been joined in earnest.

CHAPTER TWELVE

The Power Game

THE FIFTY-FIRST ORDINARY Congress of FIFA, which took place in Paris on 7 and 8 June 1998, was an unusual gathering. For the first time in twenty-four years, the delegates, drawn from over 190 member associations, had to vote for a new President to succeed João Havelange, who was at last prepared to give up the reins of power. It was to be a straight fight, a two-horse race between FIFA's Secretary General, Sepp Blatter, who had finally decided to run after his earlier prevarications, and Lennart Johansson, the President of UEFA and a member of FIFA's Executive Committee.

Unfortunately, it had been so long since democracy had been given an airing within FIFA that the assembled delegates were unsure of how to conduct the proceedings. At first, Havelange suggested that each delegation, which consisted of three members, should choose one of its number to cast its vote. This met with uproar, as some delegations felt they could not trust one person to act as agreed. They wanted all three to vote together, while others thought there should be an open show of hands. After an hour of argument, it was finally decided that there would be a formal vote rather than a show of hands and each delegation could decide for itself how many of its number would actually be present at the vote.

Another half an hour was expended on a roll call. Like children answering a school register, the associations had to respond to their countries' names being called by saying 'present'. Further time was taken up as six new member countries, including such hotbeds of football as American Samoa and the Turks and Caicos Islands, were ceremoniously ushered into the conference chamber, replete with national flags and much fanfare. As might be expected, the only thing that took hardly any time at all was the voting through of the approval of FIFA's budget. For World Cup activities, the four years to 1997 expenditure total was SFr44.6 million (£17.84 million). The four-year revenue projection to 2001, however, was SFr534.1 million (£213.64 million), more than a tenfold increase. The whole financial exercise took a mere one minute to be unanimously agreed.

The somewhat disorderly display by those charged with overseeing football's future should not obscure the fact that this election was of supreme importance to followers of the game everywhere. Beyond vague generalities, it was not easy to discern exactly how the two candidates intended to shape FIFA's policies and take the organization into the twenty-first century. This was a change from Havelange's high-profile election campaign in 1974, when he was highly specific about what was wrong with the presidency of Sir Stanley Rous and what he intended to do once he became President.

Johansson, who had made all the early running, promised what he called a new style of FIFA government, comprising 'democracy, solidarity and transparency'.

For his part, Blatter was offering something he termed 'universality', summed up by a slogan inspired by Alexandre Dumas: 'Football for all and all for football.'

Under Blatter, FIFA would become more accessible. By this he meant that the governing body ought to attract a greater input, not only from national federations, but also from the playing side – coaches, referees and footballers themselves. To this end he had declared that he would create a new post if he won the contest – Director of Football – and it would be filled by Michel Platini. Platini needed a role after France 98 and he and Blatter had worked well together on the Task Force, thus the continuation of the alliance was a natural progression. Johansson, needing to respond to Platini's inclusion on Blatter's ticket, announced that he would bring back Pele to rejoin FIFA's 'Family of Football'.

Blatter made public his decision to run only at the end of March, one week before the closing date for nominations, although he had probably been working behind the scenes for some considerable time. If he had come out into the open beforehand he would have been forced to give up his position – and thus his power base – at the top of the FIFA secretariat.

The Johansson camp had been well aware that Blatter was going to run for office and tried to insist he declare his hand early. When this failed to produce the desired result, it became increasingly apparent that Blatter was gaining the upper hand in the vital skirmishing that would carry on right up until election day. At a meeting of FIFA's Executive Committee in March, Johansson's supporters attempted to force Blatter to come out into the open by proposing a resolution that would force the issue. This move so annoyed João Havelange, who was, after all, firmly in Blatter's corner, that he decided to end the meeting. 'He may be over eighty years old,' said one member afterwards, 'but he still acts as if his whole career is ahead of him. There is no stopping him and even when he is gone, you still feel he will be there watching you.' The failure of his supporters to achieve their aim was a warning to Johansson that he might not enjoy enough support where it really mattered.

Havelange's backing gave Blatter a trump card. While he was able to propose 'universality' as a change of direction, he was also able to appeal to the desire for continuity. As Havelange's right-hand man, Blatter's way of doing things was well known and he could be relied upon to maintain the broad thrust of the expansionist policies which, underpinned by commercial contracts, had been the hallmark of the Havelange presidency. Blatter would not significantly change policy but would update procedures. Among these was the introduction of a seven-strong Executive Board acting as an inner cabinet that would speed up decision making. Johansson, on the other hand, would not wait for very long before he started making policy changes, which would be the inevitable outcome of his plans to involve more member associations and the congress itself in the decision-making process.

As a major association within UEFA, the FA always intended to support their President. However, basking in the success of Euro 96, they had become obsessed with bidding for the 2006 World Cup. For once, a slick campaign was mounted, fronted by 'ambassadors' Gary Lineker, Sir Bobby Charlton and the newly-knighted Sir Geoff Hurst, and backed by the Prime Minister, Tony Blair. With the aim of cementing an alliance with major UK companies and raising £10 million to help finance its bid, the FA began an advertising campaign based on the thought: 'The birthplace of football: there's nowhere better for 2006'. It was launched at the FA Cup Final and drew support from Marks and Spencer and British Airways. The exercise was designed to influence the key movers and shakers who sit on FIFA's Executive Committee.

However, the previous FA Chairman, Sir Bert Millichip, had apparently shaken hands in the USA on a deal with the President of the German Federation, Egidius Braun, to the effect that Germany would continue to support England in its preparations for Euro 96 while England would back the German bid for the 2006 World Cup. When reminded of this after the FA had launched its own bid, the FA claimed that it was not bound by decisions of previous administrations and called into question whether there had ever been any agreement in the first place. Unfortunately for the Germans, there was no written agreement, nor any record in minutes of UEFA meetings to back up their claim. While this does not mean there was no agreement, the Germans would find it difficult, if not impossible, to prove it in the face of English denials.

The up-front nature of the FA's campaign for 2006 set England against Germany within UEFA. The governing body wanted only one country to bid on behalf of Europe. Johansson, who was identified with the German power base within UEFA, came down on the side of the Germans and urged the FA to honour the 1993 pledge. England refused, and lost ground within UEFA. Such was the enormity of the estrangement that after Sir Bert Millichip's retirement, there was no English representative on the UEFA Executive Committee. Sir Bert's successor, Keith Wiseman, attempted to gain a seat on the committee but he suffered an ignominious defeat, gaining only sixteen votes out of a possible forty-seven. However, UEFA could not force England to withdraw its World Cup bid. In fact UEFA was at odds with FIFA on the issue as FIFA is strongly opposed to continent-wide confederations like UEFA acting as a cartel to support one bid. Once an individual nation's autonomy has been usurped, the prospect of FIFA degenerating into competing regional blocs becomes all too real.

Before the row over 2006, the FA had supported Johansson for the FIFA presidency. Indeed, along with most of the European associations, the promise had been confirmed in writing. Then, with only two weeks to go to the election, they switched sides and declared their intention to back Blatter. The move was widely seen as sharp practice. Rob Hughes wrote in *The Times* that the FA was 'more concerned with the 2006 World Cup than with honour'. The pragmatic view is that the FA could no longer possibly support Johansson given the new situation. If they did it would be voting for someone who was pursuing a major policy which directly conflicted with English interests.

The FA also reasoned that although Blatter had said that he thought the 2006 World Cup should go to Africa, and he specifically mentioned South Africa, the viability of an African bid might be called into question. If this happened, England would be ready to step into the breach. In the heady climate engendered by the English bid, any internal criticism of the FA's stance was characterized as tantamount to treason, so there was little debate over the FA's change of sides. Even the normally vociferous Premier League clubs kept their mouths firmly shut, although their interests were more bound up with UEFA than FIFA and any more disagreement with the European body, which was bound to occur after the FA's about-turn, would undermine their influence. Moreover, the FA's argument ignored the fact that the World Cup is awarded by FIFA's Executive Committee, and there were enough Johansson supporters sitting on it to ensure England's bid could be frozen out.

Objectively, it was difficult to see how England could

be awarded the World Cup given the appalling record of some of its supporters. The issue was brought into greater focus when the British government's policy to restrain troublemakers was seen to fail when English fans rioted on the eve of the national team's first World Cup game against Tunisia in Marseille. Once again, the cult of 'laddish' behaviour – drunkenness, nationalism and violence – had attached itself to the England team, this time in full view of the world's media. The fact that there were also serious problems involving German fans merely meant that both countries' hopes for 2006 suffered a setback.

As far as the English were concerned, the hard-core hooligans were seen to be spoiling for a fight and did everything they could to provoke the local population, especially the North African element in Marseille. They were determined to mount a confrontation in the racially tense city, the home of substantial support for Jean-Marie Le Pen's right-wing party and a large, disaffected minority of North African immigrants. The attempt to isolate the hooligan element by constantly referring to them as a 'mindless minority', not really connected with 'true' England supporters had once again come unstuck. All the money spent on policing and the National Intelligence Unit appeared futile as the English police seconded to France admitted that many of the troublemakers in Marseille were not known to them.

The paradox is that violence has been largely eliminated from English club grounds, although there were some alarming incidents during the 1997/98 season which showed that it had not been entirely eradicated. Linesmen were attacked at Barnsley and Portsmouth and a fan was killed in a confrontation following a game between Gillingham and Fulham. Racist behaviour has been reduced somewhat in the wake of the 'Kick Racism

Out' campaign, perhaps because for many supporters, clubs are more important than the national side and English clubs now have cosmopolitan teams. This militates against overt racism. Chelsea, for instance, where there has traditionally been a nucleus of racist fans, now has a team consisting mostly of imports and the lure of big stars transcends bellicose chauvinism. Before the 1997/98 season an Arsenal fan expressed concern over the increasing presence and influence of the club's French contingent. He felt it was at the expense of indigenous players, particularly the young ones. 'But I suppose,' he said, 'it will be okay if he [Arsène Wenger] wins the championship.'

Any England bid for the World Cup fails to meet the criteria contained in FIFA's Code of Conduct. Point four of the code requires respect for opponents, referees, officials and spectators. On this basis alone it would be difficult for England to be awarded the tournament, despite the fact that the FA pledged to promote the FIFA code in its planning for 2006. The truth is that the FA simply does not have the wherewithal to make good on such an undertaking. On international occasions Wembley can still be an unpleasant place to visit, with the ritual booing of the opposition's national anthem and the aggressive, confrontational atmosphere that accompanies the games. There is also the perennial question of how the troublemakers would behave if England performed badly in their own backyard. And as Euro 96 proved, a major tournament in England can be a catalyst for nationalist fervour which is at best overbearing and at worst xenophobic.

Perhaps it would be better, in light of such considerations, if England did the honourable thing and withdrew its bid for 2006, although this would be heresy to the FA. If English hooligans ruin tournaments held abroad, what right do we have to play host to the world? A pragmatic approach might mean FIFA is left with two choices. Either hold the World Cup far enough away from England to discourage attendance or, paradoxically, give it to England in order that the trouble is not exported.

It would also help if the British government took a stronger line and put more emphasis on coordinating its efforts. For instance, David Mellor's Task Force could be asked to prioritize racism and crowd control with regard to the national team. Furthermore, if magistrates are not prepared to extend substantially the number of restriction orders, perhaps England should consider withdrawing from all international competitions. After the trouble caused by German fans in Lens during France 98, which left a French policeman severely injured, the German authorities offered to withdraw their team from the World Cup. No such offer was made by the FA after England supporters ran wild in Marseille. Instead, the FA was offered more support from the Minister for Sport, Tony Banks, who remained fully committed to 2006. 'I don't believe,' he said, 'we should allow that thuggish minority of people who follow the national team to start dictating national football policy or whatever.' Yet that is exactly what they did as far as the government's policy towards those wanting to attend France 98 without tickets was concerned. The law-abiding were denied their right to enjoy the tournament as other nationalities could. And as Tony Banks himself admitted: 'It's very humiliating to keep apologizing on behalf of the government and on behalf of football to various people around the world.'

With such considerations seething in the background, the day of judgement arrived. At the election itself, João Havelange signed off by singing the same old song: diplomatic triumphs; expansion of tournaments; and money. 'I leave with $60 million in the bank and contracts worth $4 billion,' went the refrain.

To win on the first ballot, a two-thirds majority (144 votes) was needed. Neither side, however, reached the requisite number, the outcome being 111 for Blatter and 80 for Johansson. Rather than go through a winner-takes-all second ballot, Johansson saw the writing on the wall and conceded defeat. After his victory, Blatter immediately spoke about the 2006 World Cup, backtracking somewhat on his previous statements in favour of Africa. 'I never offered the event to anyone,' he said, 'I simply said that it appears logical to me that this continent organizes such an event after Asia in 2002.' The comment was seized upon by the English as a vindication of their volte-face.

Lennart Johansson was bitter about the way the support he expected to receive had failed to materialize. He reserved his greatest bitterness for the English. After his withdrawal, he said: 'I thought I would get a hundred [votes] ... I know, for example, that the [English] FA were for me a fortnight ago and they were no longer [for me] a fortnight later. That surprised me but I don't want to go further. If I mention England it is because I was the one who almost alone had sympathy for them after Heysel. I was the one who proposed they should host Euro 96. I was a little naive.'

Johansson had a point, and it went unanswered by the FA. Apart from being an Anglophile, he had championed England's cause when the clubs were banned from European competitions in the 1980s. At a time when most of the European federations felt the ban should continue, Johansson pushed and manoeuvred for English clubs to be readmitted. If the FA had always thought he was the wrong man for the presidency there might be an argument to make that they were right to support someone else. But this was not the case. It was a matter of self-interest. Graham Kelly, the FA's Chief Executive, confirmed this when he was reported as saying: 'Had Johansson won we would have looked like idiots. Now we look very clever but in the end it was a question of judgement of what was good for the game and good for England.'

In his victory speech Sepp Blatter thanked his family but didn't mention Michel Platini. He did, however, later confirm that Platini was to become FIFA's Sporting Director. His role would be to supervise players, referees and coaches, whose voices the new FIFA administration had promised to hear. For Platini, over and above his allotted role, there is the distinct possibility that his new position close to the centre of footballing power will enable him to establish his own constituency which could see him become Blatter's eventual successor.

Havelange, now playing the role of elder statesman, gave Blatter some advice. He should 'continue the work we have established at FIFA'. There was little chance his exhortation would be ignored. Havelange was not exactly departing, he had been elected FIFA's first Honorary President, thus, in effect, there were now two Presidents. Moreover, Sepp Blatter has been closely identified with the policy changes ushered in during the Havelange years. It is inconceivable that he would now take FIFA on a completely different path, especially since his erstwhile boss would remain in close proximity in his honorary capacity. For his part, Havelange had successfully helped to stop Johansson, thus ensuring he had an important say in the succession. His continuing presence was the best way of making sure his legacy remained intact.

Although Havelange was obviously proud of the results of his expansionist policies, the bottom line was always about money. 'In order to administrate you must have money,' was Havelange's creed. This has sometimes led to an over-exaggeration of FIFA's contribution to the world economy. Both Havelange and Blatter are fond of equating FIFA with global corporations. As a guide to their more vivid imaginings, Blatter is fond of recounting what can only be described as a preposterous claim. It is that FIFA, in addition to its direct income, demonstrates its omnipotence through its ability to generate invisible earnings. 'Thirty-seven billion television viewers' (nine times the total population of the planet), would, according to Blatter, watch the sixty-four matches during France 98. 'They will,' he continued, 'drink something, eat something. They smoke, they go out, perhaps they pay an entry fee if they watch in a restaurant for the atmosphere. One can estimate that each of the television viewers will account for a revenue of $2, so in little more than a month – 33 days – there will be a turnover of $74 billion. Now, if I can put it into the context of Switzerland, this is a turnover bigger than Nestlé, the biggest Swiss multinational company.' Football is big, of that there is no doubt. But this was as if Blatter believed that all these people would not drink, eat or smoke if there was no World Cup.

Back in the real world, when asked where all the money went, Havelange replied: 'Be certain it doesn't go into my pocket, that's the first thing. Secondly, FIFA is not a bank. It receives and returns and for that reason it has become strong.' While this is true as far as it goes, Havelange didn't see fit to mention the huge sums FIFA now spends on entertainment and travel. The budget for 'presidential activities' from 1994 to 1997 was SFr5.5 million (£2.2 million), for instance. Blatter will do even better since the projected spend on the same activities for 1998 to 2001 is SFr8.3 million (£3.3 million). When the new budget for the Executive Committee (SFr12 million, £4.8 million) is added, the full amount becomes a staggering SFr20.3 million (£8.1 million).

Of course, Johansson had not lost simply because of England's vote. It was always going to be difficult once Havelange refused to support him. Neither did Johansson's 'blackie' outburst help his cause. But some of the antagonism towards him could have come from the fact that he queried the figures. He also felt that maybe he had made a mistake in not promising gifts and money to federations. Many of them were more than happy to stick with the existing set-up, which Blatter personified, since they undoubtedly received money paid as advances against annual subsidies and for the more impoverished among them, this could have been an overriding consideration. Others put a different interpretation on events, suggesting at Blatter's post-election conference that there was widespread talk of bribes. Naturally, Blatter was dismissive. 'The game is over,' he said. 'The players have already gone to the changing room. I will not respond to this question.'

It will be interesting to see whether Blatter can deliver on his promise of 'universality'. He certainly made the right noises. 'I want,' he said, 'to bring in all those involved in football – coaches, players, referees – so that I don't have to succumb to the demands of our economic partners.' But so many promises have been made that the money-making schemes are likely to grow. Among the guests at the intimate celebratory dinner hosted by Blatter and his family were representatives of the key FIFA sponsors. After all, the only guarantees in place regarding 2006 were from Coca-Cola and Adidas and it would soon be time to get down to serious business.

These and other considerations were temporarily set aside, however, as France 98 got under way and everyone's attention was diverted to the football spectacle. The English would have to wait for six days before their first game, plenty of time for everyone to consider the merits of the other participants and prepare themselves for England's new dawn. Destiny was about to beckon to Glenn Hoddle.

CHAPTER THIRTEEN

Slipping and Sliding

A T LAST, AFTER two years of growing anticipation, Glenn Hoddle's New Model England took to the fields of France. But if anyone thought the arguments had all been debated and dispensed with when England's Gazza-less squad was announced, they were in for a rude awakening. When the team to start the first match against Tunisia was revealed, Hoddle showed again his propensity for controversy. David Beckham, who had played in all the qualifiers, was dropped in favour of Darren Anderton. And there was no place for Michael Owen, Hoddle preferring to stick with Teddy Sheringham, rather than risk the inexperience of the Liverpool striker.

In the event, England's 2–0 victory, with goals from Alan Shearer and Paul Scholes, seemed to justify the coach's views. However, although Tunisia failed to offer very much in the way of opposition England were unable to kill them off until the last minute of the game when Scholes scored with a curling shot. Disconcertingly, in the searing heat of Marseille, Hoddle's use, or more precisely, lack of use, of substitutes appeared to be some-what conservative. Teddy Sheringham created one half-chance for himself during the game (a volleyed shot from the edge of the penalty area) but apart from that his performance was no different from those that had been so ineffectual for Manchester United during the regular season. Even so, he stayed on the pitch until replaced by Michael Owen with only six minutes left, too late to be of benefit to either player. As for Beckham, he got nowhere near the action as the coach persisted with Anderton to the end.

Hoddle, nevertheless, could be pleased with the win and the three points it brought. As England have often discovered in the past, a faltering start in the World Cup leaves a team with a lot to do to qualify for the second stage. Winning was the objective and Hoddle had achieved his aim.

During England's stay in France a similar approach to the media was arranged as that in place at Bisham Abbey. Players participated in press conferences at their base camp at the Hotel Golf de Saint-Denac, near La Baule, an old-fashioned resort in Brittany which is a French counterpart of Eastbourne. In the run-up to the game against Tunisia, David Beckham was among those put up to answer questions. With everyone, including the player himself, taking it for granted that he would be in the team, the discussion concentrated on other matters.

After fending off the inevitable interest in his private life and admitting that the crowd's taunts could have an adverse effect at times, the questioning turned to football and Beckham became a little more forthcoming. He preferred playing in the centre of midfield, he said, adding the rider that 'being in the team is still the most important thing to me, both for United and England'. With no real news in the phoney war atmosphere which preceded England's first game, the coverage of him, even on the sports pages, tended to concentrate on his lifestyle rather than his football: his dyed-blond hair, for instance, and his choice of a sarong to wear during an evening out while staying on the Côte d'Azur with his fiancée before joining up with the England party.

The amount of attention devoted to Beckham's super-star status obscured what little discussion there was about the player's role in the England team, particularly now that Paul Gascoigne was no longer around. Despite Alex Ferguson's decision to leave Beckham out of the United side at the start of the season, he ended up playing in more games (forty-five in all) than any other United player. His twelve goals attested to his growing influence on United's attacking capability, yet by the beginning of France 98, Beckham was still awaiting his first goal for England. He had mainly been used on the right side for both club and country, so the obvious question was whether his lack of international goals was due to the national team not making optimum use of his talent.

Back at La Baule the day after the victory over Tunisia, the media were surprised to find that Beckham was again one of the players made available to them. He cut a sad and lonely figure and it was plain that he spoke from the heart when he said he was 'devastated' by his omission. He went on to add some details of what had occurred, saying, 'My stomach was turning over so many times it was unbelievable. He [Hoddle] named the team in front of everybody. I tried to hide my disappointment but it was pretty hard because we had training after-wards, which I found hard to get into.' It appeared from what Beckham said that the reasons for Hoddle's action had not been fully explained to him.

Alex Ferguson was more than a little concerned. It wasn't so much because his player had been dropped even though he personally thought Beckham a better choice than his replacement, Anderton. What dismayed Ferguson was that Beckham was forced to face the media, his pain exposed for all to see. Ferguson went public with his views, first in a World Cup column he was producing for the *Sunday Times*, then on ITV's World Cup panel programme, *Encore*. Hoddle responded by saying he was disappointed to hear what Ferguson had said, claiming that when he had been asked to comment on Manchester United's Champions' League campaign when things had started to go wrong he had refrained from saying anything that might interfere with United's preparations.

After the initial spat Hoddle was keen to defuse the situation, but the media had other ideas. The coach, continuously goaded over the Beckham affair, seemed exasperated. 'There are twenty-two players available and I have been quite staggered that I have been asked about David Beckham. If we had lost 2–0 and I had got it wrong there would have been some justification. But we won 2–0 and we won well.' Hoddle went on to indicate that the media, who saw the issue as a straight choice between Beckham and Anderton, had the wrong end of the stick. 'When was the last time he played on the right-hand side for England building up for the World Cup?' he asked rhetorically, before answering, 'Portugal at Wembley in April. In the last few games he has played inside. There's your answer.' So in Hoddle's mind it was not necessarily an either-or situation.

As the next game approached, against Romania in Toulouse, the only thing that disturbed the media's concentration on the Beckham saga was the possibility of further violence on the part of the English fans. There was much trepidation and a large police presence but in the event there was mercifully little trouble, although one English supporter suffered a stab wound. Given that official World Cup knives, which were supposed to have been withdrawn well before the tournament started, were openly on sale in Toulouse shops, it was a relief that more injuries were avoided. The authorities, with help from English police 'spotters', had analysed surveillance tapes from Marseille and were now confident that they were better able to identify troublemakers. English fans in the city, on the other hand, claimed that the hardcore hooligans were elsewhere, regrouping for a confrontation at the final group game against Colombia in the northern town of Lens.

On the day of the match against Romania, facilities which were available for every other game, such as the televising of the match on a big screen on the banks of the Garonne river, were temporarily withdrawn, so there would be no focal point where violence might be triggered. The citizens of the southern city were also deprived of their annual June music festival.

Emboldened by the Tunisia result, Hoddle stuck with the same team for the Romania game, except for Gary Neville coming in for the injured Gareth Southgate. This, of course, meant there was again no place for David Beckham in the starting line-up. The Romanians were always seen as England's most dangerous opponents in the group. They had kept most of their squad together from USA 94, had qualified for the finals after dropping only one point and were the group's seeded team. Having started the tournament with a 1–0 win over Colombia, it was a fair bet that their morale was high.

Disaster is the only word which adequately sums up England's night as far as the football was concerned. Romania hit the bar early on, which should have served as a warning, but attention was diverted when Paul Ince was injured after half an hour, to be replaced by none other than Beckham, who went into the centre of

England's midfield. It was in defence, however, that England's problems were most visible. They never seemed to get to grips with the game and to add insult to injury, the two goals which defeated them were both scored by players from the Premiership. The first, two minutes into the second half, was smashed home by Coventry City's Viorel Moldovan, while the winner, scored within moments of the final whistle, was poked through David Seaman's legs by Chelsea's Dan Petrescu. Graeme Le Saux, against instructions, allowed Georghe Hagi to come inside to set up the first goal and was left exposed for the second by Tony Adams's last-minute walkabout.

In between the two Romanian goals England looked ineffective going forward, despite positive contributions from Beckham and Anderton. The pace of the game was dictated by the Romanians, who gave England a lesson in possession football. That only changed when Hoddle decided to introduce Michael Owen for Teddy Sheringham with seventeen minutes left. The clamour for Owen had been growing, not only because of the Liverpool teenager's prodigious ability but also because Sheringham's form had dipped badly. Hoddle, however, was, until that moment, unprepared to ditch the Manchester United striker, despite his poor recent performances and his much publicized night on the town in Portugal immediately prior to the squad's departure for France. Hoddle's attachment to Sheringham seemed strange given the coach's attitude to the likes of Gascoigne and Beckham. Perhaps that was because Sheringham was Alan Shearer's preferred partner, and it appeared that what Shearer wanted, Shearer got. Shearer claimed that Sheringham was 'a yard quicker in his head', which, according to the England captain, enabled him to see a pass or a move before anyone else. There was, however, little evidence of this quick thinking against Romania.

When Owen arrived on the scene, England were transformed and he scored the equalizer with seven minutes left. Having got back to 1–1, England, instead of protecting their hard-won parity, which would have left them top of the group on goal difference, went for the winner. This led to the slackness at the back which was exploited by Petrescu. There was still enough time for Owen almost to save England again when he produced a shot out of nothing from long range, but the ball hit the post and the moment passed.

Glenn Hoddle put the defeat down to the defensive errors which led to the Romanian goals. They were, he said, 'schoolboy stuff'. Once again, though, Hoddle's use of substitutes left something to be desired. It is a testament to Michael Owen's class that seventeen minutes was all he needed to make his impact. In addition, England's formation, using three central defenders with wing-backs, gave Romania space down the flanks which they used to good effect throughout the match. And an inability to modify tactics once the score was 1–1 let England down badly. Writing in the *Independent*, Eamon Dunphy sarcastically commented on the coach's post-match analysis by declaring that, 'Victories are down to Glenn's tactics, defeats to his players' deficiencies.'

Instead of holding pole position in the group, an outcome which a draw would have produced, England now needed at least a point from their showdown against Colombia to guarantee qualification into the second-round knockout stage. Assuming that Romania would either win or draw their last game against Tunisia, the most England could hope for was second place. Colombia had bounced back from defeat by Romania with an encouraging win over the Tunisians. That meant

England and Colombia were locked together on three points but England had a superior goal difference. A draw would be enough to qualify but because of the way the other groups were shaping up, second place for England would result in a tough second-round tie against Argentina, rather than a somewhat easier match, on paper at least, against Croatia. By their inept performance against Romania, England had given themselves an unnecessarily difficult task when their group had been there for the taking.

Having failed to explain his decision to drop Beckham for the first two matches, Hoddle, once he was back at La Baule, decided to revisit the issue. Beckham undoubtedly played well when he came on for Ince but Hoddle launched into a critical assessment of the player's state of mind when he arrived in France. 'I don't think he's been focused coming into this tournament,' Hoddle said. 'At the end of the season, he's not been focused. Perhaps his club should have looked at that a little bit earlier, but he hasn't been focused on his football and he's just been a bit vague.' Whatever Hoddle meant – and he was taken to mean that Beckham's liaison with the world of showbusiness was deflecting his attention from football – his assertion that Manchester United, and by inference, Alex Ferguson, bore some responsibility for the situation was sure to be controversial.

While Hoddle provided no details to back up his diagnosis, he did tell the media what he had done to rectify the problem. 'We've had a good long chat,' he revealed. 'Whatever other people's opinions [are] of how it was dealt with, we've had a chat. He certainly looks more focused now and came on and did very well for us against Romania.'

Alex Ferguson responded in his *Sunday Times* column. His complaint against Hoddle, he said, had nothing to do with his inclusion or omission of Beckham. 'Selection,' Ferguson emphasized, 'is a matter for the coach and no one else.' What concerned him was that 'if Hoddle thought lack of focus had diminished Beckham's contribution to the point where his selection wasn't justified, he had every right to leave the boy out. Having done so, the coach might have been wise to make the facts known earlier than he did. Waiting till after the defeat by Romania to talk about it was a strange piece of timing.'

While Ferguson's criticism was self-evidently valid, it would perhaps have been more telling had he been candid enough to reveal how he personally handled Beckham. The United manager had himself dropped the player at the beginning of the 1997/98 season and an avuncular approach wasn't too much in evidence then. In the *Sunday Times*, Ferguson drew a comparison between Beckham and Ryan Giggs. After Giggs's much-heralded introduction to United's first team, he reached a plateau. However, Ferguson maintained that Giggs overcame his problems and had now gravitated to a higher plane. Beckham, he felt, had the potential to do likewise. But in truth Giggs was the beneficiary of a special relationship with his manager which extended to his family. He, like Beckham, had a high-profile, though short-lived, liaison with a famous woman, in his case the television presenter Dani Behr. But Giggs, less outgoing than Beckham, always enjoyed the company of long-time friends, in direct contrast to the ostentatious lifestyle Beckham seems to court. Beckham also tests Ferguson's patience and he has often been on the receiving end of critical outbursts from his manager.

The more sympathetic attitude Ferguson displayed in his newspaper article may have come about when he travelled on a flight from Nice to Heathrow with Beckham and Victoria Adams just prior to the World

Cup. Seeing the enormous pressure the couple came under, with paparazzi dogging their every step, must have opened his eyes to the fact that this kind of media attention went beyond anything he had ever seen during his forty-year career in football. 'I cannot imagine ever wanting to give even a minute of my life to the sort of nonsense that surrounded David that day,' a genuinely shocked Ferguson wrote.

Alex Ferguson was prepared to take Glenn Hoddle at face value, even if he disagreed with some of his methods, but others probed a little deeper. Frenchman Erik Bielderman, an experienced observer of English football, who was reporting on England's World Cup campaign for the daily sports paper *L'Equipe*, thought there was more to it than Hoddle had let on. 'In exposing Beckham [to the media],' Bielderman wrote, 'he [Hoddle] destabilized him temporarily. The whole of England could therefore see how difficult it was for David to come to terms with the [biggest] disappointment of his career. With Beckham unnerved from that point it would be easier for Hoddle to justify the omission of someone whom he would [then] accuse of "not arriving at the World Cup sufficiently focused".'

The 'not focused' tag baffled many other observers, including Hoddle's right-hand man, John Gorman. Gorman was quoted as saying, 'We've always felt he's been fine.' One of Beckham's closest friends, Gary Neville, revealed that Beckham had talked about the World Cup as the most important event in his life and was excited by the opportunity it afforded him to emulate Gazza's feats during Italia 90. It was left to a member of the public, one Mr S. Hartley, to come up with the most concise opinion, which he e-mailed to the Sky Sports World Cup phone-in show. 'Gazza was focused but not fit. Beckham is fit but not focused. No one knows if Anderton is fit or focused. Glenn Hoddle has lost the plot,' was Mr Hartley's view. While that may have been a bit over the top, it certainly reflected the puzzlement felt over Hoddle's selection policy.

Having reignited the Beckham story, Hoddle turned his attention to the upcoming encounter with Colombia. He intimated that Michael Owen might play from the start. The coach, as had become his style, was determined to give nothing away until he had to (which, technically, was when the team sheet was handed to a FIFA official an hour before kick-off). Hoddle's reluctance to confirm the obvious was a bridge too far for the media. Many decided to get their information direct from the numerous players with whom they were collaborating in the production of newspaper columns. Thus, on the morning of the match, headlines announced that Beckham and Owen would be in the team.

Afterwards, Hoddle was more forthcoming. The team was, he said, predetermined. He had always aspired to 'nurse' Owen through the tournament by introducing him for limited periods in the first two games. Since Colombia played square at the back, he had intended to start with Owen and Beckham in this game. As far as Beckham was concerned, his outlook, according to the coach, had been completely turned around. 'He's now a hundred per cent focused on his football and the boy's got talent,' enthused Hoddle.

The result of the Colombia game seemed to vindicate Hoddle. England tore into the opposition and, in a fine attacking display during the first half, scored two goals through Anderton and Beckham in a nine-minute spell, ending Colombia's faint hopes of qualifying in England's place. There could have been more but for some excellent goalkeeping by Farid Mondragon. This time no one could argue with Hoddle's assessment that, 'It was a conclusive and controlled performance, perhaps the best under me so far.'

After Beckham had struck a magnificent free-kick into the net to claim England's second goal, his reaction indicated something beyond joy for the team. Just as he had used his celebration against Chelsea in the FA Cup to make a point to his detractors, so this goal resulted in a demonstration of Beckham's perceived rehabilitation. There was no ear-cupping this time, rather a sexual gyrating of the hips as his face distorted into an expression of crazed delight, conveying unmistakably that this was as good as it gets.

Unfortunately for the fans, they couldn't toast Beckham's exploits. The whole of Lens, a town with a smaller population than its stadium's capacity of 40,000, was closed for the duration of England's stay. Facing a massive police operation and with only the remnants of duty-free purchases to imbibe, there was no serious trouble and the real hooligans were prevented from causing mischief. This was a considerable relief after the inhabitants' experience of the German fans' violence when they visited the town a few days earlier.

With Romania managing to obtain the draw they needed to top the group, England's 2-0 victory put them in the runners-up position. The outcome, therefore, had turned out as expected. In the second round, Romania would face Croatia, while England were paired with Argentina. Given that the Argentinians were many people's choice as potential winners of the World Cup (including Hoddle himself), there was huge disappointment at home that England had not done enough to avoid meeting them at such an early stage of the tournament. Hoddle, though, claimed he preferred to meet Argentina rather than Croatia, saying, 'We talked about it among the staff . . . I feel we're better when we're playing against the big footballing countries.' The coach was plainly unconcerned with any uncomfortable truths which contradicted his view. One such was that England had failed to beat any of the top four sides (Brazil, Germany, Argentina and Italy) in a major international tournament since the victory over West Germany in 1966.

Presumably, the coach's reference to 'preferring Argentina' was another example of Hoddle putting his particular brand of spin on events. This is borne out by the fact that he did not personally watch Argentina play during the group stage but, with John Gorman and Ray Clemence, did travel to Saint-Étienne to see Croatia play Japan.

This method of evaluating the situation was nothing new to the media. Discerning the meaning of his comments was becoming like the Kremlin experts during the Cold War. Nothing is what it seems and information must be gleaned from interpretation more than acceptance of statements at face value. No one had forgotten how they were misled before the Rome game against Italy. So when Hoddle attended his media conferences at La Baule and held forth about his players' fitness, the assembled throng greeted his words with a cynicism that grew by the day. The announcement before the Romania game that Gareth Southgate had recovered from injury was taken to mean that he would definitely not be playing. Perhaps sensing the mood, the coach then took things further with games of double bluff. Thus when he mused that Michael Owen might start against Colombia, it was taken as evidence that Sheringham must still be in favour. Owen, of course, played. After Hoddle claimed that his team selection against Colombia was planned in advance of the tournament, some reporters thought enough was enough. Colin Malam, writing in the *Sunday Telegraph*, was moved to say that 'The England coach has

235

emerged as one of the foremost revisionists in his profession's great tradition of rewriting history.'

As the day of reckoning approached, England fans, knowing their team were underdogs but egged on by the confidence of the coach, allowed themselves to hope that maybe he had really planned it this way, and they actually began to believe they might win.

CHAPTER FOURTEEN

The Way We Are

I T WAS FITTING THAT Saint-Étienne should act as host to the most dramatic encounter of France 98. It was the local club, which included such illustrious names as Michel Platini and Dominic Rocheteau, that captured the imagination of the country through its European exploits in the 1970s. In those days, when French football was emerging from a period in the doldrums, '*Allez les verts*' was a common refrain throughout the nation. Now, with the team languishing in the second division, Platini had helped bring the World Cup to this small industrial town near Lyons, a place which is often called the forgotten city of France.

The Stade Geoffroy-Guichard, named after the founder of the Casino supermarket chain, is a ground where all four stands hug the touchlines. The proximity of fans to the pitch ensured that the match between Argentina and England evoked memories of home. Since the World Cup draw had been made in Marseille the previous December, the prospect of Argentina and England facing each other in the first knockout round had been in the air. Now the stage was set for one of the enduring confrontations in international football, the third act in a sublime trilogy.

Act one came in 1966, when Argentinian captain, Antonio Rattin, was harshly sent off at Wembley in a World Cup quarter-final which England won 1–0. The sense of injustice felt by the losers was not helped when Alf Ramsey called them 'animals' and from that moment games between the countries became epic encounters. (A bitter battle for the World Club Championship, played by the winners of the European Cup and its South American equivalent, the Copa Libertadores, followed in the late 1960s, when Estudiantes beat Manchester United.) The Argentine national team turned the tables twenty years after the Wembley quarter-final, in Act Two, the 'Hand of God' epic, when, in the wake of the Falklands war, they knocked England out of the Mexico World Cup in the most controversial of circumstances.

In a press conference the weekend before the third act, Glenn Hoddle spoke at length about the 1986 game, when, as an England player, he witnessed the handball goal of Diego Maradona at close quarters. He told how upset he had been at the time and how he had tried to convince the referee of Maradona's foul, all to no avail. 'I remember the feeling then was one of total injustice,' he said. This match in Saint-Étienne, he thought, gave him the chance to 'redress the balance', although revenge was a word he preferred not to use. 'For the football people in our country,' he continued, 'we have got a chance of turning that result round and getting it out of our system.'

By reminding the world so clearly of England's 1986 defeat, Hoddle invited his audience to share in his memories at a time when the presence of English hooligans was casting a threatening shadow over the upcoming fixture. He might not have liked the word but everyone else regarded the game as a revenge match, and the emotion must also have transmitted itself to his players. The talk of 'redressing the balance' left Hoddle, a man in total control of his team, in the self-appointed role of avenging angel.

Hoddle was convinced that if Maradona's first strike had been disallowed for handball, the second brilliant solo goal would not have been scored. Argentinians find this theory bizarre and they are bemused that England are still going on about it. To them, both goals are important, a team has to score, period. Unlike Rattin's dismissal at Wembley, the first Maradona goal was a blatant piece of gamesmanship. It was not their fault the referee missed it. As Jorge Valdano, then Maradona's teammate, now a respected coach and writer, said: 'The second goal was so wonderful it was worth two anyway.' In Argentina, then, both goals are revered.

In France, the Argentinian camp was, if anything, even more of a fortress than England's and the team's coach, Daniel Passarella, was just as authoritarian as Hoddle. As a player he led the national team when they won the World Cup in 1978 and is known as the 'great captain' to distinguish him from the officers of the military junta which was in charge of the country at the time. Passarella subsequently fell out of favour as the 1978 coach, Cesar Luis Menotti, was replaced by Carlos Bilardo. He started and finished his career with River Plate, with spells in between at Fiorentina and Internazionale, his playing career bringing him seven championship titles in his home country.

After the disappointment and disgrace of USA 94, when Maradona was expelled for drug abuse, Passarella was the uncontested choice to restore pride and discipline to the national squad, his three titles as coach at River Plate giving him the managerial credentials to go with his playing exploits. Intolerant of rule-breakers, Passarella was determined to keep out anyone he considered a prima donna. At one point a comment he made about long hair, earrings and homosexuals caused widespread publicity and a whole raft of players, including Claudio Caniggia, Fernando Redondo and, of course, Diego Maradona, were cast aside. Juan Veron must have been lucky to survive the cut, given that he later said of David Beckham: 'He is too handsome to be a footballer, I don't know whether to kick him or kiss him.'

Meanwhile, Passarella built his team around River Plate players, past and present, including Hernan Crespo, Ariel Ortega, Matias Almeyda and Marcelo Gallardo. The accent was on youth, reinforced by the experience of Jose Chamot, Roberto Ayala, Nestor Sensini, captain Diego Simeone and the goal machine, Gabriel Batistuta, who was prepared to toe the line and get his hair cut in his desire to go to France.

If the English media thought that access to the team at La Baule was limited, they were taken aback at the lengths Passarella went to. At the Argentinian headquarters near Saint-Étienne the theme was 'concentration'. There were to be no late nights or nights on the town and, above all, no women. This was so important that volunteers attached to the squad or seconded from the hotel to help look after them had to be male. After their group stage game against Japan, the word went out from the players that there would be no further one-to-one interviews. There were also no insights to be gained from visits to the training ground. Whenever the media was around they were more likely to be playing volleyball than football.

The night before the England game there was a tense atmosphere in Saint-Étienne, a heavy police presence suggesting the prospect of widespread English mayhem. Yet against expectations, when match day arrived it was sunny and there was a good feeling among the two sets of fans. This, at last, was a real game for real fans. It was one match where the ubiquitous Mexican wave would find it hard to get a look in.

For Argentina, games against England always hold a special place. Usual considerations of form tend to go out of the window when they meet the nation they regard as 'pirates'. This view of their adversaries is not confined to colonial and political affairs, it extends to football itself. The first-ever true international football matches were instituted at the start of this century by the entrepreneur and retailer Sir Thomas Lipton, and they were played between Argentina and Uruguay. In England, however, it is claimed that England–Scotland matches, which were begun earlier, were the first internationals. But since they were not played by two separate nation states, they are not considered real internationals by many fans in South America.

The Argentine players and staff had no problem with motivation but nevertheless regarded their own superior form with suspicion. Yet they were favourites to emerge as victors in 1998, having won all three of their group games with ease. The team that Hoddle preferred to meet had not given a goal away in eight games and their counter-attacking style had won plaudits from all directions, including England. In Veron they had the most consistent midfielder in France and Ortega had already shown enough to suggest he was ready to assume the mantle of great playmaker. In Batistuta, they possessed one of the most feared strikers in the world. If that wasn't enough, they had recently beaten Brazil in Rio.

England fielded the same team that defeated Colombia, with both Beckham and Owen playing in an attacking 3–5–2 formation. It was totally different from the more conservative approach that had served England so well in their previous game against a world-class side,

241

the encounter with Italy in Rome at the end of the qualifying competition. With Argentina adopting a similar
attitude, the first forty-five minutes were saturated with
an intensity no other tournament game had equalled.

Two debatable penalties, one to each side, in the opening minutes, were a mere foretaste of the drama to come.
Before and after England's equalizer, Hoddle's team
produced their best attacking play of the tournament,
culminating in Owen's wonder goal, when he outpaced
Chamot and Ayala before clipping the ball into the net,
and Paul Scholes's miss from a great position which
would have put England 3–1 in front. After that,
Argentina went for their own equalizer with urgency.
When it came, their second goal was as superb in its own
way as Owen's had been, Argentina bamboozling
England's defence with a well-worked free-kick.
Batistuta dummied, Veron rolled the ball to Zanetti, and
he peeled away from the England wall before finishing
clinically. With the goal coming right on half-time,
Argentina went into the interval in the ascendant.

If the first half was memorable for the quality of the
football, the second was steeped in drama. From the
moment David Beckham was sent off in the forty-
seventh minute for kicking out at Simeone – not
viciously, but intentionally – after the Argentine captain
had fouled him, the pressure was unrelenting. England's
ten men performed miraculously and might have won
the game, while Argentina seemed to go into their shell.
Sol Campbell's disallowed goal and a handball in the
Argentine penalty box which went unpunished by the
referee cost England dear. So there was no golden goal
and in the end England's nemesis, the penalty shoot-out,
was required to settle the issue. Paul Ince and David
Batty missed and, as might have been expected, England
had lost and were out of the World Cup. After a roller-

coaster night of conflicting emotions, England were again left with the despair of yet another heroic failure.

But it had been a superb contest. *L'Equipe* put it best with the simple front-page headline: 'We shall remember', followed by the comment that it was a 'match of very high quality filled with exploits and emotions. What a night.'

Immediately after the game, Glenn Hoddle concentrated on Beckham's moment of madness, which he saw as the main cause of his team's defeat. 'It cost us,' he said, 'it cost us dearly . . . I am not denying it cost us the game.' He also found fault with the referee but did not appear to accept any responsibility himself for the outcome.

The English press similarly heaped the blame squarely on to Beckham's shoulders. 'Ten Heroic Lions, One Stupid Boy' was the *Daily Mirror*'s front-page headline. The *Daily Telegraph* portentously asked: 'Is Beckham what is wrong with this country?' and continued by castigating him as a 'sex-and-shopping, fame-schooled, daytime-TV, over-coiffed twerp'. The *Daily Star*, meanwhile, devoted its entire front page to the comment: 'Sorry lads. No tits on page three, only Beckham.' It should not be surprising that, taking its lead from that kind of abuse, the English public turned on Beckham with venom, the like of which it normally reserves for paedophiles and murderers.

In Beckham, the public had been provided with a ready-made scapegoat and Hoddle's subsequent, more reflective opinion, that Beckham's had been a 'foolish' indiscretion, which was more worthy of a yellow, rather than a red card, probably came too late.

In their devastation, the yobs and xenophobes had been handed a sacrificial victim on a plate. David Beckham and Victoria Adams were cast as successors to Hugh Grant and Liz Hurley or, to an older generation,

243

Richard Burton and Elizabeth Taylor. Never mind that their foibles can be exposed to millions, that their flaws as human beings can be played out as if on a stage or in a soap opera, their vast incomes are supposed to make up for it. But the media likes to build up the most vulnerable into stars because they are all the easier to knock down.

Already the media were planning to poll the public on Beckham's 'dastardly deed', an effigy of the player was discovered as if lynched and West Ham fans were promising a special 'welcome' when Manchester United arrived to play their first Premiership away game of the new season. What effect all this will have on Beckham is anyone's guess. Perhaps he can learn from Eric Cantona and return stronger for the experience. For the sake of Manchester United and England it has to be hoped that it turns out that way. However, Beckham is only twenty-three and doesn't possess Cantona's self-awareness, self-esteem or arrogance. It will be a grave loss to English football if Beckham is not given the space and time to recover from his mistake.

The Beckham issue ran through the entire England experience in France. Although he had shown before that he could sometimes be petulant on the field, Beckham's transgression in Saint-Étienne was not merely a repetition of some previous occasional bad behaviour. 'On the pitch and off it, I'm two different people,' he told Erik Bielderman. 'On the pitch I know there are people who hate me.' In some games, most notably against Feyenoord in the Champions' League, Beckham has slyly committed some gratuitous fouls on opposing players. Had they been spotted and Beckham punished, as Michael Owen was for an horrendous foul on Ronny Johnsen of Manchester United in April 1998, he might have been able to improve his behaviour before the spotlight of

England's most important match for years fell on him.

Dropped and accused of not being focused once he was in France, Beckham's successful rehabilitation had been loudly proclaimed by Hoddle, who took the credit for it. The player had been deconstructed by his coach, who blamed his perceived deficiencies on his club. Hoddle then, prematurely as it turned out, said Beckham's display against Colombia showed how he was now focused, the implication being that this had been achieved as a direct result of the coach's intervention.

Hoddle had tried to exert such control over Beckham's psyche that the player was stretched to the point where he must have felt, however unnecessarily, that he had to prove himself all over again. Whatever responsibility Beckham holds for his actions, his coach's psychological ploys had manifestly failed. And if Hoddle wanted to claim credit for Beckham's so-called improved state, then he must surely take a share of the blame for that moment when it all went wrong. Hoddle's programme for Beckham could not have had a worse outcome.

While Hoddle was convinced that England would have beaten Argentina had Beckham remained on the pitch, some observers saw it differently. Ruud Gullit, for instance, writing in the *Observer*, noted that when Beckham was sent off, 'the balance had swung back to Argentina ... it is a little fanciful to suggest England would have been winners but for Beckham's dismissal'. Hoddle, meanwhile, had expanded on his views of the refereeing decisions during the game, which reinforced his belief in Beckham's culpability. If his team of ten men were only denied by poor decisions (he thought Campbell's goal would have been allowed in the Premiership and that the referee was too inhibited by the golden-goal situation, and the fact that he had already awarded two penalties, to give the handball against

Chamot during extra-time), they surely would have claimed victory with eleven.

But what of the situation within the coach's control? In the game itself, Hoddle's use of substitutes was again found wanting. Passarella was not afraid to take off his captain, Simeone, or his most potent threat up front, Batistuta, because he felt the situation warranted it and he wanted to get 'his boy', Hernan Crespo, on to the pitch. Similarly, Hoddle could have taken off Alan Shearer. Michael Owen could have been left permanently up front, where two defenders would have been needed to contain him, thus nullifying the numerical disadvantage. Hoddle, however, didn't contemplate this option. But taking off Shearer would have allowed Hoddle to reinforce the midfield with a specialist, either Steve McManaman, whose ability to run at opponents would have given England a route to goal if Hoddle hoped to win the game in normal time or during the extra thirty minutes, or Rob Lee, if he wanted to be more cautious. And unlike David Batty, who was eventually brought on, both players take penalties. The tactic Hoddle decided to use, which was to rotate Shearer and Owen between the right-back and centre-forward positions, achieved nothing tangible.

Given that England had lost in semi-finals of the World Cup and the European Championships by failing in penalty shoot-outs, it would seem wilful to ignore the possibility that such an ordeal might have to be faced in France at some stage. Hoddle was rightly proud of his attention to detail but this was one detail he seemed to be equally proud to have forsaken. He revealed that apart from the recognized penalty takers and the goalkeepers, his players did not practise penalty taking. This was because, he reasoned, you could not recreate the match atmosphere in training, so there was no point. 'It is not about practice,' he insisted, 'it is about how you feel on that walk from the halfway line to the penalty spot. You can't prepare for that.' He obviously didn't subscribe to the observation of the golfer Gary Player that 'It's funny, but the more I practise, the luckier I get.' In addition to the lack of practice, England's representatives in the event of a shoot-out could have been compiled from one to twenty-two, so the order would have been predetermined, taking into account whoever was left on the pitch at the end. Instead, it was left to the players to volunteer for the task.

How could a coach who has made it his job to impose his control in such a complete manner, allow David Batty to volunteer himself for the crucial fifth spot-kick? At the time Hoddle's leadership qualities were most needed, he should have saved Batty from himself. Yet he abdicated responsibility in the knowledge that in the 'lottery' of the shoot-out, no one could be blamed for losing.

David Pleat, who is not an enthusiast for penalty kicks being used to decide games, nevertheless believes that preparation for them is vital. 'The manager is the important one,' he claimed in the *Sunday Times*. 'He must nominate his five gladiators, then look into their eyes and ask them if they are happy with the responsibility.'

In a variety of other areas Hoddle had certainly produced a well-prepared squad. Vitamin supplements, attention to nutritional requirements and meticulously planned exercise, all engendered a sense of physical well-being. There was also extensive video analysis, which was then put to practical use on the training pitch. This helps explain Hoddle's strange predilection for David Batty. Batty rarely gives the ball away but neither does he produce many penetrating passes or runs to hurt the opposition where it matters. On the other hand, the videos show that Steve McManaman, because of his penchant for adventurous play which takes the game to the opposition, is something of a risk; he sometimes loses the ball in the process. So Batty is preferred in the interests of control.

Danny Blanchflower, responding to a derogatory comment about Hoddle the player, once said: 'Hoddle a luxury? It's the bad players who are the luxury.' But would Hoddle the coach have picked Hoddle the player, a talented individual who couldn't defend and didn't work hard enough? The coach says he would pick himself because the system he was forced to play never made the best use of him. '4–4–2,' he explained, 'puts us in chains.' Hoddle implied that 3–5–2 is more flexible and provides more attacking options. In that case, why no McManaman or Le Tissier, even as substitutes (and they too can both take penalties)?

To Hoddle, control was the key. Heaven forbid that opponents might get wind of his tactics. For instance, after qualifying for France he used important set-plays sparingly in the series of friendlies before the World Cup, even if the performances suffered as a result and criticism was forthcoming. Moreover, the media only saw what the coach wanted them to see, which was often just enough to ensure they would jump to the wrong conclusion. He played Beckham in the reserve team in training at La Baule, knowing he would not be in the side to face Tunisia, then switched him to the first team when the media were allowed in. This was not done to spite the reporters but to throw the opposition off the scent.

The media, of course, were there to report what they saw to the world. This, Hoddle realized, meant that opponents could see media stories just as much as fans. Thus the media could be used to feed false information to the enemy. It wasn't that Hoddle held any antagonism for journalists, he just didn't rate their relevance very highly. There was nothing to be gained from paying them any heed because their view of the game was different from that of a coach, who has to pore over videos for hours and attempt to put the knowledge gained to practical use. The media could not devise tactics, only a coach could do that.

The information Hoddle sought out in his hours of video-watching was sifted, analysed and compartmentalized. Knowledge of the opposition bred confidence and determined tactics. Against Tunisia, for instance, Hoddle warned his defenders not to risk a last-ditch tackle, because in a one-to-one situation against the goalkeeper, the analysis proved that the Tunisians often missed the target. There was a tactical answer to everything. Thus goals conceded were due to defensive errors, except where they were the result of something unforeseen, like Zanetti's equalizer for Argentina. Hoddle could admit that the goal was a good one because he had never seen it before. On this occasion, Daniel Passarella had outwitted him at his own game of secret strategy. The biter had been well and truly bit.

When Carlos Roa saved David Batty's penalty, Passarella exploded. He ran on to the pitch but slipped before he could get to wherever he was heading. Instead of getting up and continuing his progress he lay on his back kicking his legs in the air. Juan Veron leaped over the advertising boards and climbed up the fencing to share his joy with the fans, shouting, 'We did it, we did it.' Amid the pandemonium Passarella pulled himself together enough to be able to fulfil his obligations to the media. He was happy to reveal how sweet the victory was but was also open enough to admit he had been wrong to take off Batistuta, believing erroneously that Crespo was ready to join the fray after an injury.

Players had no similar responsibility to talk to the

media. While some teams were happy to talk – the Chileans spoke for ages after their defeat by Brazil – the Argentinians deliberately walked straight past the waiting reporters and disappeared, displaying smiles of satisfaction they could not contain. They soon found an outlet for their joy. Leaving the stadium in their team bus, they waved their shirts in the air and goaded the England players, who were departing at the same time. At first, the English were baffled as to how a coachload of Argentinian supporters could have penetrated the security cordon. When they realized it was actually their opponents they were horrified.

This behaviour by the Latin Americans might seem a cheap shot but it is the sort of thing fans do given the chance and there is a strong sense of communion between the Argentine players and their fans. After they had beaten Jamaica 5–0 in the Parc des Princes, there was a feeling of oneness between players and supporters unlike anything witnessed on the part of England and their followers, where a distance is always maintained. As the Argentine bus left after the Jamaica game, Gabriel Batistuta looked at the massed supporters with a beatific gaze on his face, as if he was deliberately partaking of the moment with them. His pride and pleasure in having scored a hat-trick in the match were there for all to see.

David Beckham would never have been vilified the way he has been if he had been playing for the other side. As if to prove the point, four days later, Ariel Ortega was sent off in the quarter-final against Holland. His dismissal, for putting his head into Dutch goalkeeper Edwin Van der Sar's face, came in the final minutes. Although Argentina then conceded the winning goal to Dennis Bergkamp, fans and media were understanding in a way that would have been impossible in England. Van der Sar, they thought, was asking for trouble by standing over Ortega and accusing him of diving. Argentine journalist Marcelo Mora y Araujo put this feeling best, saying, 'As a nation, we had empathy with Ortega, in the same way that as a nation we had empathy with Maradona, who just flipped his hand because he could.' While to the English, the 'Argies' will forever be associated with gamesmanship, and while they can dismiss Maradona's second goal as Hoddle did, Jorge Valdano, despite his partisan feelings, is able to say, 'I didn't have it in me to feel bad about Owen's goal. It was too perfect to cry over.'

Maybe Hoddle will take comfort from the words of his mentor, Arsenal manager Arsène Wenger, who gave a considered appraisal. 'There are two problems when a team represents its country,' he said. 'The first and most important is to convey an image with which the fans can identify. I believe, on that criterion, England have rendered a good image of the country and fulfilled the basic requirement. The second point, naturally, is to return with a trophy because in England one is always being asked, "How many trophies have you won?" Here, England failed but in an unfortunate manner and under extenuating circumstances. Personally, I regret very much that they are out because they had shown attractive play and scored a number of goals. Moreover, they went out, unfortunately, against a very strong team, one of the favourites, and when they met each other, one obviously had to go. They left with honour.'

The confidence in his own ability probably means Hoddle does not need words of comfort. Perhaps this very confidence enables him to accentuate the positive aspects at the expense of the big picture. Certainly, the emergence of Michael Owen is one positive, the potential of Anderton another. And the prospect of these two playing with Beckham, Campbell and Neville augurs well for the future. But the bitter taste of disappointment, whether through heroic failure, bad luck or whatever interpretation the coach wants to put on it, fuelled the despondency felt back home and the overwhelming sense of what might have been.

There was nothing but praise from the FA. Chairman Keith Wiseman was certain Hoddle was the right man for the job and was prepared to suggest a longer-term contract. Hoddle's current agreement expires after the 2000 European Championships. 'There is no doubt in my mind,' Wiseman said, 'that England will win the World Cup under Glenn Hoddle. We have complete confidence in him and the job he is doing. When he wants a new agreement we will talk about it with him.' However, Wiseman's words will only be taken seriously if the true nature of what happened in France is accepted and the country does not descend into denial. The prosaic fact is that England lost to the first world-class team they faced and were eliminated as soon as the knockout stage arrived.

For all his deficiencies, Hoddle is probably the kind of manager England needs. He at least knows what he wants and is determined to shape the set-up and the team to his ideas. Difficult though he may find it to admit mistakes, if he is to fulfil his own immense potential he must have an inkling of what they are, even if only to himself. If there is one thing that needs to be accepted it is that facing Argentina at that stage of the tournament was unnecessary and could have been avoided with a different approach to the Romania game. Of course, there was no guarantee that England would have beaten Croatia, who did exceptionally well to finish third, but if it came to a choice of whether to face one of the traditional 'big four' of world football or a team from an emerging nation playing in their first World Cup there is surely only one answer.

As events were to prove, Argentina exhausted themselves in beating England. Their quarter-final conquerors, Holland, had to do likewise to make it to the semi-final. Nevertheless, once there they pushed Brazil to the limit, softening up the favourites before they met France in the final. For their part, the hosts came through the easier part of the draw. It would have been this route that England would have taken had they merely drawn with Romania.

Glenn Hoddle believed England could have won the World Cup, as any England coach must. Whether that belief was well-founded will only be seen by results in the future. With the European Championship qualifiers for the 2000 tournament in Belgium and Holland due to start a mere two months after the end of the World Cup, there will not be long to wait for an indication of the way England are going. If the man of destiny can see what is plain to many observers, namely that the early exit from France was not a question of fate or defensive errors but was due to mistakes in selection and strategy, then there may be a better tomorrow.

In compiling his own World Cup story for publication, Hoddle was uneasy at some of the questioning he was forced to endure from someone he thought to be 'on his side'. There was the feeling it was the first time his answers had been challenged. 'I understand,' he said, 'you are being the devil's advocate.' 'No Glenn, not entirely,' his interrogator replied.

CHAPTER FIFTEEN

Yesterday's Gone

REFEREE PIERLUIGI COLLINA is instantly recognizable to millions of Italians, his distinguished bearing and shaven head marking him out from his colleagues just as much as his skill and control. In the VIP room at Parc des Princes in Paris, Collina, cutting a dash in his Yves St Laurent blazer that was the uniform for all World Cup referees, was happy to talk. Until, that is, he was approached by one of the corporate guests.

'Do you speak English?'
'Yes.'
'You're well known to football followers in England, you know.'
'Yes.'
'Can I ask you about Juventus?'
'No.'
'Can we talk about football?'
'No.'
'Can I talk about football?'
'No.'

As if he sensed that the encounter was heading towards embarrassment, Collina hurriedly made for the exit and before he could be accosted again, he was gone.

Collina was forced to make such a nervous departure in case he breached rules which severely limit his freedom of expression. At the World Cup, referees were not allowed to talk. So paranoid has everyone become, they can't even listen to someone else talking about football, particularly when in the presence of their superiors.

This did not stop the new FIFA President, Sepp Blatter, from suggesting after the first week that referees had not been strict enough, despite common agreement that they had done a good job. When accused of committing something of a blunder, he said: 'A blunder, why? It is my role, my duty, to remind referees of their instructions. I didn't say I was content, I said it was good but good is not sufficient for me. Like the players, the referees must be very good.' Consequently, referees, thinking they should be tougher, became more erratic and the level playing field, to say nothing of the entertainment value of many games, was jeopardized. Now, coaches could blame officials for their team's elimination, as Glenn Hoddle did in part after England's defeat by Argentina.

While FIFA were right to ban the tackle from behind – nobody was literally kicked out of the tournament as Pele had been in 1966 – they ignored the fact that players will find other ways of stretching the rules to gain an advantage; pushing, shirt-pulling and diving were the preferred methods in France 98. Blatter's response this time was to make a joke of the problem, saying, 'Players are testing the quality of the textiles.' He then insisted that the referee is always right, even when he is wrong. 'Football must keep its human face,' he went on. 'If football starts to become scientific [by using videos to correct mistakes], it will lose all emotion, all passion. People will no longer come.'

Having trailed the attractions of France 98 around the

world in the years leading up to the t
inviting fans to attend, interest was
unprecedented levels, just as the orga
would be. However, with the supply of t
meet the demand, many French citize
taking up their allocation and selling to foreigners in a
French version of the British building society windfall.
This made a mockery of the UK government's advertising
campaign warning that tickets purchased on the black
market would lead to supporters running up against a
checking system which would prevent them getting into
stadia. Nothing remotely resembling such a scenario
occurred and checks were notable by their absence.

João Havelange called complaints over ticketing 'a
storm in a teacup', claiming there was nothing to be
done, as though the system was preordained. 'Everyone
wants to see it but there aren't places for everyone,' he
intoned. There was, though, a ready-made solution and
Havelange told us what it was. 'In every corner of the
world,' he explained, 'there is television. Why don't
people take a coffee, a beer, and watch the match? That's
the modern world.' Meanwhile, Sepp Blatter enthused
over a future where World Cup matches will be seen on
'cable and non-cable, subscription and non-subscription.
There's a place for everyone,' he concluded.

Havelange must have been taken aback when his
welcome speech before the opening match between
Scotland and Brazil was roundly jeered by the Scottish
fans. This was not in the script, they were supposed to be
there to party, to sing and to add colour. The Organizing
Committee must have wondered how they had so
misjudged the Scots, who now seemed like hooligans.
However, when they listened respectfully to the words of
French President, Jacques Chirac, then joined in the
singing of the Marseillaise, albeit their own phonetic

...ion, the doubts were cast aside. It emerged that the protest was specifically aimed at FIFA for their handling of ticket sales. The Scots were angry that FIFA, in giving priority to the corporate sector, had prevented large numbers of their compatriots from attending the game and had driven many others into the hands of the touts.

The problems over World Cup tickets became symbolic of the current divisions in football. At every turn, fans see their loyalty, their love for their teams and the game, downgraded in relation to the interests of commercialism. Football is no longer a sport, it is a business, it is argued by way of explanation. The game has been taken away from the ordinary fan and sold to the highest bidder and just as in the Premiership, many fans couldn't even get into the stadia to watch games. The actions of football's authorities, with a few notable exceptions, confirm the fans' view and they saw FIFA's response to their difficulties in obtaining World Cup tickets as merely the latest, most high-profile example of that disregard.

But fans have always been treated with disdain. It is nothing new, only the details change. When supporters, who traditionally were drawn from low-income groups, provided the chief source of income by paying to attend matches, stadia were large and facilities were poor. Now that football attracts a wealthier clientele, stadia are smaller but facilities are much better. It is not television or commercialism that are the enemies of fans, it is the attitude of owners and administrators, and that is the same as it always has been.

Yet there is no inherent conflict between the business interests which seem to be taking over football and the long-suffering supporters. In fact, they should be natural allies. Television, for instance, the new paymaster, needs large, full stadia, with committed supporters to generate

the atmosphere essential to the creation of the televisic.
spectacular.

What media hype and commercial demands actually
do is create expectations that are impossible to fulfil. It
should not be surprising, therefore, that players, who are
the receptacle of millions of hopes and dreams, should
sometimes find the pressures too great a burden to bear.
If anything summed up this aspect of the World Cup –
the biggest, most hyped tournament of all time – it was
two cameos of Dennis Bergkamp. The Dutchman produced a wonderful moment of pure skill in the dying
minutes of the quarter-final against Argentina to score
Holland's winner. It was a goal fashioned out of true
class and was the type of finish with which Bergkamp's
many admirers have become familiar. But such flashes
were rare and neither Bergkamp nor his peers produced
as many of them as might have been expected.

Bergkamp is, above all else, a cerebral player. Yet in the
game against Yugoslavia he trod on the prone Sinisa
Mihajlovic. He could not have been ignorant of the retribution this sort of behaviour would attract. A red card
and a ban would surely be the outcome. Fortunately for
Bergkamp, the referee failed to notice the misdemeanour.
Sepp Blatter felt that the World Cup Disciplinary
Commission should have banned him. 'On the next occasion,' he warned, 'you will see they will use the video.'
Blatter did not see any contradiction between this view
and his general opinions about videos. It would not be
used to correct a referee's mistake but it would be used to
punish a player whose misdeed escaped attention.

The odd flash of brilliance and momentary losses of
composure, then, were the twin characteristics of France
98. And if a seasoned campaigner like Bergkamp could
succumb to the overwhelming pressures the ever-
increasing hype brings, what chance do younger, rawer

ave? No amount of wealth or fame can
yer on this stage, as David Beckham found
st. As everyone now knows, the one player
ifies all of this is Ronaldo, for whom the
World Cup might have ended in tragedy. Ronaldo, the
world's best player, the game's highest earner, the one for
whom the World Cup was waiting, played well enough,
scored and made goals, yet so much more was wanted.
His much discussed medical problems before the final,
the reaction to his condition on the part of his Brazilian
teammates, the coaching and medical staff and the country's football administrators, culminating in the dis-
graceful decision to let him play, was symptomatic of the
way in which the demands placed on players can
outstrip any semblance of care for their physical and
mental well-being.

Moreover, football itself, for all its sophisticated tactical
plans and training methods, is not producing players or
teams which play the game in a more spectacular way than
in the past. The great World Cup teams lie in the memory
of fans. There are no contemporary equals to Brazil in 1970,
Holland in 1974 or Argentina in 1978. Neither have the
1990s produced the likes of Maradona, Platini, Cruyff, Pele,
Eusébio, Beckenbauer or Charlton. There are good teams
and fine players, of that there is no doubt, but if the
message goes out that each World Cup has to be bigger,
better and more lucrative than the last, it is not reflected in
the quality of the football served up. France 98 was a good
World Cup but there were no really outstanding teams,
only a few games that could possibly be described as
memorable and no player dominated the tournament. The
influx of money and the power of television cannot guarantee better players or more attacking teams.

If France 98 fell short of absolute greatness on the
pitch, it was nevertheless a most enjoyable tournament.

The organizers succeeded in their desire to produce a popular festival, where both the French people and the world could be lifted by the spirit in which games were played and the friendliness shown to visitors in all the host cities. Even the ugliness caused by English and German fans was transcended. Two days after England played against Romania in Toulouse, the city was back to a party atmosphere, with English fans left over from their team's game mixing freely and happily with Nigerians and Paraguayans, who were there for the next match. None of this could make up for the more unsavoury incidents – the policeman left in a coma by German fans in Lens or the death of a Frenchman, stabbed by an Englishman on a train because he was mistaken for an Argentinian – but there was a time when these terrible events would have led to something worse. Instead, the French, other nations' supporters, and even the Germans and English managed to rise above baser instincts.

So did other participants. As Laurent Blanc of France took the long walk to the bench during the semi-final, the victim of a referee who was duped into sending him off by the play-acting of Croatia's Slaven Bilic, it was too much for Jacques Lambert, the Director General of France 98. With the loss of Blanc, Lambert felt the host's place in the final ebbing away. He left his seat in the presidential box and proceeded to pace around the perimeter of the Stade de France, nervously smoking and anxiously waiting for the final whistle. When it came and the rousing chant of '*Allez en final*' rent the air, Lambert, one of the main architects of the tournament, was asked for his immediate reaction. 'Fernand Sastre,' he replied, in a poignant reference to his former colleague who was Co-President of France 98 along with Michel Platini. Sastre had died during the first week of the tournament.

It was where football and festival converged that the

1998 World Cup produced its finest hour. The ultimate victory of France added a new name to the list of World Cup winners for the first time since Argentina in 1978. For the nation which did more than any other to internationalize football, it was fitting that they should win it in their own backyard. And such was the euphoria that, unusually in the partisan world of football, few begrudged them their triumph.

From being unsure at best about Aimé Jacquet and his squad, the French nation was slowly but surely roused. They gradually got behind their side and the scenes on the streets following the 3–0 victory in the final against Brazil were phenomenal, the crowds bigger than at any time since the liberation in 1945.

There was more to it than that, though. France, for all its belief in its culture, has been unsure of its role in the modern world. The French team, '*noir, blanc, bleu*' (black, white, blue – an adaptation of the team's colours), challenged the definition of ethnic Frenchness. With over half the squad being of foreign extraction, including Armenians, Africans, a Polynesian and a Guadeloupais, they provided the most potent example yet seen of French people from all backgrounds working together for the common cause. In front of the world, this polyglot collection won and they did it in style. Theirs was the true expression of Gallic class and it gave the French something they yearned for, a pointer to the future. This was not a product of the hype, nor was it concerned with money or business.

Succeeding where the more gifted <u>French</u> teams of 1982 and 1986 failed, these genuine heroes gave the country a renewed sense of value. Only the World Cup could have produced such an outcome. The days after the final were heady indeed. Never mind Sepp Blatter's wild claims about the World Cup's economic impact, this

was something altogether more importa
provided a nation with an opportunity f
n't matter if it is a fleeting moment or
back somewhat from the high ideals fe
ate aftermath of victory. The French have now ...
experience, it cannot be expunged and the way forward
has clearly been shown. Once again, *L'Equipe* was spot
on. Having been among Jacquet's fiercest critics, the
sports paper was now as swept along on the tide of
passion as everybody else. 'For Eternity', said the front-
page headline. Jerome Bureau's editorial continued the
theme. 'Nothing will ever be the same again,' he wrote.

The pressures on players which became so obvious
during the World Cup also exist at club level. It is easy to
forget that the youngsters at Manchester United are just
that: youngsters. Now, for the 1998/99 season, they face
an even sterner test. If David Beckham has learned from
his experience United might yet confound their critics.
For their fans for whom the European Cup holds such
potent memories and hopes, they can be thankful that
they were given a second chance to make it into the
Champions' League. That chance, of course, was
provided by the expansion of the competition by UEFA,
who were driven by commercial considerations. Are
there any United fans who would forgo the opportunity
because it was brought about by the requirements of television and sponsors? The memories of the Busby Babes
and the 1968 side represent the zenith for United. There
is, once more, the opportunity to emulate past glories. If
they are to keep faith with the present, the time has come
for Europe's biggest club to win the biggest prize.

The consensus among fans now is that the game is
about money and business, not love and glory. Modern
football is awash with money and the distorted perspec-
tives it can bring. But as the World Cup showed, as the

m of Manchester United fans makes clear, football is
uch more valuable than that and there is no reason why
it should not remain so.

Do players only pull on the jersey nowadays for
money? Emmanuel Petit exemplified both Arsenal's
season and France's World Cup. In each case he was slow
into his stride, became stronger as time went on, and
provided the most telling contribution possible at the
end. Every time Petit runs on to the field he picks up a
handful of grass and throws it to the winds. The ritual is
Petit's way of paying homage to the memory of his
younger brother, Olivier, who died suddenly while playing football some years ago. As he went to collect his
winner's medal in the Stade de France, which he dedi-
cated to Olivier, he was embraced by David Dein. '*Quel
saison!* (What a season!)' Dein said.

In the hard and heartless commercial world that football has joined, the old game managed to give two gifts
of absolute purity: the experience of unity to a nation and
the opportunity to pay tribute to a brother's memory. In
both cases the business of winning was crucial to the
outcome, just as it is crucial to every football contest.

A defining moment in the biggest sporting occasion
the planet has ever witnessed came when France, breaking upfield after a period of Brazilian pressure which
culminated with Denilson hitting the bar, struck their
final, ecstatic goal. There was no more fitting scorer than
Emmanuel Petit. The last act of the most commercial
World Cup ever was provided through love, not money
and what it gave to a nation was not profit, but glory.
This is what football can do. It touches a depth of
commitment that can never be bought because, as every
football fan knows, it is a birthright that is not for sale at
any price.

CHAPTER SIXTEEN

Own Goals by the Score

A FEW DAYS after the French World Cup final triumph in Paris, a crucial meeting took place at the Royal Berkshire Hotel near Ascot. The surroundings could not have been more pleasant, nor could the conviviality of the participants. No one could have foreseen the dramatic fall from grace which would follow from this gathering's decisions.

Before England's qualification for France, Glenn Hoddle's agent, Dennis Roach, along with Alex Fynn, who helped Roach with some of Hoddle's commercial activities, had negotiated terms for the publication of the coach's 'World Cup diary'. With the tournament running into July, Hoddle and his 'ghost-writer', the FA's public relations supremo, David Davies, had their work cut out to meet the August publication deadline.

The meeting at the Royal Berkshire had been called to review the book's progress and agree the subject matter for the outstanding chapters. Present were Fynn, Davies, and representatives of the publisher, André Deutsch. Glenn Hoddle, arriving a few minutes later, was relaxed and friendly; Fynn, though, was worried by what he had seen of the book's contents. In his view the authors had

failed to deal satisfactorily with some of the most important issues arising from England's World Cup campaign.

Yet one of the first thoughts Hoddle offered was that
his main regret about his own performance in France 98
was the fact that he had not arranged for his spiritual
mentor, Eileen Drewery, to be present in the training
camp from the start of the tournament. Mrs Drewery had
been due to join Hoddle and his squad at the quarter-
final stage, which, of course, they never reached.

At last the coach had revealed something significant
that had perplexed many fans. There were any number of
dubious decisions that could be attributed to Hoddle: the
dropping of David Beckham and his subsequent treatment of the player; the preference for Teddy Sheringham
over Michael Owen; the lack of penalty-taking practice;
even Paul Gascoigne's exclusion (although this was later
vindicated by Gascoigne's poor 1998–99 displays). All
these and more could be construed as possible mistakes,
yet here was the coach implying that the absence of his
healer was all that had stood between him and winning
the World Cup.

At the time, Fynn, being obsessed with pure football
issues, failed to realize the wider impact the book would
have on those who read it. In fact Hoddle's diary would
not become just another undistinguished example of the
bland fare served up by footballers and managers. It was
set to light the blue touch-paper.

Meanwhile, Fynn and Hoddle blithely indulged in
some knockabout football banter, as if nothing else
mattered. Not only that, the two men were, in many
ways, talking at cross-purposes. Fynn was putting
forward some of the concerns expressed by media and
public about the coach's controversial decisions, which
he felt Hoddle should address. It was an exercise, according to Fynn, not in courting publicity for the book, but in

making the diary relevant to as wide a public as possible by dissecting the reasons behind the coach's tactics. To counter any reticence Hoddle might have in revealing some of his strategic thinking, Fynn told him: 'Hoddle the coach can afford to ignore the media, Hoddle the author can't.' For a worthwhile book, he argued, the coach had to explain himself.

Hoddle's response was two-pronged. On the one hand he appeared disappointed when he realized Fynn was not simply playing the role of devil's advocate. On the other he dismissed all alternative opinions as hardly worth refuting because they came from somebody who had never played the game professionally. All that remained, then, was the incredible assertion that the absence of Eileen Drewery had been the coach's only failure.

The huge public interest in England's World Cup campaign ensured that the tabloid press would be eagerly awaiting the publication of Glenn Hoddle's book. Perhaps, with hindsight, someone should have realized that selling serialization rights to the *Sun* was not such a smart move. It might have been worth a large amount of money – some £200,000 – but it pitched Hoddle right into the vicious circulation war that rages continuously between British newspapers. Moreover, since the *Sun*'s job was to seek out the most sensational angles possible, there was no doubt the paper would root out any remotely controversial elements and use them to maximum effect.

Thus the stage was set for the story of England's ill-starred French campaign and Hoddle's part in it to reach new heights of frenzied national debate. Given that David Davies had been so prompt in his concern for Glenn Hoddle's reputation at the Royal Berkshire meeting and that he is an old media hand, it could be argued

that he should have counselled against tabloid serialization, particularly since Graham Taylor had suffered
badly in the infamous 'Do I not like that' television docu-
mentary. In fact, the previous January, the publisher had
asked Hoddle and Davies if there were any newspapers
to which they objected. They replied that there were
papers they regarded as unacceptable but the *Sun* was
perfectly OK. However, to be fair, at that stage Davies
could have had no hint of the explosive nature of
Hoddle's views.

With events surrounding the serialization and publication of the book seemingly under control, there was little
thought given to any possible pitfalls. No one in the
higher echelons of the FA seemed to mind that they were
letting the England coach loose into the media bear pit.
This was probably because the world of football has
become one mad scramble for the maximum amount of
cash and the relentless pursuit of riches is now the
driving force of a game hooked on its new-found
celebrity status.

The *Sun* wasted no time in doing what it does best.
Hoddle's insistence that Eileen Drewery's travel arrangements constituted his single mistake during the World
Cup was emblazoned across the paper as soon as the
presses could roll. It seemed he had invested his team's
chances of success in the world's greatest sporting tournament in a middle-aged woman of whom no one
outside the arcane world of healing and spiritualism had
ever heard six months previously. The backlash was
venomous and it must have taken all of Hoddle's faith to
withstand the scorn heaped upon him.

The *Sun*, not about to rest on its laurels, immediately
followed up with the memorable 'Gazza Trashed My
Room' headline, as if it were a quote from Hoddle's
book, which it was not. The room in question was at the

England squad's hotel at La Manga in Spain where the coach informed Paul Gascoigne that he would be receiving a one-way ticket back to England. Hoddle was now perceived as insensitive for humiliating Gazza for a second time, having first dropped him so publicly from the squad for France and now betraying a player under his care by revealing intimate details of Gazza's behaviour under intense pressure.

The revelations in the *Sun*, which were repeated ad nauseam throughout the media, had a disconcerting effect on many England players. If the boss of the national team could tell the world confidential details through the pages of the *Sun*, how could any of them be sure that the next confidence to be broken wouldn't be their own? Suspicion and a lack of candour are the inevitable consequences of such behaviour. Commitment to the cause, without which a team becomes enfeebled, was being slowly replaced by a climate of mistrust.

Despite a damage limitation exercise by Hoddle and David Davies, the pair found it difficult to distance themselves from the *Sun*'s lurid presentation and merely succeeded in giving the various stories fresh legs in the rest of the media. By now, every word to emanate from the *Sun*'s serialization, or the full version contained in the book, was pored over for further news fodder.

A revealing epitaph to the tumult unleashed by Hoddle's diary came towards the end of the 1998–99 season, after his departure from the England scene. When David Beckham was sent off against Argentina, there was a knee-jerk reaction on the part of many to blame him for England's defeat. A ludicrous opinion gained currency, encouraged by certain sections of the media but crucially fuelled by Hoddle, that if Beckham had not aimed his kick at Diego Simeone, England would have won the game. There followed a concerted and reprehensible campaign by the mob element to intimidate Beckham, showering him with even more abuse than ever and threatening him and his family with all sorts of violence wherever he went the following season. There were many who publicly advised him to leave the country and play abroad. To his eternal credit, he stayed and toughed it out, in the process curbing some of his earlier petulant traits.

David Beckham spoke about what occurred in Saint-Étienne and paid a fulsome tribute to Tony Adams, who had sat with him in the dressing room after the game and talked him through his pain. Adams tried to bring a new perspective into Beckham's shattered world. Having realized through conquering his own problems that playing professional football was a means to an end and not the be-all and end-all of life itself, the Arsenal captain was moved to console the other players after Argentina's victory. His concern even extended beyond his playing colleagues to some new-found friends for whom he had arranged tickets for the match and who were distraught at the outcome. 'It's only a game,' he told them. Beckham expressed his appreciation for Adams's efforts, saying, 'I really needed that talk.' What, Beckham was asked, did Glenn Hoddle say to him at the time? 'Actually, he never spoke to me,' was the reply.

All of Hoddle's perceived sins might have been forgiven if the England team could have picked up the pieces in qualifying for the European Championships, due to be held in Belgium and Holland in the summer of 2000. Certainly, there was no question within the FA of Hoddle losing his job. On the contrary, the people who mattered – the members of the Executive and International Committees – were content enough with their man. According to one of their number, the prevailing view after the World Cup was that, 'Hoddle was well organized, the training methods seemed to be sensible, there was a good camaraderie amongst the team. They did play for him as well as themselves. They wanted to win. They were proud to put an England shirt on.' In other words, the FA's stance on the widespread disappointment with the World Cup campaign was that it was occasioned more by bad luck than bad judgement.

The omens for Euro 2000, however, were not auspicious. The truth was that since the 0–0 draw in Italy, Hoddle's England had been on a downward spiral. France 98 had merely continued a trend that had been evident for some months. It wasn't long before the on-field problems of the team reminded everyone that World Cup ghosts could not be exorcised simply by wishing them away. The opening games for Euro 2000 proved dismal in the extreme. A 2–1 defeat in Sweden was bad enough but the subsequent failure to beat Bulgaria at Wembley in a turgid 0–0 draw was unquestionably a major setback. A laborious win over Luxembourg in the third match hardly restored confidence and England were left trailing behind both Sweden and Poland in their qualifying group. The side's prospects of qualifying without having to go to a play-off were, to borrow a quote from the boxing promoter, Don King, 'somewhere between slim and none – and Slim has left town'. That heady night in Rome now seemed a long time ago, the joy and optimism that accompanied it a distant memory.

Astonishingly, in the midst of the disintegration of England's ambitions, Glenn Hoddle asked for, and received, a substantial pay rise. 'Until you find he cannot do the job anymore,' a spokesman said, 'he deserved the benefit of the doubt.' And a nice bonus, according to the FA. Moreover, the FA failed in the one area where they did attempt to deal with a controversial issue surrounding Hoddle. It wasn't the performance of the team, nor the furore caused by the diary. What concerned them most was the continued use of Eileen Drewery's services and they wanted Hoddle to lessen her involvement in the England set-up. Hoddle, however, flatly refused to countenance interference from any quarter in decisions over his support staff; the use of Mrs Drewery was non-negotiable. Hoddle told the International Committee – which evidently didn't see that the manager was in a somewhat weakened negotiating position – in no uncertain terms that 'if she goes, I go' and the FA didn't press the point. So Hoddle got everything he wanted while the FA got nothing. Not only had they made no inroads into his power, it had actually been consolidated.

Hoddle's loyalty to those who have served him well down the years is certainly commendable. However, the absolute power of coaches over the appointment of support staff that is a gospel truth in football is attacked as dangerous cronyism in any other business or in politics. In the case of Glenn Hoddle and Eileen Drewery, there also appears to exist a degree of mutual support that transcends almost all other considerations. Hoddle would have relinquished the job he loved rather than compromise his belief in Mrs Drewery's abilities and there was no stauncher champion for Hoddle than Eileen Drewery.

Another example of the special dispensation Hoddle granted his mentor came a couple of months before the World Cup began, when the *Sun* published a series of articles on Mrs Drewery. Hoddle's agent, Dennis Roach, who had brokered the arrangement with the newspaper, asked Alex Fynn if, as a personal favour to Roach, he would sit in on the reporter's interview with Mrs Drewery, as she was unused to dealing with the media. In the event, Fynn was hardly required, as Mrs Drewery and the reporter, Sue Evanson, struck up a cordial relationship, which culminated in a mutually satisfactory end product.

However, it was not all plain sailing. At one point the *Sun* requested an interview with Hoddle to examine his involvement with Mrs Drewery. Fynn's attempt to secure Hoddle's cooperation was rejected out of hand. He was told there was not enough time and anyway there were other priorities like an international the following week, against Portugal at Wembley. Never prepared to take no for an answer, the *Sun* tried another tack. They prevailed upon Eileen Drewery to intercede with Hoddle directly and the result was a glowing testimony from Hoddle that became the centrepiece of the series.

Since the World Cup, Hoddle had, for a while, managed the FA to his advantage. From there, his omnipotence should have enabled him to execute a turnaround in his and his team's fortunes. If he kept his head down and beat Poland in the next European Championship qualifier, the team's chances could yet be salvaged. But important though the debate about the state of the national team was, the attention of the FA's top men was directed elsewhere. After all, under-performance on the field and disaffection with the manager are perennial problems which the FA has had to contend with for decades.

In a sense, the apparent ineptitude at the heart of the FA's management of the professional game seems necessary to perpetuate the organization's continuing existence in its time-honoured form. Efficiency and success would cost jobs for the boys, or rather the granddads. Real and sustained improvements would appear to be incompatible with the ingrained procedures which guarantee the role of the FA's constituent parts – the committees, councils and various bureaucracy – as established by the organization's founding fathers.

Following Euro 96, the overriding priority for the FA

273

hierarchy was the bid for the 2006 World Cup. To the government and the fans it is a matter of national pride and English football's prestige. But behind the FA's rhetorical flourishes there is another agenda, revolving around the World Cup's massive commercial and financial potential – tens of millions of pounds. Beyond even these considerations, hosting the finals of the World Cup would give a massive boost to the repositioning of England as a leading light in the global future of football.

The importance of the 2006 bid to the FA can be seen in the aggressive and efficient way it has pursued its objective. Already the FA had angered the Germans by reputedly reneging on its promise to support Germany's own claims to 2006. Then there was the last minute switch of votes at the FIFA presidential election. In addition, it has sent out the 'Two Knights' – Sir Bobby Charlton and Sir Geoff Hurst – to criss-cross the planet continually lobbying for votes; other countries' bids have been challenged at every turn; politicians, business leaders and decision-makers have been assiduously courted, not just at home but across the world. No one has been too insignificant to visit, cajole and convince. In all these activities the FA has spared no expense. Even Prince Charles, not one of football's natural allies, was co-opted to host a formal dinner for FIFA delegates and assorted dignitaries at his home at Highgrove on the eve of the FA Cup Final. The project has also been politicized at home, becoming a totemic New Labour event, which could vie with the Millennium Experience at the Greenwich Dome in terms of public interest.

An example of what is at stake can be seen in the new national stadium at Wembley, the construction of which has long been central to the FA's plans. Having devoted enormous efforts during recent years to resolve the wrangling over the future of Wembley in its favour, the

FA finally clinched an ownership deal in early 1999. With support from the government, which chose Wembley as its preferred site for a national stadium, the FA gained control of over £100 million of lottery funding and another £100 million of City finance. The remainder of the huge Wembley complex, located on a site so close to the heart of a major capital city, is unique. It could, with the new stadium at its centre, become one of the most valuable pieces of leisure development land in Europe.

In an extraordinary attempt at a belt and braces approach, FA Chairman Keith Wiseman and Chief Executive Graham Kelly hatched what can only be described as one of Baldrick's 'cunning plans'. Without the sanction of the Executive Committee, they decided to make a financial contribution, variously described as a loan or a gift, to the coffers of the Welsh FA, purportedly to help fund grassroots development in the principality. Wiseman and Kelly did this because they believed it would secure support from the Welsh in a bid to get Wiseman elected a vice-president of FIFA. This would, according to Kelly, who was guided by FIFA insiders, assist the 2006 World Cup bid.

The British associations of England, Scotland, Wales and Northern Ireland possess an historic right to have one of their number in a vice-presidential role, a position currently held by a Scot, David Will. In what became known as the 'cash for votes scandal', the two men from the FA thought they could organize a putsch against Will and install Wiseman in his place.

However, Wiseman and Kelly's arithmetic was strangely awry for professional men. The Scots obviously did not take kindly to the English FA's attempt to oust their man and the Northern Irish, who were not on board, voted for Will. With the vote deadlocked at 2–2, Wiseman's bid failed and Will remained vice-president.

What is even more astonishing than the actual attempt is that the plan – even if it had worked – would not have substantially helped England's bid for 2006, because Wiseman would not have been permitted to vote on a bid from his own country. Moreover, David Will was himself in favour of England becoming the 2006 venue.

When the FA's Executive Committee found out about the goings-on they were outraged. In all the reports of the row that subsequently appeared, the amount the Welsh stood to receive was quoted as being around £3 million. If accurate that would have been bad enough. In fact, the actual amount Wiseman and Kelly had agreed to hand over to the Welsh was, incredibly, more than twice as much as that. When an FA councillor spoke about it some months later he still resented what had occurred, saying, 'The total committed would have cost us £7.5 million to the Welsh FA to get one vote which would not have been a deciding factor. It was done against the Executive Committee's wishes. It was immoral and it was wrong. What about Scotland or Ireland or anybody else? What about our own youth development policy?'

Wiseman and Kelly were severely censured. Faced with such a hostile condemnation, their positions became untenable. While Kelly went quietly, Wiseman refused to resign. He could not bring himself to accept that his Macbeth-like 'vaulting ambition' had run its course. The signs which should have moderated his objectives were instead treated as obstacles to be surmounted. He had been rejected in a bid to become the Premier League's candidate for the post of FA Chairman, so he got himself nominated through a county FA and became Chairman via the back door. Once installed at Lancaster Gate he turned his attention to larger power centres, first trying and failing to get himself elected to the UEFA Executive Committee. Now he had bungled the attempt to become a FIFA vice-president. Even so, Wiseman hung on in the forlorn hope that he could somehow convince the FA Council to support him.

Thus the affair dragged on into the new year, when the Council ratified the censure decision and Wiseman was forced to pack his bags. In an astonishing turnaround, unprecedented in the history of the English game, the two top men at the Football Association were out. After discussions with the Welsh, the figure paid by the English was negotiated down to £700,000, a vast reduction from the previous agreement but still an exorbitant 'gift' for no discernible gain.

The man chosen to step into the breach was greeted with great surprise and not a little suspicion. It was none other than David Davies. A member of the supporting cast had now been handed the part of the leading man. With the title of 'Acting Chief Executive', Davies, the former regional BBC reporter and Hoddle's co-author, was now in Graham Kelly's seat at the head of the English game. Meanwhile, the long-serving FA Vice-Chairman, Geoff Thompson, was asked temporarily to take over Wiseman's role of Chairman. When it was enquired of them if the scandal would adversely affect England's chances of winning the 2006 World Cup bid, the Two Knights spoke as one: of course it wouldn't, was their line, as if what happened at the FA had nothing to do with the World Cup.

Despite his elevation, David Davies still had to deal with his original responsibilities in media relations. In an attempt to recover lost ground, he and Glenn Hoddle decided to make themselves more accessible than hitherto. It was a decision that would backfire in the most spectacular fashion.

In truth, Hoddle's support among the media had been badly dented long before France 98. He had appeared from the beginning of his England tenure to have little intention of and even less interest in meeting the press halfway. After England lost badly to Chile at Wembley in the run-up to the World Cup, the reporters became increasingly impatient waiting for Hoddle to turn up at the post-match press conference. He arrived over an hour after the final whistle, accompanied by David Davies. After a couple of perfunctory questions and answers, the room began to empty. Displaying mild irritation and surprise, Hoddle said, 'Got a train to catch?' 'No,' answered one of the departing hacks, 'an edition to make.' The coach's haughty attitude had made him a hostage to fortune. The knives were poised, ready and waiting.

According to Eileen Drewery, who became Hoddle's chief defender in the weeks and months after the infamous encounter with *The Times*, Hoddle had conducted a routine football interview. After it was over, in small-talk which Drewery insisted was off the record, the reporter, Matt Dickinson, asked about the coach's religious beliefs, particularly the concepts of karma and reincarnation. Drewery said that people like Hoddle and herself would never force their beliefs on anyone but if asked about them could not refrain from going into an exposition about what they perceive as the fundamental truths about life, God, the universe and so forth. If they receive such an enquiry, she explained, it is their duty to try to answer it.

In fairness, Hoddle addressed Dickinson's interest as well as he could, but when it came to his views on how disabled people fitted into his karmic philosophy, he commented in such a way as to cause offence by implying they were paying a karmic price in the here and now for sins committed in a previous life. Whether or not Mrs Drewery is correct in that Hoddle's comments were not part of the interview and off the record hardly mattered. The fact was that his words were right there on the printed page and were therefore taken as an accurate description of his beliefs on the subject. 'You and I have been given two hands and two legs and half-decent brains,' Hoddle was reported to have said. 'Some people have not been born like that for a reason. The karma is working from another lifetime.'

Hoddle's response to the subsequent furore was to claim he had been 'misunderstood', then 'misconstrued' or 'misinterpreted'. The absence of a tape of the interview caused some doubt and Hoddle threatened legal action until *The Times'* editor, Peter Stothard, made the point that Dickinson took good old-fashioned shorthand notes which he had seen. It was also recalled that Hoddle had publicly expressed the same sentiments some months earlier. Before the World Cup, when speaking to BBC Radio 5 Live's Brian Alexander, Hoddle had enthusiastically discussed his faith, including the concepts of karma and reincarnation. At the time, the interview caused no more than a blip and Keith Wiseman's response to it summed up its relevance. 'I don't care if he consults Merlin the wizard,' he said, 'as long as he gets results.'

To those westerners who take up eastern religious ideas, the views expressed by Hoddle are by no means uncommon. But perhaps because they have not experienced the cultural milieu from which such beliefs originated, their understanding may be underdeveloped. Given the complexity of these issues it is hardly surprising that Hoddle, a sincere man, was perhaps simply not sufficiently articulate fully to explain his creed.

Hoddle was then caught in a classic media pincer movement. Radio programmes, television shows, web sites and newspaper articles rapidly confronted him head-on. Then from the flanks came politicians, religious commentators, assorted academics and charitable organizations. Each of these was armed with their own moral firepower. And when the attacks were in need of fresh impetus, the public could be relied upon to inundate phone-ins and polls, thus fuelling what quickly became, for the Hoddle camp, a relentless firefighting exercise.

With few exceptions, the demands for Hoddle's head grew stronger and more strident. He was criticized by Sports Minister Tony Banks. If that wasn't enough, Prime Minister Tony Blair fired his own televised salvo from the vantage point of Richard and Judy's sofa, saying that if the coach's words had been accurately reported, it would be difficult for him to remain in charge of the England team. Even the *Sun*, having gained much from Hoddle's contribution to its pages and having been happy to promote the beliefs of Eileen Drewery – which as explained by Hoddle to the *Sun*'s stablemate *The Times*, were now causing such a commotion – lent its support to the campaign to oust the England coach.

Amazingly, given the ferocity of feeling against Hoddle in the country at large, the members of the International Committee were prepared to back their coach and keep him in situ. Hoddle himself, after taking advice from friends, including Graham Kelly, apologized for his remarks and agreed to keep his beliefs private in future. But the International Committee wanted one more concession: Eileen Drewery had to go. Hoddle, unsurprisingly, refused to accept the one condition that would have saved his job. Even at this stage there was genuine regret in the committee. One of its number said: 'He lost some of the players (but) he didn't really get dismissed for playing reasons, that's the saddest part.'

For her part, Eileen Drewery, with some justification, blamed Hoddle's downfall on a 'witch-hunt' by the media and told a meeting in Kensington Town Hall, called to promote her autobiography, that sports journalists in particular were responsible and had 'offended God' in their treatment of Hoddle. She knew this, she said, because she had 'spoken with God a couple of weeks ago' and He had told her. He had also told her in the same conversation that He would 'put everything right', though when that would be and how He had not made clear.

The notion that in a western liberal democracy on the eve of the twenty-first century someone could lose a high-profile but non-political job for the medieval crime of expressing a minority religious belief was disturbing. We shall now never know whether Glenn Hoddle would have overcome his difficulties and fulfilled his undoubted potential. His increasingly autocratic behaviour; some poor results in important matches; the overriding importance placed on the role of the spirit: any or all of these depleted the reservoir of support Hoddle needed when the chips were down. And in the modern world, Hoddle's downfall is a classic example of the necessity for international coaches to come to terms with the demands of the media. Anything less and the media, now among the most important elements driving football forward, will await their chance. They may get mad, but they'll make sure you don't get even.

Almost as soon as the Hoddle affair became yesterday's news, the already absurdly high job-mortality rate of those at the top of the English game increased yet again. This time it was the Premier League, whose guiding lights could just not bring themselves to sit back and let the FA hog all the headlines. Anyone could be forgiven for thinking a behind-the-scenes revolution was taking place.

So it was the turn of the Premier League Chairman, Sir

John Quinton and the Chief Executive, Peter Leaver, to overstep the mark. Once again, money played a central role. An extremely lucrative consultancy contract, awarded to former Sky bosses Sam Chisholm and David Chance, against the wishes of the club chairmen, forced their departure. Another day, another dollar, or rather millions of dollars. Easy come, easy go. But while the authorities played musical chairs, a predator lay in wait.

CHAPTER SEVENTEEN

Money Can't Buy You Love

As THE COUNTRY was savouring the World Cup, those charged with overseeing Manchester United's fortunes faced a defining moment in the history of the club. Commercially, United was going from strength to strength, a success story reflected in the seemingly inexorable upward trend of its share price. However, in stock market terms, Manchester United plc remained a minnow, ripe for attack from stock market sharks. And the cost of competing with the world's best on the field was rising even faster than the share price. The end of the 1997/98 season had seen the unthinkable – no trophies in the cabinet. The one saving grace was that coming second in the Premiership now meant automatic entry into the Champions' League.

When Rupert Murdoch's BSkyB decided to make its move to buy Manchester United in the summer of 1998 the mainstream media were caught on the hop. It was diligent United observers such as the fanzine *Red Issue*, and the business newsletter *TV Sports Markets*, which anticipated the manoeuvre. Televised football is about to undergo a sea-change to compare with Sky's revolution in coverage of the early 1990s: this time through the availability of digital services which will facilitate a much wider choice, including pay-per-view and, eventually, interactivity. The problem for Sky is that for all its risk-taking, investment and pioneering efforts over the past few years, the future regulatory and commercial environment is difficult to predict. Sky could find itself losing the Premiership, arguably its most lucrative contract, either when it runs out in 2001 or through decisions taken in the British courts or by the European Union.

The Office of Fair Trading (OFT) was fighting a case in the Restrictive Practices Court, arguing that the exclusive television deals between the Premier League, Sky and the BBC were against the public interest. This was because negotiations conducted centrally restricted the availability of televised games and may have forced up the price to consumers. Meanwhile, the Competition Commissioner in Brussels had been expressing similar concerns over a number of countries' domestic deals and the contracts covering the Champions' League.

In addition to these pressures, key parts of Sky's arrangements with Hollywood film companies, which assure programming for its numerous movie channels, are due to end in 2002. Thus the purchase of Manchester United represented, in Murdoch's words, an 'insurance policy'. If the OFT lost its case Sky would be first among equals, with an important say in future television deals, even if the Premier League adopted a different strategy after 2001. If the OFT won, Sky would control the worldwide television rights of the wealthiest sports club in the world bar none.

Sky's initial public offer to the Manchester United board valued the club at £575 million. That figure was pushed up by United director Greg Dyke, the man who had masterminded ITV's exclusive deal with league

football back in 1988. Dyke, who was opposed to s͟ᵤ
at all, argued that if the board was going to recommeɪ
Sky's bid to shareholders, the club was worth more. The
final figure, some £623 million, which was accepted by
the directors, was much higher than would normally be
contemplated for a company making profits of just £25
million a year. But it would seem small beer in a pay-per-
view future when United's global television income
could be more than £100 million per year.

Although Sky executives must have known many fans
would object to the move, they did not envisage government action to refer their bid to the Monopolies and
Mergers Commission (MMC). In the first place, Murdoch
had important support within the administration. The
Trade and Industry Secretary, Peter Mandelson, whose
remit covered competition matters, was one of the architects of the New Labour–Rupert Murdoch rapprochement
in the run-up to the 1997 general election. Secondly, since
there were nineteen other clubs in the Premier League that
Sky was not seeking to buy, there was no question of the
deal creating a monopoly. Thirdly, the principle of media
companies owning football clubs had long been established elsewhere in Europe, so would surely not be ruled
out in the UK.

Bob Offen, a Manchester United supporter and Chief
Executive of the media buying company, Mediapolis,
summed up Sky's business rationale, saying, 'Whatever
Murdoch does is always misinterpreted, largely because
people assume that he's a megalomaniac. He isn't. The
truth is that he's a businessman, the best businessman in
media by a mile. He does things for solid business
reasons. I think this is a classic case of vertical integration. It is about winning entertainment content for his
television stations and in that respect it is no different to
owning rights to *The Simpsons*.'

e, was precisely why a large number of opposed the deal. Vertical integration uisition by a firm of another stage in the tribution of a commodity in which it is involved. Sky wanted Manchester United for programming, period. The only difference between United games, first-run movies and *The Simpsons* was income-related. United would probably sell more subscriptions than the others and exclusive rights to the club's matches would sustain Sky's digital development, which is crucial to its long-term future.

The pragmatic business reasoning which underpinned Sky's approach to the United board was exactly the opposite of what the company's lawyers, along with the Premier League, were arguing before the Restrictive Practices Court, where their stance was that football is a special case, different from other industries. Ironically, that very proposition would eventually scupper the deal.

When news of Sky's offer broke, there was predictable consternation. Much as Sky had the element of surprise, there was little in the way of positive messages to win over fans. The main thrust of the anti-Sky argument was that its parent company, News Corporation, is a multi-national, multimedia conglomerate; a free-market money machine with little concern for tradition or the sentimental and emotional attachments which characterize the way football supporters feel about their clubs. While News Corp was officially one shareholder among many of Sky, its 40 per cent stake gave it effective managerial control. There was a belief that United would be run to further News Corp's global ambitions rather than to enhance the club and the team. As an example, it was suggested that the timing of certain fixtures could be arranged for television viewers in the Far East. There might even be the introduction of an Asian player or two to stimulate regional interest. However far-fetched that might seem, there was a precedent.

In 1998 Murdoch bought the US baseball team, the Los Angeles Dodgers. One of the Dodgers' heroes, Mike Piazza, was summarily traded to another team, the Florida Marlins, reportedly to the complete surprise of the coaching staff. The Marlins were owned by the former Blockbuster Video magnate, Wayne Huizenga, and maybe this was a case of media considerations taking priority over playing matters. Obviously, Sky would never countenance relegation for Manchester United, but, given the Piazza example, what would happen to ready-made assets like Ryan Giggs and David Beckham in a time of need? And Sky has been through such a period as recently as the early 1990s.

Under the umbrella of two organizations, the Independent Manchester United Supporters Association (IMUSA) and Shareholders Against Murdoch (SAM), a large number of fans mounted what proved to be an extremely effective campaign to thwart the takeover. Early on, SAM weighed in with a claim that the Sky offer document circulated to shareholders was misleading, since nowhere did it state that rejection of the bid was an option. Later, SAM, in the person of journalist Michael Crick, successfully challenged the United plc Chairman, Sir Roland Smith, on this point at the annual general meeting. Crick was set to take the battle to the takeover panel, a statutory body set up to ensure that such dealings are conducted according to law, when, contrary to expectations, Peter Mandelson referred the bid to the Monopolies and Mergers Commission.

As opposition to the deal had reached a crescendo, the Culture Secretary, Chris Smith, whose department includes sport, had intervened. With the support of cabinet colleagues, who realized that Manchester United was not just another football club but a central element in the lives of a large number of voters, he had persuaded Mandelson that referral to the MMC would remove the issue from politics and avoid a potentially hazardous situation for the government. But the unthinkable had really happened because those United fans opposed to the bid were spread across the country and many were able to argue their views articulately and in a media-friendly way, which they had done at every opportunity.

SAM and IMUSA tenaciously fought their case before the MMC with submissions from a battery of authoritative advocates, including academics, lawyers and economists. They also gained public support from such diverse and influential bodies as the Independent Television Authority and the Football Association. It soon became clear that the relatively simple matter of a football club's ownership was becoming enmeshed in wider arguments concerning the future of the game and its relationship with television. The main issue for the MMC to resolve was whether Manchester United could sway television decisions by the Premier League, particularly if the dominant position of Sky in pay television continues in the new landscape of multi-channel, digital pay-per-view networks.

As Michael Crick explained, this was not a simple 'either-or' matter. For instance, United under Murdoch could leave the Premier League. 'As a company with a turnover of £90 million United would be a very small player within the much wider BSkyB empire, which is hugely dependent on the (football) television contract,' he said. 'And with a beefed-up Champions' League and a possible FIFA world club tournament, one could conceive of circumstances under which United could break away. That gives BSkyB an advantage in negotiations for the (next) television contract.'

Furthermore, whatever the result of the (
are likely to be more television rights availa
current contract with Sky and the BBC e
United owned by Sky and running its own c
would possess huge leverage over other broa̲ ̲sters. It
would then become easy for the company to sign up other
major clubs and control a huge swathe of fixtures. This
has already happened in Italy, where a Canal Plus
subsidiary, Telepiù, initially bought the rights to the home
games of four of the country's biggest clubs – Juventus,
Internazionale, AC Milan and Napoli. These clubs
dominate the pay-per-view market and were offered
guarantees of £20–£30 million each per season. When
Telepiù added five more clubs to its roster, the Italian
government felt compelled to intervene and set a 60 per
cent limit on the number of Serie A games any single pay
TV operator could buy.

To many fans, Sky's top personnel were media men,
not football men. Such an accusation could never be
levelled against the boss of Canal Plus, Pierre Lescure, or
that of Mediaset, Silvio Berlusconi, who own Paris St
Germain and AC Milan respectively. Vic Wakeling's
claim, as head of Sky Sport, that 'we have shown we
understand football' may be true as far as his responsibilities are concerned but at the very top level of the
company it has a hollow ring. Upon winning the first
Premier League contract in 1992 the Australian Chief
Executive, Sam Chisholm, was reported as saying, 'We
must get rid of these 0–0 draws.' His successor, Mark
Booth, who was in charge of the takeover bid for United,
scored an early own goal when he was unable to name
the team's left back, Denis Irwin.

Throughout the proceedings Martin Edwards was
lambasted for supporting Sky's bid. For all the opposition he has engendered over the years, however, no one

ıld ever accuse him of not being a solid United man. As Michael Crick, one of Edwards's most vocal critics (in 1989 Crick co-authored a stinging attack on the Edwards family in the book *Betrayal of a Legend*), said: 'Martin Edwards stands to make £100 million out of Manchester United. Having said that I'd much prefer (him) to carry on running the club than Sky to have it. At least Martin Edwards is a United supporter and he lives in the Manchester area. Therefore he lives under that constraint and he has to walk down the street. He is conscious of what the ordinary fan feels whereas Sky isn't . . . They know nothing of United history and some of them don't even know about football.' The outspoken American television entrepreneur, Ted Turner, who founded CNN and has had a long-standing feud with Rupert Murdoch, put it more vividly, saying, 'Ownership should be restricted to locals – even if they are bums. It's better to have a local bum, then at least you can do something to him if he steps out of line, like spit on him or punch him in the nose.'

For once, Sky's strategy and tactics were off the mark. In the past News Corp had benefited from the decisions of regulators, most notably by not being required to divest itself of any major holdings when cross-ownership of media was a hot political issue. In most cases any opposition had been propounded by the 'chattering classes' and was easily overcome. Perhaps the company underestimated the resolution of their opposition in the Manchester United case. It was true that not all fans opposed the bid and although early calls for protests at Old Trafford failed to materialize, Sky were up against a broad range of opponents among the vast United support.

In the end, the MMC rejected Sky's surprising submission that football was not 'must-have' programming for

most fans. Conversely, Sky's advocates'
countenance a series of possible scenarios
put to them, which could follow a ruling in
gave the impression that the company was
to relinquish its exclusive rights under any circumstances. Assurances that Sky would not abuse its
privileged position if it owned United were deemed
unacceptable. The MMC clearly felt that football was
indeed a special case and did not buy Sky's arguments.

The MMC, renamed the Competition Commission,
gave its findings to the government in April 1999. Peter
Mandelson had by now departed from his ministry and
the new Trade and Industry Secretary, Steven Byers,
released the decision to an astonished United board, Sky
and the City. The bid, said the commission, should be
rejected because it would give Sky too much influence in
the Premier League television negotiations and could
lead to 'decisions which do not reflect the long-term
interests of football'. In addition, it would accelerate the
widening of the gap between rich and poor clubs and
'damage the quality of British football'. In this case the
public interest was felt to be more important than the
interests of business and the media. This thinking might
well eventually be extended to the appointment of a
statutory football regulator, as it is known that the
government is concerned that the football authorities
have not done enough to combat contentious developments like rising ticket and merchandising prices,
especially in the Premier League. Nor had they tackled
the potential danger of a cadre of rich clubs creating a
new cartel, particularly if individual clubs gain control of
their television rights.

Martin Edwards was surprised and mortified. 'I don't
think there's any doubt about it,' he commented. 'Had
BSkyB bought Manchester United they would have

de more money available than we could do under our own strength . . . more money would have been available from Sky to strengthen the team and that would have given us a greater chance of success in Europe.' Edward Freedman, former managing director of United's merchandising operation, agreed when he commented: 'United could have been stronger if they had been taken over by Sky. Talk of asset-stripping was nonsense. They are a major player and would have been able to exploit United's success. I don't think you ever say anyone has enough money. This game is getting bigger and bigger and the more money people have the more they can buy the best players or have the best facilities. If it was necessary they would have made investments in the club. It would have been good for United.'

The fans, though, were more interested in whether, having lost the battle, Edwards would resign. There was, he said, '. . . no chance of that at all. All we were doing was our duty on behalf of our shareholders. If we don't do that then we shouldn't be here at all.'

Those fans who now rejoiced were dismissed by journalist Mick Dennis, writing in the London *Evening Standard*, as 'dunderheads' and 'buffoons', who suffered from 'deranged logic' and 'lunatic reasoning' which 'disqualifies them from rational debate'. Offering an insider's view, Dennis put forward the point that '. . . those of us who have worked for Murdoch know that his organizations are characterized by a ruthless determination to succeed. Murdoch United would have been expected to rule Europe.'

Dennis obviously thought that United fans should have been concerned only with their club becoming ever more successful. But, as Michael Crick realized, such a development could actually be counterproductive. 'There isn't a great deal of fun in winning the league if all

the other teams are tiny,' he stated. If United '. . . ı
many millions now, at least those millions are associatᴇ
with United itself. But here you have the prospect of
many, many more millions being pumped in by an
outsider from other activities. Therefore there would be
much less of a sense of fairness. It's only worth following
football if there are forces towards equality.' And
anyway, Crick added, '. . . it is already difficult to be a
United supporter. One is regarded as a supporter of the
biggest team with the most money. To be owned by a
huge, billion-pound conglomerate would make United
even more unpopular.'

Andy Walsh, the chairman of IMUSA, was ecstatic,
saying, 'It's a tremendous victory, not just for supporters
of Manchester United but for all football fans. It's a
fantastic end to seven months' hard work and great for
anyone, anywhere, fighting for the independence of their
club.' The *Guardian* was succinct in its verdict: 'Murdoch
0, Football 1' ran the headline over its editorial.

Predictably, News Corp papers slammed the decision
on behalf of their sister company. Vic Wakeling put a
brave face on it but failed to convince. 'This is not a blow
to Sky,' he claimed, 'it is a blow, I believe, to football
because football clubs in this country are facing increasing competition from clubs in Europe, who are allowed
partnerships of this type and who will continue to
develop them.'

For many, Sky's disappointment exposed the
company's conflict of interest. If an even richer and more
dominant Manchester United were to become like
Rangers in Scotland, how could Sky continue to claim
that the Premiership was the best league in the world?
And complete dominance at home had so far failed to
translate itself into commanding European performances, just as it has at Ibrox. Tommy Docherty called

m of 1998/99, which swept to another
th a squad full of expensive imports 'the
er seen'.

nay have been another agenda. In order
egotiating power with prospective allies
and to ensure the continuation of top-quality sports programming, Sky has embarked on a number of expansionist projects in recent times. The company acquired Champions' League rights in Germany, joined an Italian consortium which holds some Serie A pay-per-view rights to challenge the Canal Plus-owned Telepiù, and will no doubt bid for a piece of the 2002 World Cup. In what might, at first sight, appear a contradictory move but one which says much about the shifting alliances within worldwide television, Sky has also been talking about merging with Canal Plus and the German media giant, Kirsch. These talks, if they reach fruition, could prioritize European football and reduce the Premier League to the status now held by the Football League in Sky's portfolio. In that case the European Super League idea is bound to rear its head once more. And of course, Murdoch could strengthen his hand by buying a European club.

Successful acquisitions notwithstanding, Sky is also concerned by a series of global mega-deals involving the US telecommunications giant AT&T and Microsoft, the world's largest software company, which have consolidated the advance of cable television and computer delivery systems. These deals could see cable and computer providing more efficient and cost-effective transmission services than satellite. Hence the need for Murdoch to hold on to and increase his trump cards, which include exclusive programmes like major sports events. It is these areas which will give viability to the development of his pay services. In such a competitive environment the loss of United could prove to be a body-blow.

On an infinitely more prosaic level, in the wake of Sky's rejection, Martin Edwards warned that finance might not be available for large-scale purchases of players at the end of the 1998/99 season. He cited expenditure already committed – £30 million to extend the capacity of Old Trafford to 67,000, a 25 per cent stake in a new, 111-bedroom hotel adjacent to the stadium, and a new training ground at Carrington costing £14 million – as the main reason. Not only that, to offset a possible fall in profits (a drop in merchandising income had compounded the heavy capital investment costs) there would be a hike in ticket prices probably amounting to 14 per cent across the board for the 1999–2000 season. The £28.2 million spent on acquiring Jaap Stam, Jesper Blomqvist and Dwight Yorke appeared an aberration in an otherwise conservative transfer policy. Yet the dividends from the outlay were there for all to see as United were poised to achieve a unique treble – Premiership, FA Cup and European Cup – as the 1998–99 season drew to a close. The United directors didn't need Sky, they needed the courage to match the fans' convictions.

Manchester United is the world's biggest sports brand almost in spite of what the board does. The thrust of its policy is sales exploitation, which is about to reach another level through the creation of Manchester United International to franchise retail and leisure operations in overseas markets. While this is perfectly acceptable in its own right, its success depends on performances on the field, particularly in the Premier League, which, through worldwide television, has showcased United's talents. But however high United's current status is, it is made up of much more than today's successful club. It is an institution, a football icon. In commercial terms it is the number-one brand, built up over the years by triumph and tragedy: Busby and the Babes; Munich; Best, Law and Charlton; 1968; and the Ferguson renaissance. To the consumer it is comparable to Nike and Adidas, but their turnover is measured in billions, not millions.

While these sportswear giants exploit football, United *are* football. Adidas sponsor David Beckham but United owns him. Instead of hiring out its stars to promote other companies' products and services, United should use the players to promote its own brand. Edward Freedman recalled the problems he had with the directors over this issue, saying: 'I wanted players to be involved with Manchester United rather than being individuals on their own and doing their own merchandising operations.' When David Beckham wanted to make a video Freedman again had to argue the point: 'I felt it should have been done through the club's licence holder, VCI, though a United director wanted it to be done through his contacts. They (the board) may understand what is involved but they weren't prepared to tackle the issue. Why aren't boot deals done by the club as they are in France? A player can't play in his own shirt and shorts so why shouldn't he promote the boots that are beneficial to his club?'

However, marketing must be accompanied by service, a bizarre notion to most football clubs. United's directors must ask themselves: What can we do that the fans want while remaining true to our glorious heritage so there will be customer goodwill if bad times ever arrive? A willingness to communicate, if necessary through advertising and public relations, is what United should do to reflect the club's pre-eminent position as *the* football brand. It is not Sky's millions that are needed but a more wide-ranging strategy. An enlightened youth policy, a gifted and experienced manager, a sprinkling of stars and even a chairman who believes in delegation rather than egomania, would soon bring United to the pinnacle of success. Occasionally, the richest club in the richest league should speculate to accumulate.

For most United fans, the Sky saga was an unwelcome diversion from the main event, which, of course, continued to take place on the pitch. Having ended the 1997–98 season on a low point, eliminated from the Champions' League at the quarter-final stage while watching Arsenal claim the double, the following season, and especially the Champions' League, offered a challenge which manager and players now felt equal to and would surely relish.

CHAPTER EIGHTEEN

Being There

THE PRESIDENT OF UEFA, Lennart Johansson, could hardly have wished for a better finale to the 1998–99 Champions' League: Manchester United against Bayern Munich at Barcelona's majestic Nou Camp stadium. After all the upheavals, it was a wonderful appetiser for the revamped competition of 1999–2000. It seemed the biggest really were the best; how right UEFA had been to create even more big-event fixtures for the future. It was a pity the game itself hadn't lived up to its star billing but even with seedings and group stages, football being football, a great final can never be guaranteed.

With the final whistle imminent, the trophy, replete with Munich ribbons, was taken pitch-side in readiness for the presentation ceremony. Mumbling condolences to the British contingent, which included Sports Minister Tony Banks, Johansson left the VIP box and took the lift inside the stadium. When he reached ground level he was told, 'I'm sorry, Mr President, they've equalized, you'll have to go back up.' Upon his return to the VIP box for extra-time there was another message. 'I'm sorry, Mr President, they've scored again, you must go back down right away.' It was the following day before he saw the United goals. What an improbable climax to a competition which only a few months previously appeared perilously close to its sell-by date.

While Manchester United fans were fending off the unwelcome advances of Rupert Murdoch, yet another seismic shock rocked the football world. Media Partners, a Milan-based sports marketing company, had for some time been conducting secret negotiations with Europe's biggest clubs. According to Media Partners, the clubs were being held back both by their smaller brethren taking an unwarranted share of income and because of foot-dragging by UEFA in reforming its three European club competitions. What was being suggested was that the moment had arrived for revolution: nothing less than a fully-fledged European Super League, to be played mid-week, outside the auspices of governing bodies, with entry by invitation only. Media Partners were also prepared to bestow a permanent place in the Super League on the first batch of invitees. To those in this favoured group, which inevitably comprised the biggest clubs with their massive wage bills and transfer costs, it was manna from heaven.

England's representatives were to be Manchester United, Arsenal and Liverpool, who would regularly play against the giants of Europe for a likely guarantee of £20 million per club in the opening season. It was certainly a tempting amount of money – twice the amount the winners of the 1999 Champions' League would make – but it hardly seemed enough to compensate for the downside. Although the Super League was presented as an add-on to national leagues, it soon became clear that it would replace UEFA's own competitions and might entail the participants being expelled from their domestic tournaments. And there was never any question that UEFA would simply step aside in the face of this massive assault on its authority.

In addition to the predictable cries of fo[...]
opposition to the plan came from FIFA. Aft[...]
Europe today, tomorrow could bring a [...]
National associations didn't think too [...]
proposal either, since it would mean the ena of their
competitions as the only providers of entrants to Europe.
What all of these bodies had in common was that they
held a monopoly in their own spheres of interest and no
encroachment on their freedom to create and control
football's competitions would be tolerated.

English fans were for once entirely at one with the
Premier League, the FA and UEFA in their stand against
the proposed league. For supporters and administrators
alike, discarding merit as the means of European qualification and moving to membership in perpetuity, along
with entry through 'wild cards', was anathema – it just
did not reflect the spirit of the game. It was fans, too, who
made the point that the attraction of a big Euro-game –
Manchester United v. Juventus, say – stemmed from its
scarcity value. They could live with expansion in
European competitions but not at the expense of domestic rivalries. The Premier League, of course, had the most
to lose. Having spent the best part of a decade establishing its pre-eminence, it now faced the possibility of
becoming a second-rate competition in which the 'big
three' could either field sub-standard teams or leave by
choice or expulsion.

For UEFA, it was not only the spectre of the Super
League that threatened its hegemony. It faced a two-
pronged attack, with the European Union making noises
about investigating the monopoly implications of
UEFA's centralized control of television rights for the
Champions' League. To help head off any interference
from Brussels, UEFA produced a glossy publication entitled 'A Solidarity System For European Football'. The

ocument strove to show that the commercial activity engendered by the Champions' League provided UEFA with the wherewithal to 'help develop football from the grassroots upwards'. To ensure this, the Champions' League '. . . is founded on a clear principle of financial solidarity'. After favourably comparing its control of finances to the salary caps and draft picks of US sports, it explained that UEFA's own objective is '. . . to ensure financial (and therefore sporting) balance is maintained . . . between leading clubs from large and small European countries'. UEFA presented the Champions' League as having '. . . given a new dimension to European football both in terms of the provision of first-class sporting entertainment and in terms of the financial support it provides for the entire European football community'.

However, the rhetoric did not entirely accord with the facts. For instance, in 1996–97, 12 per cent of Champions' League income was spent on 'UEFA General Expenses', while only 9 per cent went to 'Provisions (e.g. youth and training pool)'. Meanwhile, 20 per cent went on 'other payments to participating clubs, national associations and organizers'. This figure includes a huge amount of money that goes to TEAM, the agency which markets the Champions' League. Moreover, the big clubs were not too enamoured of UEFA's accountancy. They saw that the sixteen Champions' League participants provided 82 per cent of UEFA's total income but those same clubs received only 49 per cent of the financial cake. It was figures like these which made the ground so fertile for Media Partners.

The big clubs had the best of both worlds, as Media Partners were making their case for them. If, as a result, UEFA came up with new arrangements for the Champions' League which took account of their griev-ances they could only gain. If UEFA remained stubborn,

they could go with Media Partners. They were runni.
with the hare and the hound and before long the pressure
told and UEFA was forced to act. A new Champions'
League format was rushed through in next to no time.
Almost before the ink on UEFA's policy document was
dry, it was redundant.

Although UEFA tried gamely to maintain that its principle of solidarity was intact, the new Champions'
League condemned more smaller countries to the
margins of the qualifying phase, which gained an extra
round. It also attempted to make sure the big battalions
are virtually guaranteed a place each year by extending
entry to third- and fourth-placed clubs in the top-ranked
countries. The result was something of an unwieldy
hybrid but it at least kept alive the concept of merit. It
also kept the big clubs in the fold and Media Partners
were sidelined. (They were soon back in the fray,
however, with plans to restructure the domestic game in
Brazil and a proposal for a European Ice Hockey Super
League.) To accommodate the revised Champions'
League, the Cup Winners' Cup was scrapped after a long
and proud history. The UEFA Cup was retained and
expanded to become a dumping ground for teams who
failed to reach the last sixteen of the premier competition.

The Champions' League is now even less a league of
champions (fourth-placed teams from Italy, Spain and
Germany have a chance to qualify, for instance). The big
teams from the high-ranked countries are almost certain
to be there every year. And if they had a really bad
domestic season and ended up fifth or sixth they could
still go into the UEFA Cup. This works against big clubs
from lower-ranked countries, such as Ukraine's Dynamo
Kiev, who reached the semi-final of the Champions'
League in 1999. They will now always have to pre-
qualify unless they actually win the European Cup. So

ll countries' representatives remain, they
ce of emulating the likes of Helsinki JK and
oth of whom came through the qualifying
ague section in 1998–99. From now on they
will be up against the extra representatives from the big
countries.

When Gabriel Hanot, a former French international
turned journalist for *L'Equipe*, helped found the European
Cup in the 1950s, there was no tradition of cup football on
the continent as there was in England and Scotland.
However, with air transport still rudimentary and domestic leagues making huge demands on time, a knockout
competition was the only practical formula to adopt. The
dynamic of league football, which underpinned the club
game everywhere, had to be rejected as a template for the
new European event – until now. Although the Real
Madrid of Di Stefano, Puskas and Gento, the Cruyff-
inspired Ajax, the Beckenbauer-led Bayern Munich and
the Milan of Gullit, Rijkaard and Van Basten were
undoubtedly the greatest sides of their respective eras,
they had to win a mere half-dozen ties to lift Europe's
most important trophy. The new Champions' League,
with a greater breadth and depth of representation in
extended group stages and a massive increase in the
number of competitive fixtures, will for the first time
since the show began almost fifty years ago allow
Monsieur Hanot's question to be properly answered.
'Which,' he asked, 'is the best team in Europe?'

After the three qualifying rounds there follows two
group stages, from which eight teams emerge to enter a
knockout phase which ends in the final. The complexity,
though, is offset by the fact that the number of teams in
any group is set at four, which will ensure that all games
are important and supporter interest will remain high
throughout. The eventual winners will have played a

minimum of seventeen games, more if they take part the qualifying rounds. The rewards will be commensurate with the increase in matches, however, with the quarter-finalists collecting some £15 million and the winners at least £30 million, matching the sort of cash which was on offer from Media Partners. Furthermore, TEAM had already quadrupled annual television income to £400 million. In UEFA's press release to announce the new format, there was an indication of what was to come. Money, as before, would be shared out, in the main, in relation to performance. But in addition, SFr250 million (£105 million) would be set aside and 'distributed among the clubs in proportion to market value factors'.

To televise the new competition, with its sheer number of fixtures, many of the free-to-air networks which bought the rights took on pay TV partners. In the UK, this meant that ITV will link up with the new digital service, ONdigital. Thwarted in the UK, Sky's parent company, News Corp, bought rights to the Champions' League in Germany through a small, relatively obscure free-to-air channel. How Rupert Murdoch will utilize this acquisition remains to be seen.

If the price of seeing off Media Partners was the new Champions' League format, so FIFA realized that a world club tournament should be advanced to prevent similar moves on the global stage. Thus the first 'proper' World Club Championship, with representatives from all confederations, was planned for the beginning of the new millennium. (Although it is difficult to believe that the champions of Asia, Concacaf, Oceania and even Africa could be ranked alongside the champions of Europe and South America who already play for a 'world cup' annually in Japan.) Europe's entrants were at first going to be Bayern Munich, a strange choice given that they were not the European champions.

pions were Manchester United. Having
gnominy of a barren season in 1997–98, they
ack in spectacular style. They not only
Arsenal's double, they went one better than any
English team before them and added the greatest prize,
the European Cup. It seemed that United could not
participate in the new 'world championship' because,
unlike the rest of Europe, England has no winter break
when the tournament is to be played. It is ironic that the
club which pioneered the European adventure for
English clubs in the 1950s, against the wishes of the FA
and the Football League, should be incapable of taking
part in what might prove to be another epoch-making
development. This time, roles were reversed as the FA
sought to encourage United to participate in order to
curry favour with FIFA for the 2006 World Cup bid.
Something will have to give.

The genesis of United's best ever season began when
the board departed from its policy of yesteryear and
splashed out big money on transfer fees, together with
salary increases for existing players. At last the club was
playing in the really big league – and it showed.

Circumstances had made it extremely difficult for
English teams to do well in the European Cup in the
1990s. The five-year European exile, during which time
clubs like AC Milan had taken the game forward by ally-
ing continental flair to English athleticism, had left
Premier League clubs with a catch-up job of huge
proportions. Then, as they re-entered the European
family, the rules on who constituted overseas players
were changed. The bedrock of many English teams –
Scottish, Welsh and Irish players – was removed at a
stroke when they were reclassified as 'foreigners', until
the Bosman ruling in 1995 lifted the restrictions on
European Community nationals.

Furthermore, the creation of the Premier League brought extra pressures. Games could now be played at any time of the week and kick-off times ranged from 11 am to 8pm to suit the Sky schedules. There were occasions when many games would take place in a short time-span followed by fallow periods to accommodate the needs of the national team. The intensity and passion of matches, which has always been high in England, were cranked up even further as clubs were desperate to challenge for the title or avoid relegation to the Football League. And the clubs didn't help their own cause by using their free time to play friendlies in far-flung places in the quest for cash. It was no coincidence that English clubs could only succeed in the least demanding competition, the Cup Winners' Cup, which was won in the 1990s by United, Arsenal and Chelsea. When it came to the main events, the teams that won the Premiership, or finished on the podium, all failed in the Champions' League and the UEFA Cup.

It really shouldn't have taken United so long to learn the harsh facts of life in the fast lane of the Champions' League. After the double of 1994, there were no heavy reinforcements and the team ended the following season empty handed, though Eric Cantona's rush of blood at Selhurst Park certainly didn't help matters. Alex Ferguson forgot the old Liverpool trick: spend when you're winning. Now he had a more difficult task: he had to spend to recapture lost ground. For United, time stood still as Italian and Spanish clubs (and even Arsenal) outspent and overtook them. It was to be different in 1998–99 when there was a new, simple strategy: the Champions' League was to be prioritized. The expensive purchases, it was hoped, would make the difference.

United also possessed young English players who had grown up together, were committed to the club and could learn from their European defeats. They had also inherited an important legacy from Eric Cantona. His emphasis on skill and the practice ethic, his charismatic appeal and star status, as well as his self-belief, which had taken United to English domination, had stamped itself on youngsters who were now ready to assume his mantle on a wider stage.

No one was more focused than David Beckham. He put in a number of splendid displays, none more so than against Internazionale in Manchester, when he supplied sublime crosses for two goals. Beckham was remarkably quick to regain his equilibrium after the World Cup. Back in the bosom of his Manchester 'family' he was a model player, in terms of both performance and behaviour. He suffered abuse but that was nothing new. At the beginning of the season he was probably the most vilified player in the history of the English game. As United's corner-taker it was impossible for him not to hear the opposition fans' view of his sexual proclivities or those of his partner. Paradoxically, he got the 'royal' treatment from the tabloids when he became a father. After knocking him down, the papers were building him up again. It was a 'double whammy' though, as with a bit of luck the destruction process could happen all over again.

Despite enjoying the material benefits of his and Victoria's wealth – the magazine *France Football* ranked Beckham second only to Ronaldo in the sport's highest earners' table – he remained first and foremost a footballer. So well did he do his day job that if the ballots had taken place at the end of the season, he, rather than Tottenham's David Ginola, would probably have won both the players' and the football writers' Player of the Year awards. No matter, he remains a front-runner for the ultimate accolade, the European Player of the Year, which no Englishman has picked up since Kevin Keegan managed it twice running in the 1970s.

The man who had brought on so many of the young players, Brian Kidd, departed in December to take up the manager's job at Blackburn Rovers. His replacement, a surprise choice, was the little-known Steve McClaren from Derby County. It was, however, as shrewd a signing as Ferguson has made. When the deal was completed, the Derby manager, Jim Smith, said, 'I had been expecting the phone to ring since Brian Kidd left.' Perhaps United saw in McClaren what Smith valued so much: at Derby, he brought individual honing to the team ethos. He was responsible for the introduction of a scientific approach to the needs of each squad member, using computers and experts in the areas of nutrition and physiology. These resources became an integral part of a sophisticated fitness and motivation regime.

Then there was Alex Ferguson. Hardworking, resilient, even inspiring, his attitude was transmitted to his players. If there was one thing that had held him back in the Champions' League it was, perhaps, coming to terms with the new world of plcs and City finance and his strained relationship with the man who held the purse strings, Martin Edwards. With the outlay in 1998, he and Edwards seemed finally to have acted decisively to secure top-level performers.

The arrival of the three extra players plus a rejuvenated Roy Keane and the coming of age of even more home-grown youngsters like Wes Brown ensured that United now possessed a squad which could survive the loss of any one or two players through injury or suspension. It also allowed Ferguson to rest players at certain times in the domestic programme without detriment to results. One away performance in particular exemplified their new-found strength in depth: an 8–1 victory at

Nottingham Forest, which was incredible. Ole Gunnar Solskjaer achieved what anyone would have said was highly improbable. He came on as a substitute with only eighteen minutes to go and scored four goals in the last ten minutes. At the start of the season United were not even the best team in England. By its end, they had shown they had the best squad in Europe.

Imbued in this squad was a quality not hitherto considered a United strength: a never-say-die streak, almost a refusal to lose matches. They began to score important goals in the dying minutes, often coming from behind. According to Alex Ferguson, this stemmed from the previous season's failure. 'For the first time in the lives of the younger players they'd lost something that mattered to them,' Ferguson explained. 'They'd been brought up through the youth ranks winning everything and now, having lost the league last year, they got to grips with the situation and decided they were not going to let it happen again. That had a lot to do with the determination they've shown.'

Although no one realized it at the time, the first match of the 1998–99 season in the Premiership was a harbinger of what was to come and bore an uncanny resemblance to how the side finished the season. They came back from a losing 2–0 position against Leicester at Old Trafford to secure a draw in stoppage time with a David Beckham free-kick. Teddy Sheringham, on as a substitute, began the comeback by redirecting a mis-hit shot into the net. That was simply a prelude. In the FA Cup fourth round, a 1–0 deficit against Liverpool was turned around after eighty-nine minutes. In the semi-final, they survived a last-minute penalty against Arsenal and the dismissal of Roy Keane to win through Ryan Giggs's goal of the season in extra-time.

It was the same story in Europe. A late equalizer from

Paul Scholes against Internazionale gave United a precious away goal and took them through to a semi-final meeting with their nemesis, Juventus. In Manchester, Ryan Giggs conjured up an equalizer in injury-time after United had lost a goal in the first half. The return leg in Turin was even more remarkable. 2–0 down after twelve minutes, the team stormed back to level the score and win the game through Andy Cole's strike right at the end. At last the Italian hex was cast aside. It was nerve-racking but the message was clear: this team refused to accept defeat when the odds were stacked against them. Across Europe, indeed the world, the public loved it. Even in England, fans were seeing the light, many of them albeit reluctantly.

United also managed to find extra reserves when the final sequence of pressure games arrived at the end of the season. The Premiership was secured at Old Trafford against Spurs. A week later, in the FA Cup Final against Newcastle United, they overcame an early injury to Roy Keane to win 2–0, through Teddy Sheringham – again coming on as a substitute – scoring an early goal and Paul Scholes's second-half strike. Suddenly the loss of captain Keane did not seem such a deadly blow. This was a vital fillip since Keane and Scholes would be out of the encounter to come four days later: Bayern Munich in the European Cup final, in the fitting arena of Barcelona's Nou Camp. (It was really the runners-up final, since neither side had won their respective leagues to qualify for the Champions' League. There will certainly be more of those in the future.)

In this game the players attained a higher level again, if that was conceivable. They managed to overcome their manager's bizarre tendency to cock up his selection and tactical policy for crucial European games. Just like past gaffes, such as the dropping of Peter Schmeichel in

Barcelona and playing Eric Cantona as a lone striker against Juventus, this time he compounded the absence of Keane and Scholes by playing Giggs out of position on the right, which had a disadvantageous domino effect on the team's pattern. Moreover, Ferguson decided to play David Beckham in central midfield. Beckham had performed brilliantly in that role after Keane went off in the FA Cup Final but his incisive crosses from the right had been a major source of United's attacking play throughout the season. This asset was now lost as Giggs took Beckham's role on the right and Jesper Blomqvist played in Giggs's position on the left. He had a poor game, as did Dwight Yorke and Andy Cole up front. United looked unbalanced and although Beckham slipped into the centre with ease and confidence, his teammates seemed off the pace and on a different wavelength. At least, better late than never, Ferguson again used substitutes to great effect. The more surprising the substitution and its timing, the more it appeared to pay off.

Bayern should have won the game. As well as going a goal up early in the first half, they hit the woodwork twice late in the second. For the influential Peter Schmeichel, who had earlier announced that this was to be his final season at Old Trafford, his final game was an encapsulation of his last months with United. He went from villain to hero as first he was hopelessly wrong-footed when Bayern scored; and then he pulled off some characteristically brilliant saves as Bayern pressed forward. Nevertheless, as the final moments approached, the German fans celebrated and the Bayern players, prematurely as it turned out, believed the match was won.

It was just as well Sky were not broadcasting the match otherwise it is likely that viewers would have been subjected to prolonged overkill. Just as the

Premiership is not the best league in the world,
Manchester United are not the best team in the worl‹
They may not even be the most entertaining. What
United have is a side capable of regular dramatic
denouements which are compulsively watchable. This
could even surprise Sir Bobby Charlton, who wrote in
the *Daily Telegraph*: 'I should have learned never to
underestimate this Manchester United team, even I
thought the season had caught up with us at last in the
final five minutes in Barcelona. Somewhere along the line
I feared one test would be beyond us but once again they
proved me wrong. The manner of the victory over
Bayern was sensational: the players never know when to
quit and what happened in those final, unbelievable
minutes is down to more than mere tactics or substitu-
tions. It is about having the guts to keep going. Never has
the phrase "making your own luck" seemed more appro-
priate.' Charlton had discerned that United's triumph
was one of team spirit rather than teamwork, a demonstration of self-belief that belied a below-par performance
on the day.

For this, everyone at Manchester United has much to
thank Alex Ferguson for. Overriding tactical errors was
the belief in the power of the collective that the manager
had instilled into his players. His motivational powers
were never so great as they were that night. His half-time
team talk at the Nou Camp was a case in point. Teddy
Sheringham revealed the story, saying, 'He told us that if
we lost, "you'll have to go up and get our losers' medals
and you will be just six feet from the European Cup but
you won't be able to touch it. And for many of you that
will be the closest you will ever get. Don't you dare come
back in here without giving your all."' Ferguson's words
recalled those of Alf Ramsey when England faced extra-
time against West Germany in 1966, having conceded an

last minute. 'You've won it once,' Ramsey
've got to go out and win it again.'

lona, Ferguson's contract was renegoti-
nanager in a position of strength. The new
deal was worth £1.5 million a year for three years,
although there were misgivings among some board
members that the salary rise was too steep. Having no
intention of emulating Sir Matt Busby after 1968 by
moving upstairs or allowing the team to stagnate, the last
of the old-style British managers can look forward to his
sixtieth birthday safe in the knowledge that his control of
the playing side is as total as it is possible to get in the
world of modern football.

There was no doubting Ferguson's ambition but
Edward Freedman, who created United's merchandising
phenomenon, believes that the treble can also revive a
somewhat depressed commercial sector. If this is true it
means the board must learn the financial lessons of the
season of destiny. Any retreat to the previous conservative ways will eventually reflect itself in the share price
and the balance sheet. It is no coincidence that the
winners of all three European competitions – United,
Parma and Lazio – were among the continent's biggest
spenders.

The Italian, Spanish and German giants will rejoin the
battle with renewed purpose and financial muscle.
Having got their noses in front, United need not fall
behind again as they did once before. Already, however,
it seems Martin Edwards is leaning towards caution.
After the Sky deal collapsed he warned against expectations of large amounts of money becoming available for
new players. Edwards having considered selling his
stake in the club on four separate occasions – to Robert
Maxwell, Michael Knighton, the media company VCI
and Sky – the future direction is not predictable.

At last the spectre of 1968 had been laid to rest in the most spectacular way possible. Of course, there was delight at United's triumph but to the dispassionate observer the real victory had been gained before a ball was kicked in the final. The Champions' League presents the ultimate test for a club side and United had failed that test too often. But success is not necessarily measured only by winning the Champions' League. Any team playing in the rarefied atmosphere of Europe's elite can lose to any other team on the day. What is important is to be there, to reach the final, or at the very least the semi-final, on a regular basis. If a club can do this, it will consistently be regarded as one of the few great clubs of the moment, with the consequent effect of increasing its fan base, its income and its ability to attract the world's best players. Juventus, in a season of low achievement by their own high standards, nevertheless reached the semi-final of the Champions' League, following three successive appearances in the final.

With the team becoming more consistent in Europe, supporters, who supply the foundation of love for their club, will always be replenished with each new generation. For United, winning the European Cup was a magnificent achievement. But just as with the national team, an obsession with recapturing the glory of one great triumph which took place thirty years ago is not enough. Getting there and staying there is the peak that remains to be conquered.